How to Do Everything with Your iPhone®

About the Authors

Jason Chen is a freelance technology and consumer electronics/gadgets writer based in San Mateo, CA. He graduated from the University of California, Berkeley, with a degree in Electrical Engineering and Computer Science. Before starting as an Editor at Gizmodo, a major technology Weblog, Jason worked at various startups as a software engineer in the technology industry. Since April 2006, Jason's been giving his views of gadget news on Gizmodo. In addition to reporting the news, Jason also performs in-depth reviews and analysis of the newest gear—often before it's released to the public.

Adam Pash (http://adampash.com) is a freelance technology and consumer electronics writer and programmer based in Los Angeles, CA. He is the senior editor of Lifehacker.com, a software and technology weblog, where he posts daily tips, downloads, and reviews of the best productivity wares on the net, along with in-depth how-to articles. Born and raised in Harlan, IA, Adam graduated from the University of Iowa with an interdepartmental degree in the Philosophy of Science, Arts, and Ethics in 2003. He now resides in Los Angeles, CA.

About the Technical Editor

Raphael Liberatore has worked for the past 11 years as technical editor, contributing editor, columnist and freelancer for a variety of computer print and online magazines, including *Computer Gaming World, Computer Games Magazine, GAMES, GameDaily, Gamespot,* and *Gamespy.* He's authored hundreds of technical articles, including computer, hardware, software, and game reviews, and has written about home theater and convergence topics. In his spare time, he designs and builds high performance computers, diagnoses and builds personal and business computers and networks, and runs a long-time Mac gaming website (www.clanmacgaming.com). Raphael is a former US Army Special Forces soldier and military contractor. When he has free time, Raphael enjoys cruising Southern California in his 1969 Chevy Camaro, hiking the Rocky Mountains, working as a fighting arts and tactical combat instructor, and hosting LAN parties at his renowned computer lab, dubbed "The Cave" by Tech TV. He also writes horror fiction, which he hopes to get published in the near future. He currently resides in Southern California.

How to Do Everything with Your iPhone®

Jason Chen and Adam Pash

New York   Chicago   San Francisco
Lisbon   London   Madrid   Mexico City
Milan   New Delhi   San Juan
Seoul   Singapore   Sydney   Toronto

*The **McGraw·Hill** Companies*

Cataloging-in-Publication Data is on file with the Library of Congress

McGraw-Hill books are available at special quantity discounts to use as premiums and sales promotions, or for use in corporate training programs. For more information, please write to the Director of Special Sales, Professional Publishing, McGraw-Hill, Two Penn Plaza, New York, NY 10121-2298. Or contact your local bookstore.

How to Do Everything with Your iPhone®

1234567890   DOC DOC   01987

ISBN: 978-0-07-149790-9
MHID: 0-07-149790-0

Sponsoring Editor
Mcgg Morin

Editorial Supervisor
Patty Mon

Project Manager
Madhu Bhardwaj
(International Typesetting
and Composition)

Acquisitions Coordinator
Carly Stapleton

Technical Editor
Raphael Liberatore

Copy Editor
Julie Smith

Proofreader
Bev Weiler

Indexer
Kevin Broccoli

Production Supervisor
Jean Bodeaux

Composition
International Typesetting
and Composition

Illustration
International Typesetting
and Composition

Art Director, Cover
Jeff Weeks

Cover Designer
Pattie Lee

Contents at a Glance

Contents

Acknowledgments

Thanks to everyone at Gizmodo and Lifehacker for all the help—technical or otherwise—during the writing process. This includes, but is not limited to (in alphabetical order): Brian Ashcraft, John Biggs, Adrian Covert, Jesus Diaz, Adam Frucci, Joel Johnson, Brian Lam, Noah Robischon, Wilson Rothman, Gina Trapani, Charlie White, and Mark Wilson. Thanks to Erica Sadun for all her cool iPhone applications (especially the screenshot application), and thanks to Nate True for all his iPhone work as well. We'd like to thank the iPhone Dev Team for breaking the iPhone wide open (in a good way).

We'd also like to thank our parents for getting us hooked on technology way back when, as well as Ellen and Dixie for being patient while we were elbow-deep in our iPhones.

Introduction

We've written this book with the intention of walking you through setting up and getting to know your iPhone from the start—which is why the first chapter is dedicated to activating your phone, the second to general usage, and so on. Once we've covered basic setup and usage, we start diving into individual applications until we've covered every nook and cranny of your iPhone.

Then we move on to more advanced usage, laying out some of the best tips and tricks for using your iPhone—from getting good with the onscreen keyboard to troubleshooting any iPhone problems you may run into.

Finally, in the Spotlight section, we cover hacking open the iPhone in order to install third-party applications from developers other than Apple. According to Apple, doing this will void your warranty, but should not prevent you from using your iPhone with iTunes.

Part I

Make Calls and Sync Contacts with Your iPhone

Chapter 1

Get Your iPhone Up and Running

How to...

- Familiarize yourself with the iPhone
- Activate your iPhone
- Prepare your iPhone for use
- Sync your data to your iPhone

You've made a wise choice in purchasing your iPhone. Besides being both a revolutionary phone and an iPod, the iPhone can send and receive email, look up turn-by-turn directions, plan your week, play videos from YouTube, and so much more. Your new iPhone is the phone of the future.

You've also made a wise choice in purchasing this book. Naturally, you want to know everything there is to know about this groundbreaking device (and clearly there is a lot), and this is the place to get all the details. In this first chapter, we'll show you the steps to get your iPhone up and running to the point where you can actually start using it. We'll go through activation, syncing, and how to best prepare your phone for everything you're going to do with it. If you already started working with your iPhone by yourself, feel free to jump around to the topic that you want to know the most about.

You may be wondering whether buying the iPhone or this book has thrust you further into the future we mentioned previously. While your humble authors consider this book to be the authoritative source for all things iPhone, we can't help but give at least a little credit to Apple. The iPhone is truly the coolest gadget we've ever used (and we've used a *lot* of them), and in terms of the current mobile phone market, it has no equal. The iPhone is the future. But remember, the keys to a Ferrari aren't all that useful if you don't know how to drive, and a cool car sitting immobile in your driveway can only impress your friends and neighbors for so long before the charm wears off.

The iPhone is the most stylish mobile device in the world. But you didn't buy it because it looked good. You bought it because you wanted the power that lies inside. This book not only hands you the keys, it gives you all the driving lessons you need to squeeze every last bit of functionality out of your iPhone.

What's an iPhone, and How Is It Different from Other Cell Phones?

The iPhone is, first and foremost, a cell phone. However, as Apple Inc.'s CEO Steve Jobs said when unveiling the iPhone at MacWorld 2007, it's actually a three-in-one device: a cell phone, an iPod, and an internet communicator. It's these three devices integrated together that makes the iPhone such a remarkable piece of hardware. More specifically, the thing that makes the iPhone as such so great isn't even in the hardware itself—the secret sauce is in the software.

That's right—it's the software that makes the iPhone such a revolutionary phone. Not only does the iPhone have easy-to-access speed dial lists, call history, and contacts, but there's a giant traditional dial pad as well. But most phones have this already, you say, so what's different here? In one word: integration. It's in the way that you can easily bring up your friends' addresses in Google Maps, the flawless way they sync with Address Book on the Mac and Outlook on the PC, and the convenient way you can quickly assign unique ringtones and pictures to all your contacts. These functions are present on other phones, of course, but they require a Batman-like level of technical knowledge to get to.

Then, of course, there's the iPod in your iPhone. Apple's taken everything that was great about the music player you (most likely) already own and they've made it even better. Seriously. Instead of the touch-sensitive Click Wheel, you've got an entire screen to frolic around on. If you tilt the iPhone to the side, you get the beautiful Cover Flow mode, which lets you flip through your album covers like you would on your shelf (assuming you own both albums and a shelf to place them on). Plus, there's gigantic album art whenever you're playing a song, one-click access to many functions that were up to four-clicks away on an iPod, and convenient integration with the rest of the iPhone's features. What do we mean by that? How about automatically pausing a song when you've got an incoming call?

Lastly, the iPhone ventures into territory previously only explored by hard-to-use smartphones. What do we mean? We mean that it's a full-featured internet communicator as well. There's Safari, Apple's internet browser, which gives you desktop-quality web browsing as opposed to the shrunken and dumbed-down browsers on other phones. Then there's the Mail application, which is as close to desktop quality as we've seen on a phone this side of BlackBerry communicators. Add to that mini-applications like Google Maps, weather, stocks, and YouTube, not to mention web-based applications and the inevitable future software updates and new applications from Apple, and you'll feel comfortable leaving your laptop behind wherever you go.

So why go with an iPhone when you could go with a smartphone that has similar functionality? For one, there's never been a phone with an iPod built in. Using an iPod compared with using the media players on other phones is like the difference between flying from LA to New York first class and driving there in an old Pinto. Both will get you to your destination, but one gets you there in class, style, and comfort, while the other makes you want to give up and go home before you even start. Expand this concept to the all the iPhone's features, and you'll understand why the device is so innovative.

Activate Your iPhone

You've made the purchase and you made it home—with a quick stop at the book store to pick up the book you're currently holding—and you're ready to start using the phone. Not so fast, hot shot. You've got some setting up to do. Your first step is activation. Instead of waiting inside a cell phone store, you actually set up the iPhone yourself using Apple's music management software called iTunes. Here's how you do it.

1. If you're already running an Apple OS X machine purchased in the last couple of years, you probably already have iTunes installed. Windows users may or may not have already installed iTunes. Never mind that, because you want to make sure you have the latest version anyway. Open up a web browser and type this into the address bar: `http://www.apple.com/itunes/download/`.

2. Once you're there, click the Download button in order to start downloading the iTunes installer. Apple asks for an email address, but if you don't feel like giving yours away you don't need to. The iTunes website should automatically detect the right operating system (Mac OS X versus Windows XP or Windows Vista) and send you the correct version. If you're using a Linux machine, you'll have to borrow another computer or install a version of Windows in order to set up your iPhone.

3. Done downloading? Good. Now find the file you've just downloaded and open it. Once you have iTunes installed, it's time to start up the program. Under OS X, the iTunes app shows up in the dock as a CD with a music note on top. In Windows, you have to go into your Start Menu, find the iTunes folder, and then click on iTunes.

If this is your first time running iTunes, you may not be familiar with the interface. Don't worry. We'll get to its intricacies in Chapter 5. For now, we just want to get you to a point where you're up and running with an activated iPhone.

Connect the iPhone to Your Computer

Your next step is simple: connect your iPhone to your computer. First, take the iPhone connector out of the box. That's the cable with the fat flat end that fits into the bottom of the iPhone, and the rectangular USB end that fits into your computer. You need to find a spare USB port on your machine (they're the ones that your mouse, keyboard, and iPod plug into) so you can plug your iPhone in as well. Try and find a USB 2.0 port so you can transfer music and movies faster. If you don't know whether the ports on your computer support USB 2.0 or USB 1.1, don't worry too much, because both work—but check your computer's documentation if you get a chance. It's the difference between drinking a gallon of milk through a straw or holding it upside-down above your mouth and going at it.

If you've connected your iPhone correctly, iTunes will start automatically, and you'll see the activation screen you'll be using to give life to your iPhone. This is also where you're going to have to make some tough decisions about how many minutes a month you're going to need and whether or not 200 text messages are enough. But first, you'll have to enter in your information.

First you'll need to choose whether you're activating one or more iPhones and whether you're a current or new AT&T customer. We won't go through all the steps, such as getting a new number or transferring your old number because it's straightforward and iTunes does a good job of guiding you through. However, there are some things you may need to watch out for:

- ■ Transferring your old phone number from another carrier (Verizon or T-Mobile, for example) will deactivate the phone that was previously using the number.

- ■ If you're transferring a number from a landline, your transfer process may take up to a week. Transferring from another cell phone number can take anywhere between a couple of minutes to a couple of days, depending on the day of the week that you do the transfer and how busy your provider is.

- ■ When entering in your billing information, make note of the zip code you're using for your old, existing phone number and the zip code you're using for your new billing address. If they're different it may cause delays, and you should contact AT&T to check.

Pick a Plan for Your Needs

Not all plans are created equal, and you should think carefully before you pick the one you want. Luckily, the iPhone activation process can be completed at home and at your own pace, so you have hours, or even days, to think about what plan you want. We recommend you look at your last three to six months of cell phone bills and count up how many anytime minutes, night and weekend minutes, and text messages you send. Keep in mind that your old mobile-to-mobile calls will not be counted as mobile to mobile if you're switching providers. All those calls to your spouse that were free before may now be eating away at your minutes if you aren't both using AT&T!

With these factors in mind, it's time to choose a plan. If you're a new AT&T customer, the lowest priced plan at the time of this writing has 450 anytime minutes and 5000 night and weekend minutes. The other features of the plan, like unlimited data, Visual Voicemail, 200 text messages, Rollover Minutes, and Unlimited Mobile-to-Mobile are included in all the other iPhone plans as well. Your only concern should be whether you have enough anytime minutes to go around. Also, keep in mind that AT&T's night hours start at 9 PM and end at 6 AM, which actually almost matches up perfectly to sunrise and sunset times here in California. Unless you're working the night shift, these probably aren't the hours you place most of your calls.

If you're a fan of text messaging—and who wouldn't be, with the iChat-like SMS application on the iPhone—you may find that the 200 text messages allotted for you a month isn't enough. You have the choice of adding 1500 messages for an additional $10 a month, or unlimited text messages for an additional $20 a month. The rate for text messages is the same on every plan.

What about if you're already a current AT&T customer? All you have to do is add a $20 monthly data plan on top of your current minute plan. Everything else is the same as before.

Solve Possible Activation Troubles

After you enter all your information, iTunes will send your activation details to Apple and AT&T for processing. iTunes should come back with an activation confirmation almost immediately and you'll be ready to use your iPhone. If you received a message saying that your activation may take more time to complete, or a message saying that there are problems with your activation, we recommend calling AT&T and conferring with their support team.

> **NOTE** *Adam's iPhone activation with AT&T took less than a minute. Jason's took close to 48 hours. Jason claims it had something to do with porting his number from another service to AT&T (Adam went for a whole new number). Adam likes to think he's just that much better at using the iPhone.*

Prepare Your iPhone for Use

Now that you've patiently and dutifully walked through the activation process like a good iPhone owner, you're probably anxious to dive into all its cool features. Before you do, there are a handful of things that you, as a responsible iPhone owner, should consider before you take your precious iPhone out into the world.

Condition Your Battery

The first thing you should do before even using your iPhone is condition your battery. Doing so will ensure that your battery lasts as long as it possibly can, both between charges and from the day you buy your iPhone to the day the battery draws its last useful charge. Step one in conditioning your battery: let it charge fully before you start using it. Step two: don't plug your iPhone in again until the battery has completely drained. Finally, the third and most harrowing step in Battery Conditioning 101: Charge your phone until it's reached its full capacity yet again. Simple, right?

NOTE

Like the iPod, the iPhone doesn't have an easily replaceable battery. In fact, it's nearly impossible to replace the battery yourself, and even if you did, don't count on Apple to hand you a new iPhone if something goes wrong. But, if you're under warranty (AppleCare), battery replacement is free. If you don't have AppleCare, or it ran out, Apple will charge you $79 and a $6.95 shipping fee to replace it. On the plus side, the iPhone's battery life is impressive, even if you do a lot of talking, iPodding, and web browsing. Just remember, a properly conditioned battery is a happy battery.

Protect Your iPhone from Damage

Now that your iPhone is powered up, you may want to protect its beautiful look and feel to ensure your iPhone stays brand new inside as well as out.

The iPhone, in contrast to the iPod, has a brushed metal back, which doesn't scratch or smudge easily, if at all. The front of the iPhone isn't quite so durable. Basically you've got one gorgeous slab of glass lying atop your iPhone. This glass is actually quite durable, and after logging hundreds of hours with my iPhone nestled in my pocket, I've yet to incur any scratches, nicks, dents, or anything else that could fall under the damage category. However, that's me, and I admittedly handle my iPhone with kid gloves. Depending on what kind of an owner you are, you might want to consider one of many screen protectors available for the iPhone. Screen protectors provide a transparent shield of plastic between your gorgeous slab of glass and the harsh world of pointy things surrounding it.

TIP

For a look at a few iPhone cases and other accessories we like, check out Chapter 15.

No matter how careful you are with your iPhone, the biggest danger is an unprotected drop onto a hard surface. The most compelling reason you might want to grab yourself some sort of iPhone case is to ward off—or at least partially protect against—the internal and external damage that dropping your iPhone could cause. Cosmetic damage is a bummer; your iPhone won't look as new and shiny. Internal damage can mean the end of your iPhone.

Sync Your iPhone to Your Computer

If the iPhone is a little portable computer, your actual computer is like the big mothership it has to dock with from time to time to stay up-to-date with your constant flow of information and media. Yes, your iPhone can keep track of appointments and contacts, but you'll want to keep those synced up to the same information you've got sitting on your computer as well. And, syncing your iPhone with your desktop computer is the only way you can get music and movies onto your iPhone. The point is: syncing is quite important. If you're going to take advantage of all your iPhone has to offer, you'll learn to love the sync. We'll teach you how to get data both from your computer onto your iPhone and from your iPhone onto your computer.

In the next section, we'll set up iTunes so that whenever you plug in your iPhone and hit Sync, all of your contacts, appointments, music, photos, and videos will sync between your phone and your computer. So let's get started.

Sync Your Contacts

Let's get started by syncing your contacts. Your iPhone is a robust and impressive contact management tool, but if you've got a lot of contacts, it's going to make your life a lot easier to sync them from your computer to your iPhone than to try to create them all on your phone. Luckily for you, it's simple. You'll be creating contact entries on your computer and moving them onto your phone using iTunes.

Sync Your Contacts (Mac)

There are three ways the iPhone can sync contacts with your Mac. The first is with Address Book, the default contact handler for Mac OS X. The second is with Yahoo Address Book, the contact portion of Yahoo Mail. You can actually choose both if you like the idea of backing up your contacts with your Yahoo account in addition to your local Address Book. If you're comfortable with your Mac's Address Book and you want to stick with virtually the same contact format as your iPhone uses, we recommend using Address Book. But if you like to manage your contacts in multiple places, or often use Yahoo's WebMail service to store and manage your contacts, then Yahoo Address Book could be the choice for you.

> **TIP** *If you sync your contacts to both your Mac Address Book and Yahoo Address Book, you can access your contacts from anywhere at any time. If you edit your Yahoo Address Book online when you're away from the computer you sync your iPhone to, all of your contacts will be updated. Handy!*

The third option is Microsoft Entourage, the Outlook-like program Microsoft included with Microsoft Office 2004 for Mac. This is actually still syncing from Address Book, but it syncs Entourage with Address Book beforehand to pipe your contacts through.

> **NOTE** *Do you have an old cell phone? Do you want to keep your old contacts? Then you should try to sync your old phone to your Address Book first. If your phone supports it, you can do this using your old phone's USB cable or wirelessly via Bluetooth. Syncing your old phone is beyond the scope of this book, but you should be able to find some guides online if you search Google. Once you have that set up, we're ready to rock.*

It's not a huge deal if you don't have any contacts in your Address Book yet. If you don't, it'll be easier—not to mention quicker—to create them on your computer rather than on your iPhone. To do this, start up Address Book and begin entering in contacts. Feel free to assign contacts to different groups as well (friends, work, family), since the iPhone can handle multiple contact groups. For in-depth details on how to set these up, see Chapter 3.

To set up a sync with Entourage, open up Entourage, go to the Preferences screen, and then click on Sync Services. Make sure the checkbox next to Synchronize Contacts with Address Book and .Mac is checked and click OK. Once that's done, your contacts will copy themselves into Address Book (and .Mac, if you're a subscriber).

All your contacts ready to go? Good. Now all that's left to do is plug your iPhone in to your computer, select your iPhone on the left-hand column of iTunes (under Devices), and then click

FIGURE 1-1   The iTunes syncing screen where you sync Contacts, Calendars, Mail Accounts, and Bookmarks

on the Info tab. Figure 1-1 illustrates the Info tab inside iTunes. Once you're there, check the box next to Sync Address Book Contacts.

You have the choice to sync all your contacts (in which case you should select All Contacts), or only a portion of your contact groups. If you want to limit your contact sync, click Selected Groups and then check the groups you want to sync to your iPhone in the box below. Syncing only some of your contacts is a good way to keep the iPhone a work-only or a home-only device. It'll save you a ton of embarrassment by avoiding an accidental call to your boss when you meant to call your mother (Jason loves his mother). After this is done, all that's left is hitting the Apply button on the bottom right of iTunes, which will automatically sync your contacts. If you've made a mistake anywhere along the line (or you've changed your mind entirely and don't want to sync your contacts after all) hit Cancel. Alternately, if you want to sync more information and media, you can forge through the sections ahead before applying your settings. That way everything will sync in one fell swoop.

Assuming you did sync now, you're done! All your contacts are now on your iPhone. If you want to get into more advanced contact syncing and management, check Chapter 3.

Sync Your Contacts (Windows)

Let's get those contacts from Windows onto your iPhone. Like the Mac, there is more than one way to sync contacts to your iPhone. In fact, there are three. The first involves Microsoft Outlook, the second syncs with the new Microsoft Address book, and the third syncs online with Yahoo Address Book through iTunes.

The main difference between the three is that, while Microsoft Outlook and Address Book are a bit more robust and local (that is, the information lives on your computer), Yahoo Address Book lives on the Internet. The plus side to Yahoo's offering is that you can access and edit your contacts from any browser, any time. Let's start out with the first two: Microsoft Outlook and Address Book.

If you've already taken the time to fill out and organize your contacts using Microsoft Outlook or Address Book, this should be easy. On the other hand, if you've got a large contact list but your contacts reside entirely on your old phone, you'll probably want to move them into Outlook or Address Book using a USB cable or via Bluetooth before you sync your iPhone for the first time. There are a number of ways to do this, and since the one you'll choose depends on the brand of your old phone and the application you want to import your contacts to, we won't discuss them here. Suffice to say, you might need to sit down and spend some time at your computer with Uncle Google to see what you can find.

If that doesn't sound appealing, you might find it both quicker and easier to start from scratch, adding contacts to Outlook or Address Book from your desktop. You can get intimate with your iPhone really quickly by creating each individual contact directly on your iPhone, but you're new here, and chances are you'll have better luck building your contact list with your trusty desktop than with your iPhone at this point.

> **TIP** *It's actually quite easy to add and edit contacts on your iPhone, but until you get down with the speedy two-thumb peck, the big computer is the way to go. However, the time will come (in Chapter 3) that you will learn to love tweaking your contacts on your iPhone.*

If you'd prefer to manage your contacts online with Yahoo Address Book, you'll need to register for a free account with Yahoo (if you don't already have one). Their Address Book is an extension of Yahoo Mail, and it allows you to add and edit contacts at http://address.yahoo.com/.

Once you've finished filling out your address book, you're ready to sync. Plug your iPhone into your computer, open up iTunes, and then click on the iPhone icon in the left column of iTunes. Now, in the main window, click on the tab labeled Info. Figure 1-1 illustrates what you should be seeing in iTunes at this point. Now just tick the checkbox labeled Sync Contacts From and then select your preferred syncing source (Outlook, Windows Address Book, or Yahoo Address Book).

At this point, you're ready to sync. If you want to sync more info to your iPhone, like calendars and media, you can move on to the next section before performing your sync. If not, just hit Apply on the bottom right of the iTunes window whenever you're ready to finish off your sync. When you do this, just sit back and watch in wonder as your iPhone sucks all of your contacts from either your desktop or the Internet right into its internal storage.

You now have access to all of your contacts—including their phone numbers, addresses, email, and more—all in the palm of your hand. You'll want to start washing your hands more.

Sync Your Calendar

You may not use your calendar much on your current phone, but the usability of the iPhone calendar may just change your mind. And if you're already a control freak like Adam, and you have every little detail of your day programmed into your calendar, you'll want to keep the appointments with you at all times as well. Here's how you sync your iPhone's calendar with the one on your computer.

Sync Your Calendar (Mac)

First, plug your iPhone in and make sure iTunes is open. Click on your iPhone in the left-hand column, and then go to the Info tab; just like you did when you synced your Contacts to your Address Book (as shown in Figure 1-1). Now check the box next to Sync iCal Calendars, and select whether you want to sync all your calendars or only a few. Perhaps you want to keep only your important work appointments—and not personal appointments such as "have that hairy lump checked out"—on your iPhone. Or maybe you want to mix them together. The choice is yours.

If you use Microsoft Entourage to organize your calendar instead of iCal, you can still get your events onto the iPhone. To sync with Entourage, you have to first sync Entourage with iCal. To do that, open up Entourage, go to Preferences, and click on Sync Services. Make sure the Synchronize Events and Tasks with iCal and .Mac checkbox is checked, and click OK. All your scheduled events will duplicate themselves into iCal so you can easily sync them into the iPhone.

You have other options as well, such as not syncing appointments that are older than 30 days, or selecting which one of your many calendars (if you have more than one) you want to put iPhone-created events into. Of course, if there are no events on your actual iCal calendar, there's not much syncing to be done. If you want to know more about how iCal works and the intricacies of organizing events on both your computer and your iPhone, head to Chapter 8.

If you're done tweaking settings and you want to hurry up and sync already, hit Apply and watch as iTunes and iPhone make sure that your life—as much as you've programmed in, anyway—is in sync. If you've got more syncs you want to set up, like music, videos, and photos, you can wait to apply your sync until later.

Sync Your Calendar (Windows)

When it comes to syncing appointments and other calendar-related information to your iPod on Windows, you've just got one choice: Microsoft Outlook. If you use Outlook's calendar function, syncing your iPhone will dump all of the appointments from all of your calendars to your iPhone. If you don't currently manage your appointments with Outlook, the iPhone's excellent Calendar application may give you reason enough to start.

Either way, syncing your Outlook calendars to the iPhone is easy. Just fire up iTunes, plug in your iPhone (or if it's already plugged in, navigate to your iPhone under the Devices section in the sidebar), and click on the Info tab—just like you did if you synced your contacts with Outlook. Figure 1-1 illustrates the Info tab in iTunes.

Now scroll down to the section labeled Calendars, tick the checkbox labeled Sync Calendars From, and choose the source you'd like to sync your calendars from. iTunes makes this an easy choice, since, like we mentioned, the iPhone only syncs with Outlook calendars as of its first release. You can also choose how stale your backlog of appointments needs to be on your iPhone with the Do Not Sync Events Older Than X Days option, which defaults to 30. Unless you have a good reason for living that far in the past, I'd recommend sticking with the default.

If you're ready to sync your appointments, click Apply. Once it's done syncing, your calendars and every appointment therein should now have a home on your iPhone.

Sync Your Music (Windows/Mac)

Yes, first and foremost the iPhone is a phone (hence the name), but it's also the latest and greatest in the hugely popular iPod line. And just like the iPod, syncing media to your iPhone is a cinch. We'll start with your music.

When you sync your music, the process is the same for both Windows and Mac users. We're going to step through the same process (this is soon to become very routine): run iTunes, plug in your iPhone, and select your iPhone under Devices. Now just select the Music tab and tick the checkbox labeled Sync Music. You can see the Music sync tab in iTunes in Figure 1-2.

FIGURE 1-2   The iTunes music syncing screen

Now you have the option to either sync All Songs and Playlists or just Selected Playlists. Since the largest iPhone hard drive can only hold about 7.24 GB of data, chances are you won't be able to sync all of your songs to your iPhone (unless you have a fairly humble digital music library). Even if you could fit your whole music library, you probably don't want to. After all, you've still got photos and video to think about later on!

There are a lot of ways you can slice and dice your iTunes library to get a good selection of music on your iPhone, but for now you can just pick two or three of your favorite playlists to sync. If you want to learn how to get your best songs onto your iPhone with a minimal amount of fuss, head to Chapter 5, where we get down into the depths of iTunes.

When you're finished, you can sync your music by hitting Apply. If you've still got more syncs you want to set up—like photos and video—you can wait and sync them all at once. If not, go ahead and sync your music now and you're set to go.

Sync Your Photos

What good is having a phone with a great big display if you can't carry around all your vacation photos to flip through while you're riding the bus? Read on to find out how to get photos from your computer onto your iPhone. Mac users have the option of syncing from either iPhoto or from a set of folders, but Windows users can only sync from a folder. Either way, you can organize photos into different albums so they're not all in a giant jumble on your phone.

> **TIP** *When syncing photos to your iPhone, iTunes will create smaller, iPhone-optimized versions of the photos on your computer, so make sure you've got some free space on your hard drive for these extra photos. If you want to know how much space the resized photos are taking up on your computer's hard drive, just look at how much space iTunes says is devoted to photos when your iPhone is plugged in.*

Sync Your Photos (Mac)

If you're a Mac user, you can sync your photos directly from iPhoto, Apple's photo management program. iPhoto offers a good way to manage your photos into albums as well as perform some touchup work. If you're using the high-end photo-editing program Aperture, you can sync from that as well.

Not only can you bring these albums intact onto the iPhone, but you can create smart albums that contain, say, only photos that have a user-set rating of 4 stars or higher. To get a deeper look at the options you have for syncing your photos from iPhoto to your iPhone and vice versa, see Chapter 9. For now, we'll show you how to get started with a basic sync.

First, connect your iPhone and select it under iTunes. Browse over to the Photos tab and click the checkbox next to Sync Photos From. You'll want to pick either iPhoto, Aperture, or a folder on your hard drive. In this example, let's select iPhoto. Once that's done, you can select individual albums present in iPhoto. Even if you don't have any albums present, you'll still have the option of syncing your last roll (the last batch of photos you've imported into iPhoto), or the last 12 months, which contains every picture you've imported in the last year. After choosing the albums you want to sync, click Apply. iTunes will grab the photos out of these albums and resize them down to optimize storage space on your iPhone, while still keeping enough quality that you can zoom in when viewing them on your iPhone. The first sync will take a little while—thanks to the resizing—but future syncs won't need to re-resize unless you're importing new photos.

In the event that you don't like to use iPhoto or Aperture to manage your photos—or if you use some other photo album tool entirely—you're going to have to sync from a folder. In this case, follow the instructions for Windows users.

Sync Your Photos (Windows)

Unfortunately, Apple hasn't developed a photo management application like iPhoto for Windows that works with your iPhone, but you can still sync your photos from Photoshop Elements, Photoshop Album, or by using the folder method. It's much the same process.

First, connect your iPhone to your computer. Browse to your iPhone under iTunes, and then click on the Photos section. Figure 1-3 illustrates the Photos tab in iTunes. Now, you're going to want to choose a folder to sync photos from. Select any folder on your computer, and iTunes will give you a list of sub-folders. You can sync all photos in these folders, or select Selected Folders and pick and choose the folders you want synced. Once you're done, hit Apply and iTunes will start resizing the photos for a best-fit compromise between quality and space onto your iPhone.

FIGURE 1-3   The iTunes photo syncing screen

It may take a few minutes depending on how many photos you've got and how fast your computer is, but the whole process shouldn't take too long. To sync from either Photoshop Album or Photoshop Elements, just select that option instead of a folder, and choose the albums you want to sync.

If you're looking to sync photos that you've actually taken on your iPhone to your computer, see Chapter 9.

Sync Your Videos (Windows/Mac)

You've never seen a handheld gadget worth watching video on until the first time you watch a video on your iPhone's clean, crisp widescreen. Whether you've bought TV shows or movies through iTunes, or you've downloaded or made your own videos, syncing them to your iPhone is a snap.

> **TIP**   *Apple doesn't go out of its way to make it easy for you to convert your DVD collection or digital camera videos to use on your iPhone. Luckily there's a lot of free software available for both Windows and Mac that will do the trick, which we detail in Chapter 5.*

Plug in that iPhone, launch iTunes, and select your iPhone in the sidebar. Now locate and click on the tab labeled Video, as illustrated in Figure 1-4.

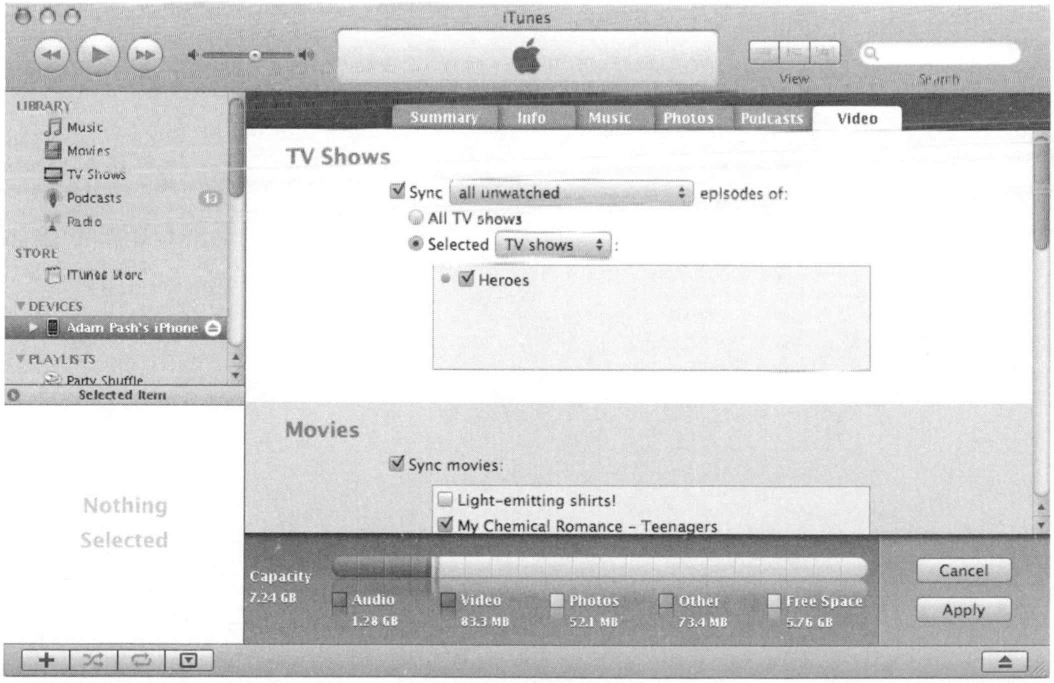

FIGURE 1-4   The iTunes video syncing screen

As you can see, iTunes lets you choose to sync TV shows and movies. In the TV Shows section, you can choose to sync a variety of combinations of unwatched or recent episodes. You can also sync only specific TV shows or video playlists.

If you're looking to sync other videos, you can pick and choose individual movies to sync to your iPhone in the Movies section. To do so, just tick the Sync Movies checkbox and pick and choose the movies you'd like to sync. Yes, it's that easy.

Finally, click the Apply button and wait as your iPhone fills up with every contact, appointment, song, photo, and video you've selected in iTunes. All of that information and media is now awaiting you on your new iPhone. Once you're done syncing, you'll be ready to disconnect the iPhone and take it out into the world.

In Chapter 2, you'll learn all the ins and outs of using your iPhone in its marquee capacity: as a full-featured cell phone.

Chapter 2

Learn to Use Your iPhone

How to...

- Turn your iPhone on and off
- Launch your iPhone's applications
- Make calls
- Type with the iPhone's keyboard
- Navigate, scroll, and zoom with multi-touch gestures
- Control the volume with hardware buttons
- Connect to a Wi-Fi hotspot

Now that you've got your iPhone up and running, you're ready to start using it. In this chapter we'll teach you everything you need to dive right in, from powering up your iPhone to connecting to a Wi-Fi hotspot and getting online. Let's start by turning it on.

Turn Your iPhone On and Off

Although the iPhone looks great even when it's not powered on, you'll find it's a lot more useful when it's turned on. Here's how you do it.

Switch Your iPhone On

To turn the iPhone on, hold the top power button for half a second (this is the top button shown in Figure 2-1). When the Apple logo shows up on the screen, you'll know the phone is on and you can let go of the button. It takes a few more seconds for the iPhone to get to a state where you can actually do anything with it, but it doesn't require any more user-input until then. Unlike other phones, which sometimes require you to hold the power button down until you're sure the phone is on, it only takes a half a second to see that the iPhone is on.

Switch Your iPhone Off

Turning your phone off follows the same basic steps as turning it on, but there's an added step. From any screen (even if the phone is locked and there's nothing on the screen), hold down the power button for three seconds. A new screen will pop up with the words "slide to power off" and a red arrow. Place your finger on the arrow and slide it to the right—all the way to the end— to turn the phone off. If you accidentally held down the power button by mistake and didn't mean to turn the phone off, it's OK! Just hit the Cancel button on the bottom of the screen to go back to whatever you were doing.

NOTE   *The On/Off button can also be used to direct calls. This is an advanced feature we'll talk about in Chapter 3.*

FIGURE 2-1   The iPhone's hardware buttons. The On/Off switch sits on top, and the mute switch is on the side, above the volume up and down buttons.

Lock and Unlock Your iPhone

Locking your iPhone is a great way to save power and to reduce accidental key-presses, which can still occasionally happen even though your iPhone uses cutting-edge multi-touch technology instead of traditional hardware buttons. To lock the phone, press the On/Off button (the top button in Figure 2-1) and then let go immediately. That's it! Simple!

To unlock your phone, either press the On/Off button again or press the Home button (see Figure 2-4). The standby screen will come up, displaying the time, the date, and a slider with the words "slide to unlock." as shown in Figure 2-2. Take your finger, place it on the gray button, and then slide it all the way to the right side of the screen. Make sure to keep your finger on the screen until you reach the end of the slider. Lifting your finger before you reach the end of the slider will send the button back to the starting position.

You don't have to remember to lock the phone all the time to avoid unintended key presses or to save battery. After a minute, the iPhone locks itself. If one minute is too short for you, you can adjust the automatic lock time in one minute intervals; the minimum is one minute and the maximum is five minutes. Or, you can turn off auto-locking completely, which means the phone will only lock when you manually lock it.

How to ... Reset an Unresponsive iPhone

If your iPhone locks up and is unresponsive for any reason, there are a couple of ways to remedy the situation. First, try holding the Home button for six seconds until the application quits. If that doesn't work, you can reset the phone by pressing and holding both the On/Off button and the Home button simultaneously for 10 seconds or until the Apple logo appears on the screen.

TIP *If you want an added level of security on the phone to prevent unauthorized calls, you can also set the iPhone to ask for a four-digit PIN when it's unlocked. See Chapter 12 to find out how to do this.*

FIGURE 2-2   The unlock slider

Launch Your iPhone's Applications

Apple took great pains to make the iPhone work as intuitively as possible, and nowhere is this more evident than your iPhone's home screen. You can think of the iPhone home screen like you do the desktop of other operating systems; the icons you see on the home screen are like shortcuts for running the applications on your iPhone. Here's how you launch an application.

Launch an Application

You can launch any of the iPhone's 16 default applications from the home screen, and doing this is as simple as a press of the finger. If you just turned on your iPhone, the home screen is the first screen you will see. It contains 16 small icons representing all of your iPhone applications and looks just like Figure 2-3. To launch an application, just tap any of those icons with the tip of your finger. The application icon will dim when you first press it, then launch the instant you release your finger. If you pressed the wrong application icon by mistake, just slide your finger to the side—without lifting it—until the icon is no longer dimmed and then let go.

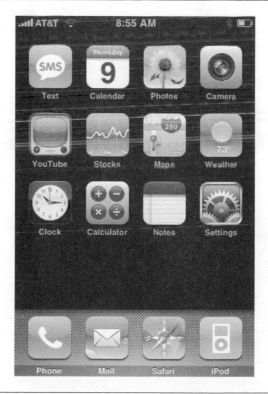

FIGURE 2-3   The iPhone's home screen

Yes, it really is that simple. There's no reason for you to go digging through menus or searching through folders for the appropriate application on the iPhone. All you need is right there on the home screen, and each application will launch as soon as you tap the respective application icon.

Return to the Home Screen

After you've launched an application, you may notice that there's no Close button anywhere in the application interface; at least not in the traditional sense you've gotten used to with desktop operating systems like Windows and OS X. That's because you never need to close applications on your iPhone. So how do you get back to the Home screen?

Actually, you've got an entire hardware key dedicated to your Home screen located at the bottom center of the front of your iPhone (see Figure 2-4). Any time you want to leave the application you're currently viewing, launch another application, or check out some of the other information available on the home screen (like the number of missed calls, unread emails, and SMS messages—more on this later), just press the Home button.

The application that you were viewing will shrink into the distance with a slick animation, and your Home screen will return to the foreground. From here, you can go ahead and launch any of your iPhone's other applications. What you've done is effectively minimize the application, in the traditional sense, because the next time you launch that first application it will remember where you were working—and even what you were typing.

FIGURE 2-4   The iPhone's Home button

NOTE

It's common among Windows and Mac users to close applications we're not using to save memory and keep our computers running smoothly. Though this is a good habit on a traditional computer, it's one you need not worry about on your iPhone. Programs are never closed, and you shouldn't worry about closing them to save memory. In the interest of simplicity, you needn't worry about anything other than launching whatever application you want when you want it. Leave the memory management to other smart phones!

Make and Take Calls

Now that you know how to launch an application, we're going to show you how to make and take calls.

Make a Call

To make a call, unlock your iPhone, go to the home screen, and press the green Phone button with the image of a white phone receiver on the bottom left. To get to the screen where you can actually dial a number, take a look at the bottom row of five icons. You'll see Favorites, Recents, Contacts, Keypad, and Voicemail. Hit the Keypad button and a large numeric dial pad will show up (see Figure 2-5). This is where your iPhone simulates the hardware keypad found on traditional phones.

Making a call from this screen is simple. Just press down on any key, just as if you were pressing an actual physical button, and the number will register on the screen above the keypad. It's easy to see what number you're dialing because the iPhone will display all the numbers you've previously punched in. If you make a mistake, it's also easy to go back and delete numbers by pressing the delete button, which looks like an arrow with an X through it on the bottom right (again, see Figure 2-5). Press it once and let go to delete one digit; hold it down to delete multiple digits. Once you have the number you want to call up on the screen, click the green Call button. To hang up, hit the giant red End Call button on the bottom.

Take a Call

It's just as easy to take an incoming call. If your phone is locked when it starts to ring, you'll see a call screen with a green slider button on the bottom that says "slide to answer." Use your fingertip to slide the green button all the way to the right to accept the call and then start talking. If you're already using your phone when a call comes in, you'll see two buttons instead: a red Decline button and a green Answer button (see Figure 2-6). To take the call and start talking, hit Answer. To decline the call and send it directly to your voicemail, hit Decline.

CAUTION

If you're actively using your Internet connection over EDGE, you run the risk of missing incoming calls. While you're transferring data over EDGE, any incoming calls will automatically be routed to your voicemail. This is why we recommend connecting to a Wi-Fi network when possible, because this is an EDGE-only problem. See the section at the end of this chapter to learn how to connect to a Wi-Fi hotspot.

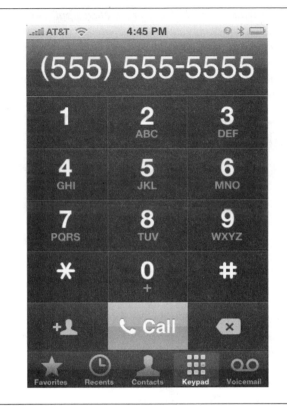

FIGURE 2-5   The keypad

We've just scratched the surface of making and taking calls with your iPhone. See Chapter 3 to learn how to set up your Visual Voicemail, make calls from your contact list, and much more.

Type with the iPhone's Keyboard

Your iPhone keeps close tabs on what you're doing, and any time you need to input text, the iPhone's adaptable software keyboard will slide up from the bottom of the screen with a truly brilliant touch-sensitive keyboard. Typing with this software keyboard works much like launching applications on your iPhone. It's just a matter of pressing your fingertip to the keys one by one.

To start out, we recommend that you type holding the iPhone with one hand and press the keys with the index finger of your other hand. When you press down on a key, you'll see a magnified version of the key above your finger, which is designed to give you a better view of the key-press that will be made if you pull your finger off the keyboard. If the magnified key isn't what you meant

FIGURE 2-6   The incoming call screen

to press, you can reposition your finger on the keyboard until the appropriate key is magnified. Just make sure you don't lift your finger from the keyboard until you see the key you want.

TIP   *Actually, your iPhone's keyboard is smart. Even if you mis-key a letter or three, your iPhone's predictive text feature will make its best guess at what you meant to spell. This makes typing quickly on your iPhone an easy prospect... it just requires a little trust. See more on predictive typing in Chapter 14.*

The advantage of the software keyboard is that it adapts to the environment in which you're using it. In the Safari web browser, for example, you get a key dedicated to typing **.com** at the end of URLs. (I'd like to see the iPhone's hardware keyboard counterparts compete with that!) Your keyboard will change slightly depending on the application and context, but in all of your typing environments, the first keyboard you'll see uses the ubiquitous computer-style keyboard (called the QWERTY keyboard after the first six keys in the top row) you're used to using on your PC or Mac. If you need to type punctuation or numbers you don't see on the first keyboard, you can access more characters at any time by pressing the button to the left of your space key. In most cases, the key will have .?123 on it, as you see in Figure 2-7. After you toggle keyboards, the new keyboard will remain on screen until you toggle back to the QWERTY keyboard (the button will now have ABC on it) or you hit the space bar (in which case it automatically returns to the QWERTY layout).

Once you've mastered these basic steps, you should be more than proficient enough with your iPhone's keyboard to get around easily on your iPhone.

NOTE *A lot has been said about the iPhone's software keyboard, some of it good, much of it bad. If you're like me, the keyboard was a source of some stress when you decided to buy your iPhone, since a good hardware keyboard can be a wonderful thing. If you've worried like I did, lay your fears to rest. The iPhone's adaptable software keyboard is fantastic. However, if you've spent a lot of time with the keyboard but you don't feel like you're getting the hang of it—or you just want to check out various methods for honing your keyboard skills and speed—check out Chapter 14.*

FIGURE 2-7   The standard iPhone keyboard

Navigate, Scroll, and Zoom with Multi-Touch Gestures

One of the reasons why the iPhone is so easy and intuitive to use is the multi-touch gesture system, which lets you interact with your iPhone using just the tips of your fingers. Here is how you use gestures (beyond basic pointing) to get around the iPhone.

> **TIP** *The iPhone uses a conductive technology to detect presses on the screen. That means it works great with your fingers, but not at all with a pencil or a stylus, which is the pointer you usually use on other smartphones.*

Swipe and Flick to Scroll

Any time you're looking at a list on your phone—the recent call list, SMS messages, emails, or a web page, for example—you'll have to scroll. But there's no scroll bar like on your computer! Apple's made it even simpler than that. You can simply just swipe or flick your finger across the screen to scroll around.

Swipe Your Finger to Scroll

Swiping is the basic way to navigate lists and menus in your iPhone. Here's an example of how you swipe.

First, open up Google Maps. Once the map is finished loading, place your finger onto any part of the screen (in the map section) and then move it in any direction. You'll notice that the map moves along with your finger, as if you're sliding it around on your desk. If you move your finger to the right, the map moves to the right and what was left of the map before will come into view. You can do this in any direction and the map will scroll with you, such as your Contacts list in the Phone app, you'll only be able to scroll up and down. But the theory is the same. Just hold down on any part of the list and move up and down to scroll, as shown in Figure 2-8. The arrows indicate an upward and downward motion one would use when swiping.

> **TIP** *If you have a hard time getting the hang of the swipe, just think of the map in the previous example as a piece of paper on your desk. Swiping your iPhone works just like putting your finger on that piece of paper and moving it around your desktop.*

Flick Your Finger to Quickly Glide Through Lists

To get around even faster than scrolling, you have the option of *flicking*. This is how flicking works.

Open up any application where you've got a big list of items, such as your phone contacts. Like swiping, you start by putting your finger down on any part of the list. Now, quickly move your finger either up or down and let go. You'll notice the list zooming either up or down in the direction that you just flicked. It can be hard to see exactly where you're going, so flicking is best for getting from one place in a list to another very fast. However, the speed at which your iPhone will scroll when you flick depends on the speed of your flick, so a quick flick will jump through content quickly, while a slow, gentle flick will scroll slowly when you let go. If you want more precision in your navigation, you'll have to switch to the swipe method.

FIGURE 2-8   Swiping the screen to scroll

Zoom In and Out by Pinching

Although the iPhone's screen is large, it's still quite small if you compare it to an actual computer monitor. This is why Apple made it easy to zoom in and out of photos, maps, and web pages, so you can get a better iPhone-sized look at content.

To give it a try, open up your Photos application, choose one of your albums and open up a photo. If you don't have any photos, open up Google Maps instead. Once you're in, take your thumb and pointer finger and place them onto the screen. To zoom out, pinch your fingers together, as shown in Figure 2-9. To zoom in, spread your fingers apart. You can continue doing this as long as there's enough room on the screen to move your fingers. If you run out of room, lift up, place them on the screen and then spread/pinch again. There's usually a maximum and minimum limit that you can zoom in and out, and you'll notice when you've hit the cap when the map or picture stops getting bigger or smaller.

FIGURE 2-9   Pinching to zoom out of a picture

Some people aren't comfortable with the thumb and index finger pinch. If you're one of those people, you can just as easily perform the "pinch" by using your index and middle finger—or any other combination of fingertips on either hand, for that matter. As long as you spread your fingers apart or bring them closer together, the iPhone will still zoom the content.

Control the Volume with Hardware Buttons

Like any cell phone worth its salt, your iPhone comes with dedicated hardware buttons along the left side of the phone dedicated to volume control. However, Apple has thrown in a few creative takes on how you can manipulate the volume on your iPhone.

Volume Rocker

Quite simply, the Volume Rocker button on the left side of your iPhone (see Figure 2-1) adjusts the volume of the currently active application. That means that the volume rocker can adjust the volume of your iPhone's notifications (including ringtones for incoming calls, alarms, and email and SMS notifications), as well as for the iPod and YouTube.

As you would expect, pressing up on the Volume Rocker will increase the volume, while pressing down will decrease your volume. Unless you're playing media with your iPod or videos with YouTube, any volume adjustments you make with the volume rocker will apply to the system-wide notifications mentioned previously. However, you can be sure you're changing the notification volume when you see the word Ringer on the top of the volume graphic that appears when you adjust the volume, as shown in Figure 2-10.

If your iPod is playing, the volume rocker will adjust the iPod volume regardless of whether or not the iPod application is active. On the other hand, the volume rocker will adjust the volume in YouTube only if YouTube is active and playing a video. No matter what volume needs adjusting, the volume rocker button will generally be the quickest and easiest way to adjust the volume on your iPhone.

FIGURE 2-10   The volume meter and mute

Silence Your Phone with the Mute Switch

At one point or another, we've all been that unlucky person in the movie theater who forgot to turn off our ringer and ended up embarrassing ourselves and our loved ones. To facilitate a quick and easy mute of your iPhone's ringer, Apple has integrated an ingenious mute switch to the iPhone just above the Volume Rocker (see Figure 2-1). Flicking the switch down mutes your ringer volume instantaneously, like in Figure 2-10; flicking it back up restores your volume.

CAUTION   *The Mute switch only mutes certain notifications, namely your ringer, SMS, and email alerts. By default, an incoming phone call, new text message, or new email will vibrate your phone when the mute switch is flipped. However the mute switch will not mute the iPod, YouTube videos, or alarms. That means that if you have an alarm set to go off in the middle of a movie, the mute switch won't silence it. If you set a lot of alarms, be sure to keep this in mind.*

If you want to turn specific alerts like email, voicemail, or text messages on and off, see Chapter 12.

Connect to a Wi-Fi Hotspot

Several of your iPhone's applications connect to the Internet in order to work—it's a breakthrough Internet communicator, after all. Connecting to a Wi-Fi hotspot—either at home, at work, or at an Internet cafe—is simple.

TIP   *When you're on-the-go, AT&T's EDGE network gives you access to the Internet when a Wi-Fi hotspot is unavailable. We recommend that you use Wi-Fi instead of EDGE whenever possible, because it's tens of times faster and won't interfere with incoming calls like an active EDGE connection will.*

Did you know?   Wi-Fi Is Much Faster Than EDGE

AT&T's EDGE (Enhanced Data Rates for GSM Evolution) is a modified 2G network protocol with data speeds of up to 200 kbit/second; whereas, Wi-Fi (Wireless Fidelity) or Wireless Local-Area Network (WLAN) can support data speeds from 4 Mbits/second up to 74 Mbits/second. Essentially, Wi-Fi can be up to 30-35x faster than EDGE, but typically averages closer to 15-20x. As you may already know, distances and signal strength directly influence Wi-Fi data transfer speeds.

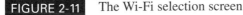

FIGURE 2-11 The Wi-Fi selection screen

First, go to the iPhone Settings app (third row, last icon on the right in Figure 2-3) and select Wi-Fi. Then make sure the switch to the right of the Wi-Fi setting says ON. Next, a list of Wi-Fi access points will show up below, allowing you to access the one you want, as shown in Figure 2-11. Choose the network you want and, if it's a secure network, you'll be prompted to enter a WEP, WPA, or WPA2 key. If you don't know the password, ask your network administrator or the person responsible for the Wi-Fi hotspot.

Once you're connected, you should see the EDGE icon (a letter E) on the upper left of your iPhone change to a Wi-Fi icon, which looks like a series of waves or a slice of pizza. The number of waves, or bars, determines how strong the connection is (just like cell phone signal bars), and if you're only getting one or two, you can try to move closer to the access point or connect to a stronger one.

NOTE *Your iPhone can support WEP, WPA, and WPA2 encryption, and will automatically detect the type of encryption that your access point is using. In the case of WEP encryption, you may have to change between a WEP Password and a WEP hex or ASCII password. See Chapter 12 for more information on advanced Wi-Fi connections.*

Now that you're familiar enough with your iPhone to start using all the applications, let's find out how to make calls like a pro.

Chapter 3

Organize Contacts, Make Calls, Use Voicemail, and More

How to …

- Sync, manage, navigate, and call contacts
- Manage and return recent calls
- Manage and call favorites
- Receive calls
- Set up and use Visual Voicemail
- Adjust call settings to suit your needs
- Use advanced calling features

By now you have already activated and learned the basics for navigating your iPhone. That means it's time to dive into each of your iPhone's applications in-depth, starting with the phone application. In this chapter, we'll show you how to work with your contacts, make and answer calls, and set up and use Visual Voicemail. Finally, we'll cover several advanced tips for making the most of your phone.

Sync, Manage, Navigate, and Call Contacts

Your iPhone provides access to your contacts in ways no other phone has ever dreamed of. In the following sections, we'll discuss several ways to get your contacts from your computer onto your phone, navigate and organize your contacts, edit contact information, and perhaps most importantly, actually call your contacts. To get started, open your iPhone's Home screen and launch the Phone app (the green icon with the white image of a phone on the bottom left of the phone, shown highlighted in Figure 3-1).

Sync Contacts Between Your iPhone and Your Computer

We covered the basics of syncing in Chapter 2, but now we'll dive into the details of managing your contacts on your computer and then syncing them onto your iPhone.

Set Up Sync Options

Before you perform your first sync, you need to set up when and how you're going to sync your iPhone to your computer.

Set Up Automatic/Manual Sync Options   To make iTunes automatically sync your iPhone whenever it's connected to your computer, connect your iPhone, open iTunes, and go to the Summary tab. Then check the option that says Automatically Sync When this iPhone is Connected. To prevent iTunes from automatically syncing, make sure this option shown in Figure 3-2, is unchecked.

FIGURE 3-1 The phone app icon

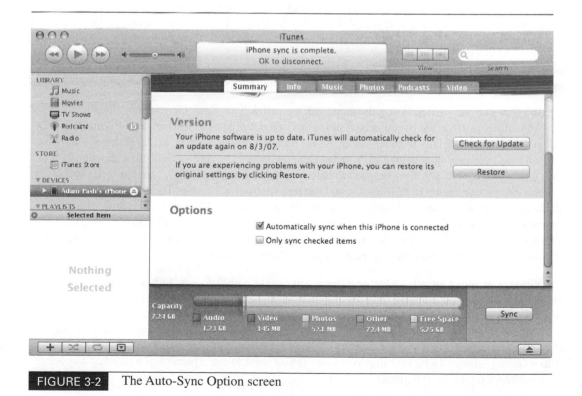

FIGURE 3-2 The Auto-Sync Option screen

If you want to ensure that no iPhones are automatically synced to this computer, open up iTunes preferences and go to the iPhone tab. Then, check the option that says Disable Automatic Syncing for All iPhones. Since you need to now manually sync your iPhone, you will need to go to one of the tabs in iTunes that belongs to your iPhone (such as Summary, Info, Music, Photos, and so on) and click Sync when you want to sync.

TIP   *You can stop iTunes from automatically syncing with your iPhone for the next sync by holding down a set of keys while you connect the phone. On Macs, hold down Command and Option. On Windows, hold down Shift and Control.*

Sync Contacts from Address Book on the Mac

For those of you not familiar with it, Address Book is the default contact management software for all Macs, and it comes pre-installed with every copy of OS X. If you want tight contact integration with other applications in OS X, this is the application you should use. Here's an example of what we mean by tight integration. If you create a contact for your Mom and add her picture to her contact picture section, whenever you receive an email from Mom, you'll see the same picture of her in the top right corner of the message. Also, if you're using iChat to talk to your mom, her icon will show up there as well. Naturally, your Mom's picture will also appear on your iPhone whenever she calls you!

First let's start up Address Book. Make sure you're in the correct view, as shown in Figure 3-3, by clicking View in the top menu bar and then by clicking Card and Columns. You'll notice that each contact is called a Card, and your Address Book is made up of a series of cards (like cards in a Rolodex).

NOTE   *You can actually sync contacts from multiple computers onto the same iPhone. This is covered later in the chapter, under Sync Contacts with Multiple Computers.*

Create a New Contact   Click File in the menu bar, then click New Card. Or you can click the + button underneath the list of contacts. A new empty card will appear, as you see in Figure 3-3, and you can enter in details like their name, phone numbers, email address, postal address, job title, and the company they belong to. You can even customize the type of fields that show up in each contact card, so if you have no need to enter in information on people's assistant's names or the phonetic pronunciation of their names, you can remove those altogether. The good thing is that all the contact fields present in Address Book are supported in your iPhone. So everything you enter here will be visible in their contact entry on the iPhone as well. Once you're finished entering in information, click the Edit button below your contact to finish editing. If you decide you want to add or change some details, click the Edit button again and resume editing.

Add Pictures to Your Contacts   One neat thing you can do with Address Book is to add a contact picture to each of your contacts. The result is that whenever you make or take calls from a contact with an assigned picture, you'll see that picture on your iPhone. Seeing pictures of your contacts when they call is an easy way to quickly know who's calling (and to avoid accidentally answering the call if you owe them money). Contact pictures don't have to be of the person who's calling—they can be anything you want. If you want to use a picture of a monkey as your boss's contact photo, be our guest!

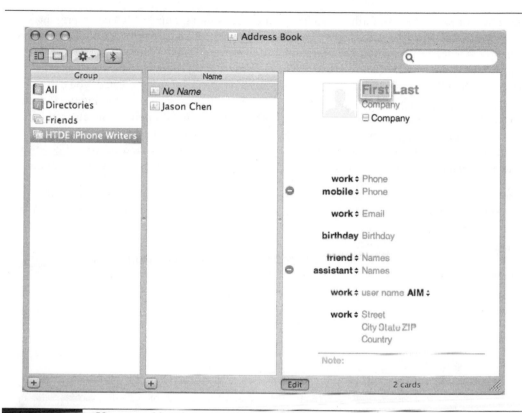

FIGURE 3-3   You can add and manage your contacts on your Mac using Address Book.

To add a picture, open up the contact entry in your Address Book and click the Edit button. Now double click on the outline of a person next to the contact's name. This will pop up a new window that lets you either drag a photo in or, if you have a newer Mac with a built-in iSight webcam, take a snapshot of something in front of your computer with it. In this case, we want to choose a picture. Open Finder and go to the location where you've stored the picture you want to use. Drag the file over to the square above the words Drag Image Here. Once you drop the image there, you'll get the option of choosing exactly how you want the image framed. You can either have the picture cropped tightly to a person's face, or have it contain their whole body.

TIP   *Adding contact pictures with Address Book works, but actually results in a smaller picture than if you add a contact picture on your iPhone. If you add a picture in Address Book, the icon will only be small enough to show up in the top right corner during a call. If you add it on your iPhone from the Photo application, the picture will take up the entire middle portion of the screen. It's up to you to decide whether you want large or small pictures. See Chapter 9 if you want to find out how to assign contact photos from your phone.*

Create a New Group You can further organize your contacts into groups, which can represent anything you want. Possible groups could be your family, your friends, your work, the members of your sports team, or a bunch of local restaurants around your home. We'll make a new group.

Click File in the menu bar and click New Group. Now a new group will be created and the name will be highlighted so you can type in a new name. Once the group is created, you can rename the group by double clicking on the group name or clicking once and pressing the Return key. You can add a new contact to your group either by dragging and dropping contacts from all contacts to your new group or by selecting the group and then clicking the small plus sign (+) under the list of contact names. Using groups is a good way to filter your view on your iPhone so you can see a list of your local restaurants if you're trying to think of a place to eat, for example.

Choose Which Contacts to Sync Once you've created enough contacts to represent everybody and everything you know, you're ready to sync. It's much the same process that we've detailed in Chapter 2, but now you should actually have groups to sync. Connect your iPhone, go to iTunes and click on the Info tab as shown in Figure 3-4. Here you can choose to either sync all your contacts or just specific groups. Even if you decide to sync all your contacts to your iPhone, you can filter your view by groups later, so don't feel that you'll have to wade through hundreds of contacts every time you want to find a specific person.

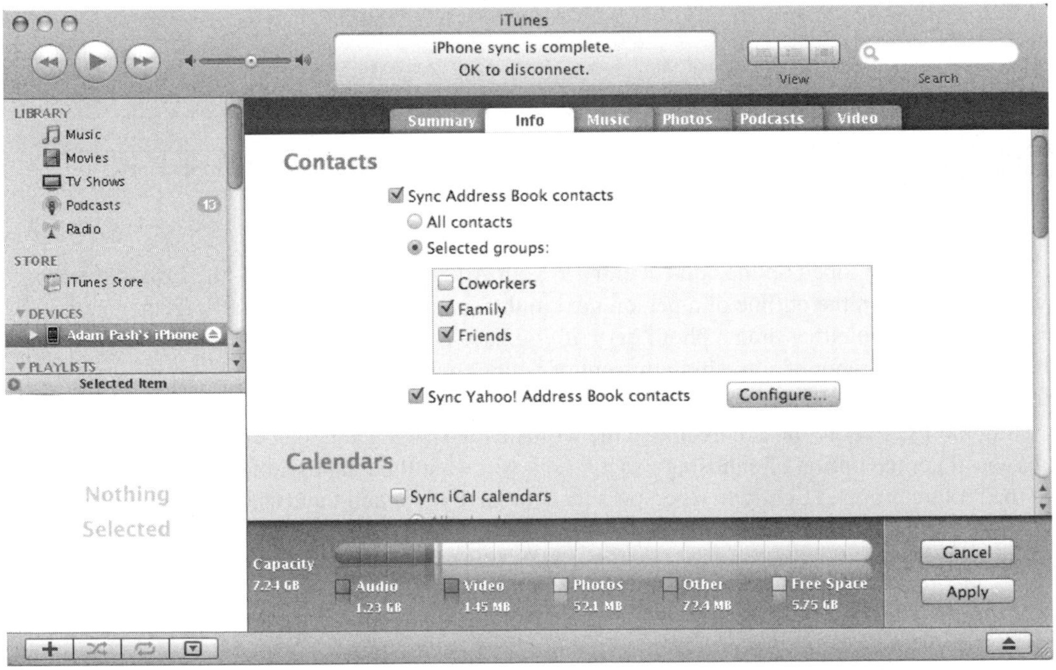

FIGURE 3-4 You can choose which contacts to sync in the iTunes Info tab.

To sync, click the Sync button on the bottom right (or Apply button, if you've changed settings). Once it's done syncing, you'll have all of the contacts you created on your Mac on your iPhone.

> **NOTE**   *We've run into some instances where moving contacts between groups in Address Book won't move them around on the iPhone, even after multiple syncs. If this happens to you, check the box labeled Override contacts on next sync and iTunes will wipe out all contacts on your iPhone and do a fresh sync. This will make sure the contact list on your phone is an exact duplicate of what's on your Mac.*

Sync Contacts Back to Your Address Book   If you've made changes to your contacts on your iPhone—or added an entirely new contact—you'll want that to be duplicated on your Mac as well. This is simple. Just plug your iPhone in and initiate a sync. If you have automatic syncing enabled, your iPhone will automatically sync contacts between your iPhone and your computer.

Sync Contacts from Entourage on Mac

Entourage is Microsoft's Outlook-like suite for managing contacts, emails, calendars and tasks. It works well with Word and Excel, which are all a part of Office 2004 for Mac. In order to get Entourage to sync with your iPhone, you actually have to go through Address Book first. Don't worry, though; it's simple.

Configure Entourage to Sync with Address Book   To sync Entourage with Address Book, just open it, click Entourage in the menu bar, and then click Preferences. Once the Preferences window is open as shown in Figure 3-5, click on Sync Services and check the box next to

How to ...   Use Address Book Keyboard Shortcuts

You can use Mac OS X's shortcuts to get around Address Book faster. Here are some convenient ones you might find useful:

- **COMMAND + N**   Creates a new contact
- **COMMAND + SHIFT + N**   Creates a new group
- **COMMAND + OPTION + N**   Creates a new smart group
- **COMMAND + L**   Toggles Edit mode
- **COMMAND +], COMMAND + [**   Goes to the next and previous contact in your contact list

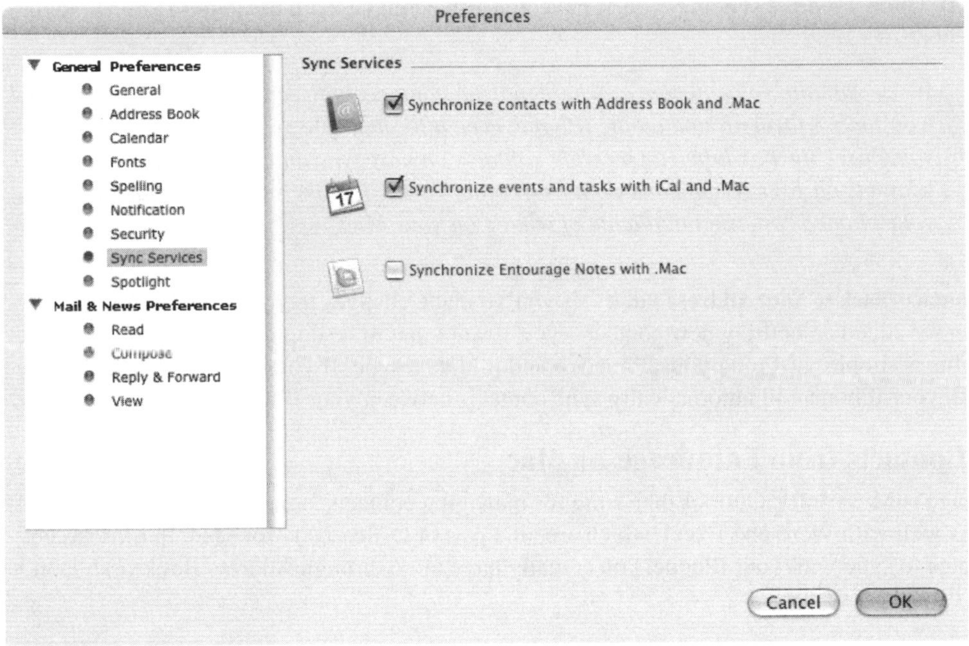

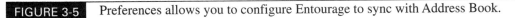

FIGURE 3-5 Preferences allows you to configure Entourage to sync with Address Book.

Synchronize contacts with Address Book and .Mac, then click the OK button. You'll be asked whether you want to replace all contacts in Entourage with Address Book, whether you want to replace all contacts in Address Book with Entourage, or merge the two together. You usually want to choose to merge the two unless you're sure you want to get rid of contacts in one (perhaps they're outdated). In that case you should overwrite that one with the one you pick. Choose carefully, as this could wipe out your contacts if you accidentally pick the wrong option. After a minute or two, it will be finished syncing, and you will have copied your contacts from Entourage into Address Book and be able to sync them to your iPhone.

Create a New Contact Creating new contacts in Entourage is easy, and is usually much faster than creating them all in your iPhone—even if you have mastered typing on its virtual keyboard. To start, open Entourage and click on Address Book. Now click on the File in the menu bar, then New, and then Contact. A new contact form will pop up, where you can type in the name, email, phone number, and address information. When you're finished, either click the Save & Close button at the top, or the Save & New button if you want to enter in another contact immediately afterwards. We'll assume this is the only contact you want to add for now (feel free to keep adding if there are more). After a few seconds, your new contact will automatically show up in Address Book. If you're done and want to move on to sync your contact to your iPhone, you can close Entourage and the two programs will immediately sync.

Did you know?

Entourage Doesn't Do Everything Address Book Can

Although Entourage can match Address Book's basic functionality in creating and editing contacts, there are some things it can't do. For example, if you add a contact picture to Entourage, it won't sync through and duplicate into Address Book. Contact groups (either Groups or Categories in Entourage) won't sync over to Address Book either. We recommend using Address Book to organize your contacts in order to get a better sync with the iPhone, but if you need to use Entourage for certain reasons, you can also do some rearranging in Address Book after the fact to accomplish the same goals. It's just slightly more of a hassle to have to manage your contacts in two places.

Choose Which Contacts to Sync   Even though you're using Entourage instead of Address Book, you can still choose between syncing all your contacts or only specific groups. To do this, you'll have to use Address Book to manage your groups. See the section covering Address Book syncing to learn how to do this.

Sync Contacts with Your iPhone   You're all ready to sync your contacts with your iPhone. All you have to do is plug in the iPhone, go to iTunes, and click on the Info tab. Now click on the Sync button and wait while your contacts are first swapped between your phone and Address Book, and then synced to Entourage. If you've made changes in your iPhone, such as adding or editing a contact, those changes will be imported into your computer as well.

Sync Contacts with Outlook 2007 on Windows

Microsoft Outlook comes bundled with the Microsoft Office suite of software, so if you've got Office installed and you're using it to manage contacts and/or email, this is the program you'll want to use to sync contacts to your iPhone.

Create a New Contact   To create a new contact in Outlook 2007, go to the File menu, select New, and the choose Contact (or press CTRL + SHIFT + C). In the new contact window, as shown in Figure 3-6, add all of the information you want to your contact. While not all of the info will sync to your iPhone (some of the more esoteric fields are left out), the important stuff like email and phone number definitely will. When you're finished, click the Save and Close button.

NOTE   *Unlike most of the other sync options, Outlook 2007 does not sync contact groups as of this writing. If you want to organize contacts with groups, consider using Outlook Express or Windows Mail to manage your contacts.*

Sync Contacts with Your iPhone   To sync your Outlook 2007 contacts to your iPhone, plug in your phone and open up iTunes. In the Info tab of the iPhone section, check the box labeled Sync Contacts From and then choose Outlook from the drop-down list.

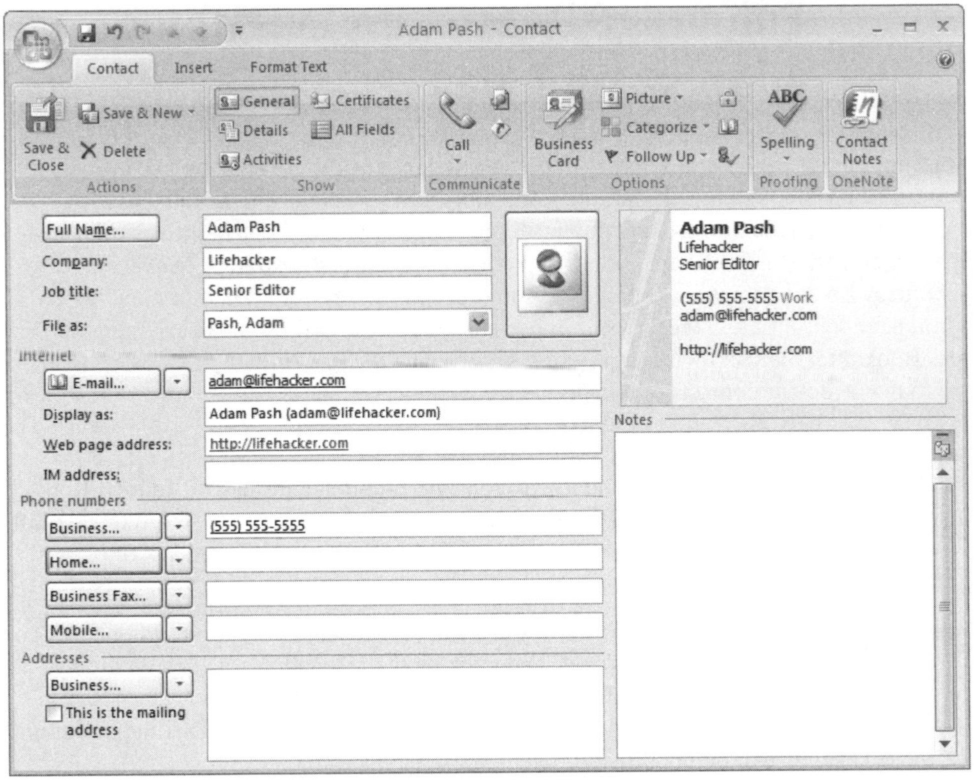

| FIGURE 3-6 | Creating multiple new contacts in Outlook is faster and easier than creating them on the iPhone. |

Sync Contacts Back to Outlook 2007   Any time you make changes to your contacts on your iPhone, you can easily sync this information back to Outlook as soon as you plug your phone back in. If you've set up automatic syncing, Outlook and your iPhone will sync as soon as you plug in the phone. Otherwise, select the Info tab and click the Sync button to manually initiate a sync.

Sync Contacts with Outlook Express and Windows Mail on Windows

Windows XP and Windows Vista both come with free contact and email applications called Outlook Express and Windows Mail, respectively. Either program works nicely with your iPhone for syncing and managing your contacts—and they work in basically the same way.

Create a New Contact   To create a new contact in Outlook Express or Windows Mail, go to the File menu, select New, and then click Contact. You can now fill in the information in the New Contact Properties window. The first tab of this window is for name and email address information; you can enter addresses and phone numbers for your home and business, as well as other pieces of data in subsequent tabs. Most of this contact information will incorporate with your iPhone (with the exception of a few more esoteric fields), so fill out as much as you can to create robust contacts for your iPhone.

Create a New Contact Group Contact groups offer a simple way to organize a large contact list into more granular, easy-to-access lists on your iPhone. You can organize groups in simple terms, like Friends and Coworkers, or you can get more specific and create contacts for restaurants or movie theaters.

To set up a contact group in Outlook Express, go to Tools and select Address Book (or press CTRL + SHIFT + B). If you're on Windows Vista with Windows Mail, select Tools and then Windows Contacts (or press CTRL + SHIFT + C). You'll now see your desktop address book full of your contacts. Click the button labeled New and select New Group... from the contact list. Then give your group a name and begin selecting and adding members to the group by clicking the Select Members button. You can see this process in effect in Figure 3-7. Next time you sync your iPhone contacts, you'll see a separate group from All Contacts which contains your newly created group and group contacts.

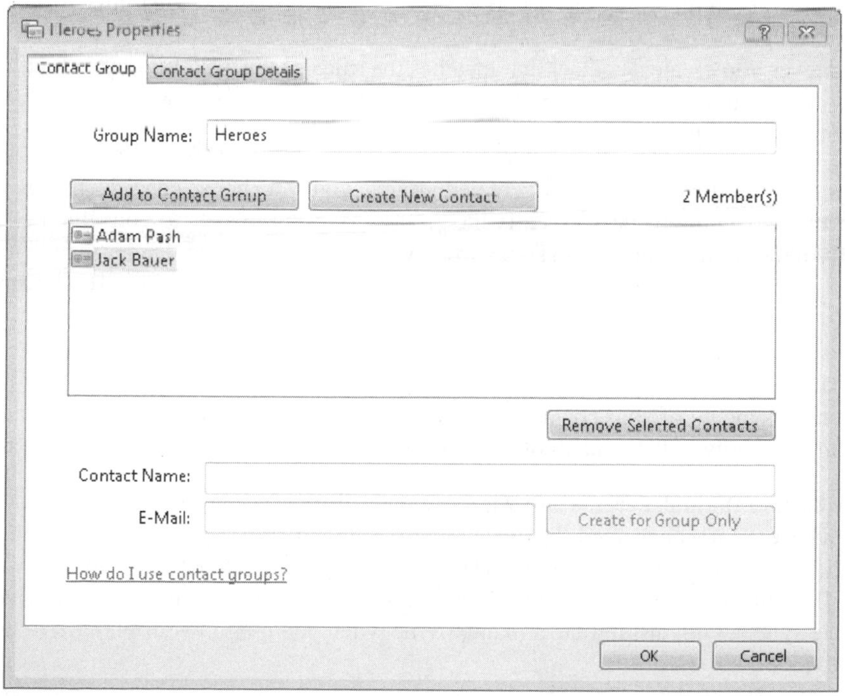

FIGURE 3-7   Windows Contacts is the only place in Windows Vista that you can make and assign groups to your iPhone contacts.

TIP

Under Windows Vista, Windows Contacts are stored inside a folder structure. When you open Windows Contacts, make sure you're inside the Contacts view or you won't be able to create new contacts or contact groups. To confirm, right-click on any blank portion of the right side of the contacts window (where the contacts reside), then click Customize This Folder.... Once there, click on the Customize tab and make sure the Use This Folder Type as a Template: dropdown says Contacts.

Create a New Smart Contact Group   In addition to having static, regular contact groups, Address Book can create smart contact groups as well. What's the difference? For example, smart groups can automatically be set to include all of your contacts with a specific company field, allowing you to easily have a group that always includes your company's contacts as long as you set their field correctly. Other examples are creating contact groups that filters by specific city, phone numbers, or names.

To start, click File, then New Smart Group. Now pick a name for your group and enter it in. Under Contains Cards Which Match the Following, you have the choice of picking one or more rules that Address Book will match when it decides which contacts should belong in this group. Choose an entry in the first drop-down, an inclusion/exclusion type in the second dropdown, and type in what you want in the third box. If you want another row to further customize the rules, click the + button on the right. Click OK when you're finished.

Now whenever you create a contact that matches the rules of this smart group, it will automatically be added. If you've chosen the option to highlight the group when updated, you'll get a small notification when this happens as well.

Choose Which Contacts to Sync   If you've created groups, you can choose specific groups you want to sync and leave out others. To specify the groups you want to sync to your iPhone, go to the Info tab in the iPhone section of iTunes when your phone is docked. Under the Contacts section, check the box labeled Sync contacts from and choose Windows Address Book from the drop-down list if you're syncing Outlook Express; choose Windows Contacts if you want to sync with Windows Mail contacts in Vista. Next select the radio button labeled Selected Groups and check the boxes next to all the groups you want to sync.

If you want to sync all of your contacts, just select the All Contacts radio button. Whatever you choice, hit the Apply button and all of your chosen contacts will sync up to your iPhone.

Sync Contacts Back to Outlook Express and Windows Mail   If you've chosen to automatically sync your iPhone whenever it's connected (by checking the Automatically Sync When This iPhone Is Connected check box in the Summary tab in iTunes), any time you edit or add contacts on your iPhone, they'll seamlessly sync back to your desktop when you plug in your iPhone. If you don't have automatic sync set up, just initiate a manual sync when you plug in your phone by clicking the Sync button.

Sync Contacts with Yahoo Address Book on Mac and Windows

Another option for syncing your contacts, besides using the desktop software mentioned previously, is Yahoo Address Book. Yahoo's Address Book is tied into Yahoo's Webmail program, and is an online-only system for managing your contacts. It's possible to sync with Yahoo Address Book in addition to the Mac contact managers, making it a convenient way to back up your contacts as well. If you're running Windows, you'll have to choose between Yahoo Address Book and your other desktop solutions.

Enable Syncing with Yahoo Address Book   To turn on Yahoo Address Book syncing, plug in your iPhone, go to iTunes, and click on the Info tab. Now check the box next to Sync Yahoo Address Book contacts on your Mac or choose Yahoo Address Book from the drop-down menu next to Sync Contacts From on your Windows PC. You'll now get a pop-up window asking you to type in a username and password for Yahoo Address Book. This actually doesn't have to be the same account that you're using to send and receive Yahoo mail in the iPhone's Mail application. If you want to change the account that you sync contacts to, click the Configure... button and then type in a new username and password.

Create a New Contact with Yahoo Address Book   To add a new contact in Yahoo Address Book, go to `http://address.yahoo.com`.

Then, log in with your user name and password (if you don't already have one, you can register for a free account now). Click the Add Contact button and then type in the appropriate details for your contact. Once you're done, click the Save button.

> NOTE   *Yahoo Address Book is a decent address book, but unlike OS X's Address Book, it can't do groups and it can't manage contact photos. If you use Yahoo Address Book to manage your contacts, you'll be missing out on these features, unless you go into Address Book and create groups and add pictures there. See the earlier section on Mac Address Book Contact Syncing to learn how to do this.*

Sync Your Contacts with Yahoo Address Book   To sync your contacts between your iPhone and Yahoo Address Book, open iTunes, click on your iPhone, and click the Sync button. iTunes will ask whether you want to merge the data between this computer and Yahoo, or replace the data on this computer with Yahoo's data. In most cases you'll choose merge, but if for some reason you want to make Yahoo's contacts override your computer's, you can select that too.

> TIP   *If you're using Address Book on the Mac, you can duplicate your contacts on your iPhone as well as in Address Book and Yahoo Address Book. How's that for backing up your data?*

Sync Contacts with Multiple Computers

You can actually sync contacts with multiple computers at the same time. To do this, just sync your iPhone normally, and then take the iPhone and plug it into a different computer. When you sync your contacts, iTunes will ask you whether you want to overwrite or merge contacts with the set of contacts already on your iPhone. If you choose Merge, you can actually have two sets of contacts existing on your iPhone simultaneously. This is useful if you have, for example, a work computer and a home computer, and want both groups on your phone at the same time. You can even sync with three or more computers, if your contacts are spread all over the place.

NOTE   *You can sync calendars, music, video, and more with multiple computers too, which we'll discuss in the chapters covering those topics.*

Resolve Sync Conflicts

Occasionally you'll run into some conflicts while syncing your iPhone to your computer. Here's a scenario when this might happen: You sync your iPhone, then change a contact's phone number on your computer, and then change the same contact's phone number on your iPhone to a totally different number. When you sync the next time, iTunes will ask which one of the two contact versions you want to take as the official version (illustrated in Figure 3-8), and you'll get to choose to either deal with this conflict now or put it off until later. If you choose to deal with it now, you'll pick one of the two and that will override both locations.

Navigate Contacts on Your iPhone

Your iPhone can navigate contacts in a number of ways. After you launch the Phone app, look for the Contacts icon on the bottom row of your screen (it looks like a silhouette of a bust with Contacts underneath it, as shown in Figure 3-9). If it's not already selected, press the Contacts button (if it's active, it will glow blue). You should now see every one of your contacts arranged in alphabetical order by first name.

TIP   *You can change the order that your iPhone sorts contacts from the Settings application. See Chapter 12 for more information on tweaking the Phone Application settings.*

FIGURE 3-8   An example of a sync conflict

FIGURE 3.0   The iPhone Contacts screen

Swipe and Flick to Navigate Contacts

Most of the time, you'll navigate the Contacts screen by swiping or flicking your contacts (if you don't know what this means, see Chapter 2 for a description). If you want a nice and controlled scroll of your contact list, just swipe your finger in the direction you want to scan your contacts. To move more quickly through a long list of contacts, flicking your contact list up and down will do the trick (again, flicking involves quickly moving your finger across the screen and letting go). Flicking is generally less controlled than swiping, but it's useful when you want to get somewhere fast.

TIP   *It can be hard to keep track of where you are in a list when you quickly flick through it. One good way to keep track of where you are in a list is to keep your eye trained on the letter showing on the top left of the contact list. This letter displays the current letter your list has reached. Watching it instead of trying to watch individual contacts makes flicking much more user-friendly.*

Use the Alphabet to Browse Faster

While flicking provides a good method for moving through a large contact list, it's still not the quickest way to jump from A to Z. Luckily, there is a better way. Along the right side of your contact list, you'll see a column of letters A through Z. This alphabetical index lets you jump directly to any point in the list by simply pressing the appropriate letter. You can press the letters individually, but they're small and a bit difficult to pinpoint. Instead of worrying about hitting the letters with laser-precision, we recommend dragging your finger up and down the alphabet until you get to the letter you want.

View Contact Info on Your iPhone

To actually view a contact's info once you've found it, tap that contact's name. The contact's Info panel will slide onto the screen and you'll see phone numbers, email addresses, and the various other bits of information you've entered in. As you can see in Figure 3-10, you can also send text messages and add your contacts to your Favorites list from here.

Manage Contact Information

You could manage all of your contacts by first editing them on your desktop computer and then syncing them using one of the contact management applications mentioned previously. But, you're not always at your computer; and besides, any cell phone worth its salt can add and edit contacts. The nice part about the iPhone is that every change you make on the phone will sync seamlessly with your desktop, so you can manage contacts both on the desktop and your iPhone to your heart's content and always be confident that they'll both be synced with the same information. Previously we discussed managing contacts from your desktop. Now, we'll show you how to manage contacts from your iPhone.

Add Contacts

To add a new contact to your iPhone, go to the Contacts section of the Phone application and tap the plus sign (+) button on the top right of the screen. The New Contact panel will slide up from the bottom of the screen, and will look like Figure 3-11. Next tap the field with the text First Last inside. You'll see the Edit Name screen, where you can enter your contact's first and last name along with company (if applicable) using the software keyboard. When you're done, press the blue Save button.

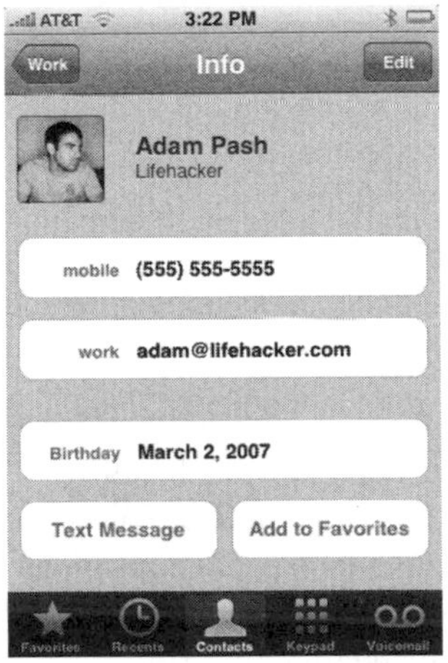

FIGURE 3-10 A contact's info pane

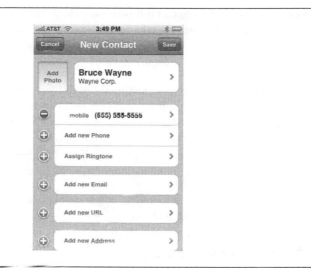

FIGURE 3-11   The add contact pane

Now you're back at the Info screen. To finish adding the contact, just hit the blue Done button. Of course, you most likely want to add more information to your contact than just her name—like phone number and email address, for starters—so read on to learn how to add to and edit your new contact's info.

Edit Contacts

To edit the information of a contact you've already got on your phone, go to the Home screen, launch the Phone application, and then go to the Contacts section. Find the contact whose information you want to edit and tap that contact. The contact Info panel will slide onto the screen; there you can see all of the information you've assigned to this contact (see Figure 3-10). A fully fleshed-out contact can contain lots of information, including your contact's

- Name
- Picture
- Phone number(s). In fact, you can add virtually any amount of phone numbers. Okay, so I stopped adding numbers at 37, but who could possibly need more than that for one contact?
- Custom ringtone
- Email address(es). Again, you can add a lot of email addresses.
- Web address(es) related to your contact
- Street address(es)
- Other information for a number of additional fields, such as Prefix, Middle, Suffix, Nickname, Job Title, Department, Birthday, Date, and Note

Adding and editing any of the contact information follows the same workflow. If you want to edit an existing contact's info, just press the Edit button on the top right of that contact's Info screen. Plus (+) and minus (−) icons will fill the Info screen, and all of the contact information will become editable, as you can see in Figure 3-12.

Edit Existing Contact Info To change any existing field, just tap that field. For example, if you wanted to change an existing phone number, you'd tap that number. You can delete the old number using the keypad on the Edit Phone screen, and then type in the new number. Next, you can assign a new label to the number (like mobile, home, work, main, home fax, work fax, pager, other, or a custom label). When you're done, press the blue Save button on the top right of the Edit screen. Your newly edited phone number should have replaced your old one.

Add New Info to a Contact On the other hand, if you want to keep the contact's existing info but add something new—like a new email address, for example—you can do that by pressing a field with a green plus sign next to it (you should still be in the Edit mode described above). Use your iPhone's software keypad to enter in the new contact data, and when you've got it, just press Save.

Delete a Contact Field While you're in Edit mode, you can remove a field from a contact altogether by pressing the Delete icon (a red circle with a white minus sign through it). The red circle will rotate and a big red Delete button will appear inside that field. If you want to get rid of the contact, go ahead and press Delete. If you've changed your mind, that's okay, too—just tap anywhere *but* the red Delete button to cancel the delete process.

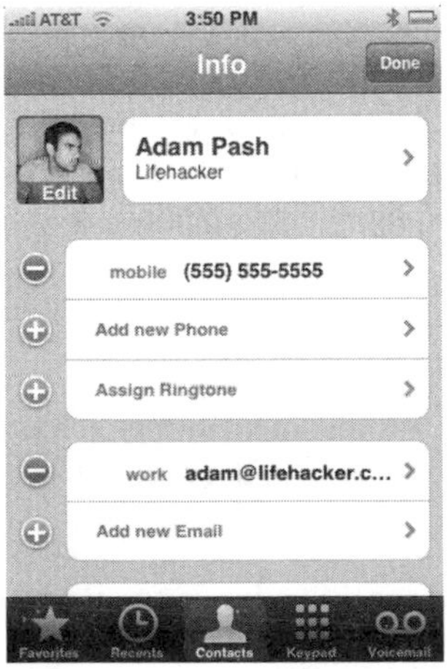

FIGURE 3-12 The edit contact pane

Assign a Custom Ringtone   One bit of contact data that differs slightly from the rest, at least in terms of how it works, are custom ringtones. To assign a custom ringtone to a contact, enter Edit mode (by hitting the Edit button on that contact's info screen) and tap the Assign Ringtone field. The Ringtone screen will slide onto the display with a list of all available ringtones. By default, the ringtone will default to None, meaning that no custom ringtone has been assigned. When this contact calls, your default ringtone will be used. (To change your default ringtone, see the section on managing your phone's settings later in the chapter.)

To assign a custom ringtone, select the ringtone you want to use from the list. Every time you tap the name of a ringtone—say, Piano riff (one of my favorites)—you'll hear a preview of what the ringtone sounds like. Once you find the one you like (it will have a check mark next to it when it's selected), tap the Info button on the top right of the Ringtones screen and that's that. You've assigned your contact a custom ringtone.

Assign a Custom Picture   You can also add a custom picture for each contact, which will show up whenever you talk to them. In fact, it's actually better to add contact photos on your iPhone instead of on your computer, because you can only get large contact photos by assigning pictures on the phone (ones assigned on the computer are tiny thumbnails). To add a photo, tap Add Photo. Now you can choose to take a photo with your iPhone's camera, or choose a photo from your library. Either one will work. Once you've taken or selected a picture, you have to move and scale the image to fit best inside the frame. This will be the photo you see when you call your contact or you contact calls you, so choose a photo that helps reminds you of the person, rather than just some abstract photo.

Delete Contacts

If you're viewing a contact, you can delete it in three simple steps:

1. Tap the Edit button on the top left of the Info panel.

2. Scroll down to the bottom of your contact and tab the big red Delete Contact button.

3. A confirmation dialog will slide up from the bottom of the phone containing two buttons: Delete Contact and Cancel. If you're sure you want to get rid of this contact, tap Delete Contact.

Add Contacts to Your Favorites

You may have noticed the Favorites button on the bottom of the Phone screen (it's the button with a big star that says Favorites on the bottom left). Your favorites provide you with quick-and-easy access to your most-used contacts. You can add any contact to your list of favorites through the contact's Info screen.

You can also add contacts to your favorites list through the Favorites screen. See the "Manage and Call Favorites" section for more information.

That means you need to launch your Phone app and go to the Contacts screen. Find the contact you want to add as a favorite and then tap the contact. The Info panel will slide onto the screen. Now just go to the bottom of the Info panel and tap the button labeled Add to Favorites. If your contact has more than one number assigned, a dialog will slide up from the bottom of the screen asking you which number you want to assign as a favorite. Tap the one you want and you're done. That contact will now show up on your favorites list.

NOTE *A contact cannot be added to your Favorites unless they have been assigned a phone number. If not, the Add to Favorites button will not be visible on that contact's Info pane.*

To verify your success, just tap the Favorites button on the bottom row. Your contact will now show up on this list. You can also check to see if the contact's number has been added to the favorites list by checking for a blue star next to their number. Numbers that are on the favorites list have this star.

Call Contacts from the Contact Screen

Now that you've added plenty of contacts to your phone, it's time to take advantage of all that work. Like almost everything else, calling a contact using the Contacts list on your iPhone is easy.

First, launch the Phone app and go to the Contacts screen. Find the contact you want to call (using the swiping, flicking, and alphabetical navigation we discussed previously), tap that contact, and then tap the number you want to call. The Info screen will fade away and the In-Call screen will take its place. You're officially making a phone call.

Manage and Call Favorites

Since the iPhone doesn't have a traditional keypad to speed dial from, the Favorites screen is the easiest way to access your most-called contacts on one screen. To get here, launch the Phone app and click on the Favorites tab (the first one on the left with a star). Figure 3-13 shows the Favorites screen selected. Once you're here, you have a few options. You can call your favorites, add new favorites, delete old favorites, or just look at their contact information.

Call Your Favorites

To call your favorites, just tap on a Favorites entry and the iPhone will automatically call that number. That's it!

Each Favorites entry actually represents a phone number and not a contact. If you've got only one number per contact, this makes no difference. But if you had two numbers for someone, a work and a home number, each Favorites entry will represent only one of their numbers. To have both, you'll have to add each number to the Favorites list individually. You can see what location each number is by the note on the right, which should say home, mobile, or work, if you added those numbers to the Favorites list.

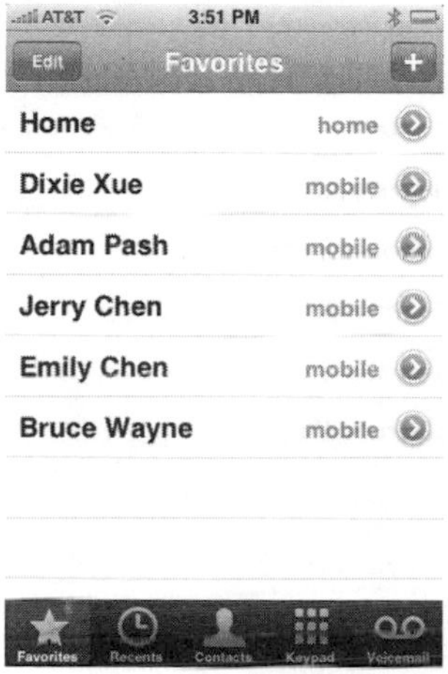

FIGURE 3-13   The favorites screen

Add a New Favorite

To add a new favorite to your Favorites list, click the + button in the top right. This will bring up a list of contacts. You can filter contacts by group type if you want to narrow down your search, and you can also use the alphabet on the right hand side to jump to a letter quickly. Once you find the contact you want, click on it and the contact will automatically be added to your favorites list. If your contact has more than one number, you'll be prompted to choose one as the one you want to add.

Feel free to add as many contact numbers as you like, but if you add too many you'll have to scroll a bit to see them on the list (which sort of defeats the purpose of having a Favorites list).

Manage Favorites

If you decide that someone's not important enough to be in your Favorites list, you can remove a contact from your Favorites. First, press the Edit button on the top left, and your Favorites list will change into something like Figure 3-14. A – symbol will show up next to each entry, allowing you to press on it to remove the entry. Once you do, a Remove button will show up on the right side of the entry, and will remove the entry when pressed.

To re-order Favorites, press the Edit button, then press and drag the drag strips on the right side of each contact. This way you can list your more frequently called contacts on top.

View a Favorite's Contact Information

Assigning contacts to Favorites isn't just an easy way to call them up; it's an easy way to access their contact information as well. Press down on the blue arrow to the right of each contact to zip over to their contact cards. This is the same contact info that's stored in your Contacts menu, so

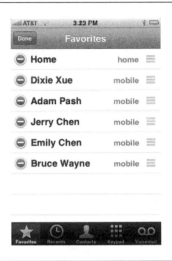

FIGURE 3-14 Rearrange or remove your favorites in the edit screen.

it's really just another door into the same room. However, you should make sure that you hit the blue arrow when you're trying to see someone's contact information from the Favorites section. If you accidentally tap the entry itself, you'll call it—which is what the Favorites menu is for!

NOTE *If you change a phone number for a contact which has been assigned to a Favorite, either on your computer or on your iPhone, the number in the Favorites entry will change as well. You don't need to add the number to your Favorites list again.*

Manage and Call Recents

The Recents list is a convenient way to see whom you've called and who's called you. It's also an easy way to make calls as well, since the more recently someone's called, the more likely you are to have a reason to call them back.

Navigate Your Recents

To browse your contacts, just take your finger and scroll up and down, like we showed you in Chapter 2. Your Recents list will grow fairly long, like the list in Figure 3-15, as you make and take calls, so flick-scrolling to get around faster could be useful if you want to find a call you made a couple weeks ago.

You'll notice that the iPhone groups calls made and received from the same contact into one entry, if the calls are right next to each other. To see the times of the individual calls, press the

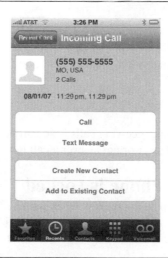

FIGURE 3-15   The Recents list

blue arrow on the right, and you'll see contact details, as well as the time and date when they called (for that entry). See Figure 3-16 for an example of this. If that contact has more than one phone number, the number highlighted in blue is the phone they called from.

The default list shows all calls, whether they're outgoing, incoming, or missed. If you want to only see the missed calls, hit the Missed tab on the top. To switch back to all calls view, press All.

FIGURE 3-16   The Recent Call Detail screen

If you get a phone call from a person not stored in your contacts, the entry in the Recents list will show the number instead of their name. The iPhone has a neat location feature that shows the general vicinity of where the call originated. If you press the blue arrow on the right, you'll see the city name and state located underneath the phone number.

Call Recents

To call a number on your Recents list, just scroll to the entry, press it and start talking. That's all! If the person you're calling has more than one phone, and you want to make sure you're calling the right one, press the blue arrow on the right to view their contact information, and then choose a number to dial from there.

Add Recents to Contacts

It's simple to add new people who've called you as a new contact. Just find their entry in the Recents list (which should just be their number at this point, since they're not yet a contact), press the blue arrow on the right, and then press the button at the bottom labeled Create New Contact. If this is a new phone number from someone you already know—say, if your friend saw your iPhone and just had to get one for their own—you can select the button labeled Add to Existing Contact as well.

Clear All Recents

To clear all your recent calls and then start again with a fresh slate, click the Clear button on the top right of the screen. A confirmation will pop up asking whether you want to Clear All Recents or Cancel. If you confirm this step, there's no easy way to go back and retrieve your recent call list, so be careful.

If you really do want to retrieve your Recents after you've deleted them, see Chapter 16's troubleshooting tips. We'll show you how to restore your phone to a previously synced state, which can possibly get your old data back.

Receive Calls

Now that you know how to make calls, receiving calls is actually even easier. Let's take a look at all your different options to either answer or not answer a call in various different situations.

Receive Calls When the Phone is Locked

If you get a call when the iPhone's locked—such as when the screen's off and the phone's sitting in your pocket—two things will happen. One, the phone will either ring, vibrate, or both, depending on the settings you've picked. Second, the screen will turn on and show you who's calling (including their contact picture, if you've assigned one), and give you the option of answering the call. To answer, just slide the slider all the way to the right, just like you do when you unlock your phone. Once that's done, put the phone up to your ear and start talking.

Using the iPhone's hardware power button, you can decline incoming calls in two ways. See the "Advanced Calling Features" section later on in the chapter for more information.

Receive Calls When You're in Another App

If you're enjoying the iPhone as much as we are, you're probably using it all the time—which means you're going to be getting calls when you're using another application. If this happens, the current app you're using will zoom into the background and the Call screen will appear. Unlike the slider that appears when you're getting a call when your iPhone is locked, you get two buttons (shown in Figure 3-17), prompting you to either Answer or Decline. Press Decline if you don't want to answer it, and press Answer if you do.

NOTE
You can be doing just about anything with your iPhone and still receive a call with no problems. However, if you're actively using your EDGE data connection—for example, checking your mail, browsing the Internet with Safari, searching for something in Google Maps, updating the data in Stocks and Weather, or viewing a video in YouTube—then incoming calls will be sent directly to your voicemail. If you can, we recommend you use Wi-Fi instead of EDGE when possible so that you don't miss calls.

FIGURE 3-17   The Receive Call screen has buttons instead of a slider when you're using the phone.

TIP *If a call comes in when you're listening to music in the iPod app, your music will slowly fade out and the ringtone will slowly fade in. This is your chance to either take off your headphones (if you want to put the phone up to your ear) or answer the call from your headphones (see how to do this in the "Advanced Calling Features" section later on in the chapter).*

Receive Calls When You're Already in a Call

If you get a call when you're already in a conversation, you'll get the three onscreen options shown in Figure 3-18: Ignore, Hold Call + Answer, and End Call + Answer. Ignoring sends the new call to voicemail; Hold Call + Answer holds the current call and starts the new call so you can switch back when you're done; and End Call + Answer ends the current call before picking up the new one. If you do Hold Call + Answer, you can swap between the two calls by hitting the Swap button, and combine the two calls with the Merge Calls button. See the later section called "Conference Calling" for more details on this.

Receive Calls with Your iPhone's Call-Capable Headphones

If you've got your iPhone headphones in when you get a call, you will actually use the headset to answer. When the call comes in, it will ring in both your headphones and on the phone's speakers. To answer the call with the headset, click the inline button once. When you want to end the call, click the button again. In case you want to decline a call, hold down the button for two seconds before letting go. You'll hear two beeps to know you've hung up.

FIGURE 3-18 The three call-waiting options help you decide what to do when a call interrupts your conversation.

Set Up and Use Visual Voicemail

You're familiar with regular voicemail on cell phones, but Visual Voicemail shown in Figure 3-19, lets you access any message in any order you want, and even lets you fast forward and rewind to separate parts of the message like you can in a song. To set it up, open the Phone application and click on the Voicemail button in the bottom right corner. If this is the first time you're accessing the Voicemail app, it will prompt you to create a password and record your greeting. You have to create a password, but creating a greeting is optional.

Set Up a Voicemail Greeting

To create a greeting, press the Greeting button and record your greeting. Press Stop if you're finished, and Play to listen to your greeting. Once you're done making a greeting, press Save. If you want to revert to the default non-personalized greeting, press Default instead.

Play Back Voicemails

Playing back voicemails is much like playing back music on your iPhone's iPod. To play back a voicemail, either double-click on the one you want to listen to immediately start playback, or select the one you want by pressing it and then pressing the Play button to the left of the entry. To pause playback, hit the Pause button. To start it up again, hit the Play button. You can also listen to a message on speaker. To do this, hit the speaker button in the top right. Once you're done, you can delete or call the person back by pressing the Delete or Call Back buttons on the bottom.

To fast forward or rewind to a part of the message you want to hear again, just drag the marker to a section and let go. You can do this as many times as you want in order to make out a name or a phone number.

FIGURE 3-19   The Voicemail screen

If you want to see the contact's information—or add the caller as a new contact—just press the blue arrow on the right. Here you can see the contact card; or if it's not an already added contact, create a new contact or add the number to an existing one.

TIP *Voicemails can only be kept for 30 days after your first listen. This should be long enough for you to save the details of the message somewhere if it's really important to you.*

Use the Old-Fashioned Non-Visual Voicemail System

To use the old fashioned, non-visual voicemail—which can be useful if you're not on your iPhone but still want to hear your messages—just call your own phone number and punch in your voicemail password. If you're on your iPhone but want to hear messages the old-fashioned way, either call your own number or hold down the 1 key in the Keypad.

Once you're in, the voicemail prompts will tell you about the erased messages recovery option (you can listen to messages you've deleted on your iPhone before you delete them permanently here) by going to the menu and pressing 1 9, or you can play back your messages. The options here are the same as on other AT&T phones. Pressing 1 lets you hear your messages, pressing 4 changes personal options, and pressing * disconnects. Once you're in a message, pressing 7 deletes the current message, pressing 9 saves it, and pressing 4 replays it. You'll notice that all the messages you have on your Visual Voicemail list are saved messages once you've listened to them already.

Adjust Call Settings to Suit Your Needs

Although the default settings may be perfect for some people, you can tweak the settings to customize your phone experience even further. To do so, go to the Home screen and press the Settings button.

Change the Default Ringtone

In addition to being able to set a ringtone for each contact, you can change your default ringtone for all contacts. In the Settings application, press Sounds, and then Ringtone. Here you can scroll through the list of ringtones and find one you like by clicking on it. Each ringtone will play and you can judge whether or not it's right for you. Keep in mind that this will be the sound you hear for all your contacts (unless you've assigned a custom ringtone to that contact), so you want to pick one that's not annoying to you or the people around you (this is why we wouldn't recommend choosing the Alarm ringtone). Make sure the ringtone you want is the one currently checked, and then press the Sounds button to get out of this screen and back to the screen shown in Figure 3-20.

You can customize the ringtone volume here as well, by dragging the volume slider. Louder is to the right, softer is to the left.

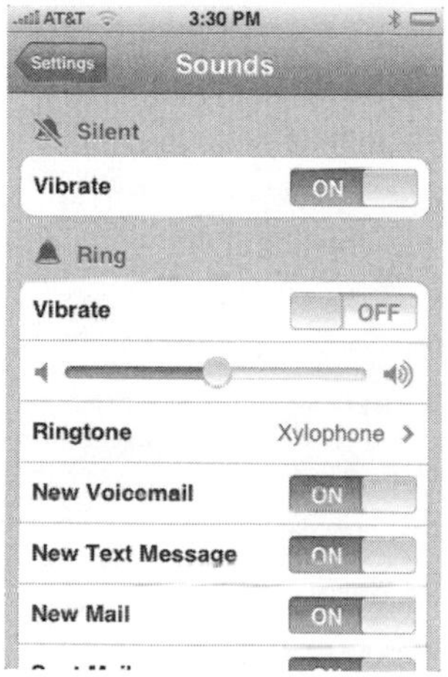

FIGURE 3-20   The Sounds Settings screen lets you change your ringtone.

Change Vibration Settings

You can customize vibration settings for both regular mode, which is your standard operating mode, and silent mode, which is activated when you flip the physical mute switch on the side of your phone. You independently set vibrate to On or Off on both modes.

Tweak Miscellaneous Settings

Under the Phone section of the Settings app, shown in Figure 3-21 you can change quite a few little things to make your iPhone behave the way you want

- **Sort Order**   Do you want to sort your contacts alphabetically by last name or first name?

- **Display Order**   You can actually sort your contacts by last name and display by first, meaning Jason Chen would come before Adam Pash in your contact list.

- **Call Forwarding**   Forward your calls to another phone number. This is useful when you don't have cell coverage or your phone's running out of batteries. Note that call forwarding still uses up your anytime minutes.

- **Call Waiting**   If this is turned off, the calls you receive when you're already on the phone will go directly to voicemail instead of ringing through.

- **Show My Caller ID**   This displays your name and phone number to the people you call when it's on. Turn off if you want some privacy.

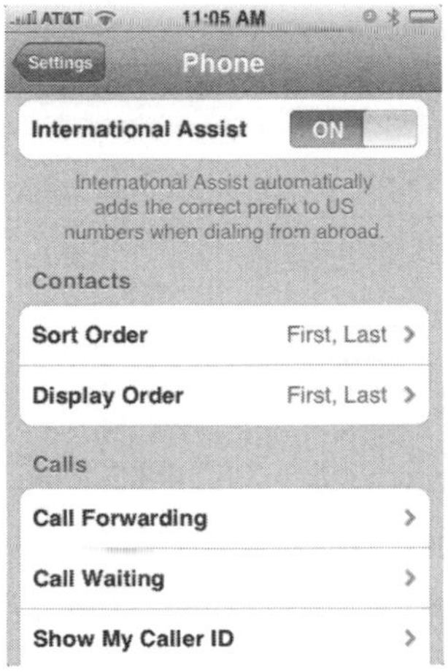

FIGURE 3-21 The Phones Settings screen

■ **TTY** Turn this on to enable teletype machine compatibility, which is used by the hearing-impaired to communicate textually.

■ **SIM PIN** If you turn this on, your SIM chip (the small, removable card inside your iPhone) can't be taken out and used in another phone without the password. This may save you a headache if your phone's been stolen.

■ **AT&T Services** This allows you to quickly check the status of your AT&T account right on your phone. You can view how many minutes you have left in the month, check your balance, or get directory assistance. Clicking AT&T My Account loads your AT&T account page in Safari, but you still need to have signed up for an online account and you will also need to enter your phone number and password.

Use Advanced Calling Features

Now that you're familiar with the basics of taking and making calls, here are some advanced calling features that let you get the most out of your iPhone.

Manage Onscreen Options During a Call

You have a couple of options to consider after you've accepted the call. Figure 3-22 shows the onscreen options.

Items like Hold, End Call, and Mute are obvious (these put the call on hold, end the call, and mute the call, as you would guess). But some of the other options require a little explanation.

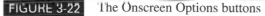

FIGURE 3-22   The Onscreen Options buttons

Use the Keypad in a Call

When you press the Keypad button during a call, the buttons flip over to reveal the standard iPhone dial pad. This is where you'll go to type in the numbers needed when you call automated support lines, for example, that require you to press 1 for sales, 2 for technical support, and so on. There's no way to delete the numbers you press, because you're sending them over a live call, so be slightly more careful when you hit digits. To go back to the regular button view hit Hide Keypad, or to end the call hit End Call.

View Contacts in a Call

The Contacts button gives you an easy way to bring up your list of contacts during a call. This feature is handy to have whenever someone asks you for another person's phone number or email address over the phone. Just click the Contacts button, browse your contacts for the right contact, and you'll be able to see all the contact details right on the screen. If you're not in a public environment, you can even put the call on speaker so you that don't have to swap back and forth between reading the numbers and repeating them into the phone.

Use the iPhone's Speakerphone

Pressing the Speaker button puts your phone in speakerphone mode. If you look at the bottom of your phone, you'll see two speaker-like sets of holes. Only the set of holes to the left of the dock adapter is the speaker; the ones to the right are the microphone. When you're in speakerphone mode, be careful not to cover up the left set of holes or you will have a hard time hearing the other party.

TIP   *If you cup your hand under the speaker at just the right angle, you can somewhat amplify the sound of the speaker. This helps a little if you think the volume is too soft.*

Talk to Multiple People with Conference Calling

To set up a conference call, you first need to establish a call. Then, to add someone to your call, click the Add Call button and dial a number from either your Recents, your Favorites, your Contacts, or the Keypad. Once this is up, click the Merge Calls button to combine the two phone calls into one big conference call. To add more calls, just repeat the process by pressing Add Call again and picking another number. The process works the same way if someone calls you. You can answer their call and then press the Merge Calls button to add them to the conference. To end the conference, hit End Call.

Talk Hands-Free with Bluetooth Headset Calling

The iPhone works with most Bluetooth headsets on the market now. To use a Bluetooth headset with your phone, the first thing you have to do is pair them.

Pair Your Bluetooth Headset with Your iPhone

To pair the phone, first go to the iPhone's Settings application. Then choose General, and then Bluetooth. Make sure the Bluetooth option is set to ON.

Now put your Bluetooth headset on Discoverable mode. Consult your headset's documentation and follow its instructions to do this. Once it's on discoverable mode, the headset will show up on the iPhone under the Devices list, as shown in Figure 3-23, and will indicate Unpaired to the right of the entry. Select this entry.

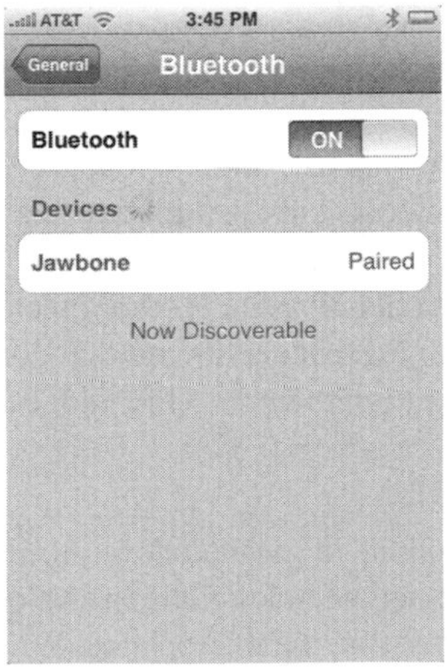

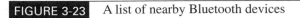

FIGURE 3-23   A list of nearby Bluetooth devices

The iPhone will prompt you to enter in a PIN number. Again, check your Bluetooth headset's manual to see what the PIN is. It has to be the exact same PIN that's specified there—it isn't prompting you to enter in any old PIN. Once you enter in the correct PIN, the headset entry in the iPhone will switch to Paired, and the Bluetooth icon in the top right of your iPhone, to the left of the battery, will be blue (it's white on the Home screen). If this doesn't work, repeat the steps again. Sometimes you'll find that the Discoverable mode for certain headsets times out before you can enter in the PIN.

> **TIP** *If you have the official Apple iPhone Bluetooth headset, you can actually skip all this pairing stuff! By plugging your iPhone and your headset into the included iPhone + Headset dock, the two will automatically pair to each other. That means you can start making and taking calls on the headset immediately afterwards.*

Make Calls with Your Bluetooth Headset

Here's how you make calls with your Bluetooth headset. First, go to the Home screen and make sure the Bluetooth icon in the top right corner is white, not gray. If it's gray, you'll have to press the Call button on your headset to connect with your iPhone. Once this is white, open up the Phone app and call a contact.

When you call a contact, the iPhone will give you three options. The first will be the name of your headset. The second will be iPhone, and the third will be Speaker. These options are there so you can choose, before the call is established, what method you want to use to have this conversation with—either the Bluetooth headset, the iPhone itself, or the iPhone's speakerphone. If your headset is paired, it will be the default option.

Once the call is established, the previous Speaker button in the top right row of buttons changes to an Audio Source button. Pressing this button allows you to choose, once again, the audio source you want to use to take this call. If you want to switch from your Bluetooth headset to the Speaker Phone, hit Speaker Phone. If you want to go back to your iPhone's default call screen, hit Hide Sources.

Take Calls with Your Bluetooth Headset

Taking calls with your Bluetooth headset as easy as making them. When a call comes in, you'll have the same options to either answer or decline the call. Both the phone and your Bluetooth headset will ring. If you tap your headset's Answer button, the iPhone will pick up the calls. If your Bluetooth headset is currently attached to your phone (in this case the top right Bluetooth icon will be blue or white), the audio will default to your headset when you answer a call. If the headset is not currently paired to your iPhone, or if the headset is off, the default audio source will be the iPhone itself.

To change between audio sources, just push the Audio Source button on your iPhone and select the one you want. You can switch back and forth to the headset even after a call's been established. You can use your headset's End Call button to end the call as well (assuming your headset has an End Call button; most should).

Listen to Voicemails with Your Bluetooth Headset

You can also listen to your voicemails with your Bluetooth headset. When your headset is paired with the iPhone, the Voicemail screen has an Audio button instead of a Speaker button in the top right. When you press this, you can switch between your iPhone, the Speaker iPhone, and your headset.

TIP *If you're not going to use a Bluetooth headset, turn the Bluetooth option Off in your settings. This will save battery life and protect your phone from potential attacks using Bluetooth (none have been found for the iPhone at the time of this writing).*

Make Calls with Your iPhone's Headphones

Handling calls with the call-capable iPhone headphones is easy. When a call comes in, click the inline button once to answer, and then again to hang up.

If you want to get really fancy with your headphones, you can also control calls when you're already in a conversation. When you get a call, press the button once to answer the new call and put the current call on hold. Press again to switch back and forth between calls. To pick up the new call and end the current call, hold down the button for two seconds before letting go. To end the call your conversation's done once, hold the buttom down for two seconds again.

Send Calls to Voicemail Using the On/Off Button

To send an incoming call directly to voicemail, just press the On/Off button twice while the phone is ringing. This is convenient if you're in the middle of a meeting or a movie and have forgotten to silence your phone. Note that sending your call directly to voicemail will let the caller know that you're around (or on the phone), but that you've sent their call to voicemail. To just silence an incoming call, see the next section.

Silence Incoming Calls Using the On/Off Button

If you receive a call you don't want to answer immediately, you can silence the call (but not send it to voicemail) by pressing the On/Off button. Doing this will let the caller hear the ring as usual, but the iPhone itself won't vibrate or ring after you press the button. This is useful if you're avoiding someone, but don't want them to know that you're in front of your phone and sending their call directly to voicemail.

Adjust the Volume During a Call

During a call, you may feel the need to raise or lower the volume, depending on how loudly or softly the other person is talking. Instead of taking your phone away from your ear and digging through the menus, just use the side volume buttons! The hardware buttons can increase or decrease the volume easily, and you can press them with your fingers even during a call.

Multitask During a Call

Since the iPhone is one part phone and two parts computing device, you can actually multitask and do a bunch of stuff while you're in the middle of a call. To do this, just press the Home button to go back to your iPhone's Home screen. You'll see a green bar at the top of your screen that tells you to press it to go back to the call, just like in Figure 3-24. When you're here, you can pretty much do anything you can do when you're not in a call. The only restriction is that you can't use your EDGE connection to download data, so if you're not in range of a Wi-Fi hotspot, you can't browse the Internet or check your email.

Make and Take Calls Internationally

The AT&T account you use with the iPhone actually lets you take your phone internationally and use it in any country that supports the GSM standard. All you have to do is call AT&T support and tell them to activate international roaming, a service that's off by default for security purposes. You don't want someone stealing your phone and racking up charges overseas!

Be careful when you're taking the iPhone abroad though. When you make phone calls while you're in other countries, you'll get charged outrageous roaming fees to the tune of many tens of cents per minute. This is fine if your office is footing the bill, but you should probably pick up a native cell phone in the country you're visiting instead of taking your iPhone with you. You won't be able to take calls using your regular number, but you will save a hefty sum. The same rule exists for data as well, so unless you're only using the Wi-Fi connection in other countries, be prepared to be charged large data roaming fees as well.

FIGURE 3-24   The Home screen while you're on a call—note the green bar on top that lets you go back to your call.

TIP

AT&T has an international travel guide that lets you plan your itinerary and see whether the iPhone (and any other phone you may have) is compatible with that country's cellular network. AT&T World and AT&T's international rates sites are also useful in helping you figure out how much you'll have to pay when roaming internationally.

`http://www.wireless.att.com/travelguide/`
`http://tinyurl.com/yvrvft`
`http://tinyurl.com/2xka7v`

Now forge ahead to Chapter 4 to learn how to take advantage of the iPhone's iPod functions.

Part II

Manage Music and Video with Your iPhone and iTunes

Chapter 4

Use the iPod on Your iPhone

How to...

- Navigate and play music on the iPod
- Play podcasts and audiobooks on your iPhone
- Play videos on your iPhone
- Customize the bottom row
- Buy music with the iTunes Wi-Fi Music Store
- Tweak your iPod settings
- Use the headphones and other accessories

Now that you've mastered your iPhone's calling capabilities, you're one step closer to calling yourself an iPhone pro. Next up? The iPod: the second of the three revolutionary devices that make up the iPhone. You've no doubt heard of the iPod and may even own one, so you know what a great music and video player it is. The iPod on your phone isn't exactly like the iPod you're familiar with as shown in Figure 4-1—there's no scroll wheel for example—but it's actually even easier to use! Read on to see how you can get the most out of the iPod inside your iPhone.

FIGURE 4-1   The iPod's Now Playing screen

Navigate and Play Music on the iPod

First and foremost, the iPod is and always has been about your music. We'll focus on that first. From the Home screen, tap the orange iPod button on the bottom right. You'll see an interface similar to what you see when you open the Phone application—a list of items (this time of songs or playlists rather than contacts) and five black buttons across the bottom of the screen: Playlists, Artists, Songs, Videos, and More, by default.

> **TIP** *You can customize the bottom row to fit your preferences. Find out how in the next section.*

Navigate the iPod

The first time you open the iPod application, Playlists, the first of the five buttons shown on the bottom of Figure 4-2, will be selected. To get to another section, just tap its button on the bottom row. For example, tapping Artists shows you a listing of all the artists you've got on your iPhone. There are actually more categories than just the default four you see on the bottom row.

.ılı AT&T 🛜	6:28 PM	▷ ✳ 🔋
	Playlists	Now Playing

Stereophonics - You Gotta...	>
Suede	>
The Killers	>
The Killers - Sam's Town	>
The Smiths	>
The Smiths - Meat Is Murder	>
The Smiths - The Queen Is...	>
25 Playlists	

Playlists   Artists   Songs   Videos   • More

FIGURE 4-2 The default setup lets you access playlists, artists, songs, and videos on the top level.

To access these, press the More button on the bottom right. Here's a brief description of what each category contains.

- **Playlists**   These are all the playlists (both regular and smart) that you created and synced from iTunes, along with your On-The-Go playlist.

- **Artists**   This is a listing of all the artists for the songs currently synced to your iPhone. Each artist will have multiple sub-entries (songs) if they have multiple songs, and will even have album listings if you have more than one album from the artist.

- **Songs**   These include all the individual songs on your iPhone. This list is the longest list you have in the iPod app, so you'll want to use the alphabet method or the flick method to get around quickly.

- **Videos**   This section contains movies, TV shows, and anything else that's in video form.

- **Albums**   This is a list of all the albums on your phone.

- **Audiobooks**   This contains all the audiobooks you've downloaded from iTunes, Audible, or that you've created yourself.

- **Compilations**   This is a list of albums that are compilations (for example, movie soundtracks that have a several different artists on the same album). You can manually set albums as compilations in iTunes.

- **Composers**   This is the list of all the different composers for all your songs. Not all songs have composers, so unless a track explicitly has information in the composer field, it won't be listed under this screen.

- **Genres**   This is a listing of all the genres present on your phone. If a song doesn't have the genre field selected, it won't show up at all under this listing.

- **Podcasts**   All of the podcasts you've downloaded on iTunes and synced to the iPhone will be here, including video and audio podcasts.

NOTE   *If you launch a video podcast from the podcast screen, it will display a still image from the video and play back the audio only. This feature allows you to listen to the podcast audio while doing other stuff, like reading your email or browsing the Internet. If you want to watch the podcast in its full-motion glory, go to the Videos section and launch the video there.*

Now that you know what each category holds, you should get a handle on the interface conventions Apple's created to make navigating the iPod app super simple.

- Any time you see a gray arrow on the right side of the screen, it means you can press the entry to go to a submenu. You can see this in effect under Playlists and Genres. You can also go into submenus from virtually any view that will generally contain more than one song, such as Albums or Artists.

■ Whenever you're in a submenu, you'll see a left-pointing blue arrow button in the top left corner. This always takes you back to the previous screen. The text inside the arrow gives you a hint as to what the previous screen is if you've forgotten where you came from.

■ If you've got a song playing and you navigate out of the Now Playing screen, there will always be a right-pointing arrow on the top right that takes you back to the Now Playing screen.

Play Music in the Now Playing Screen

Once you've selected a song you want to listen to and started playback, you'll see the iPod's Now Playing screen (Figure 4-1). This displays the current track's title, artist, album, and the album's artwork (if it's been assigned) in crisp, full screen glory. From the Now Playing screen, you can change tracks, pause playback, adjust the volume, rate your music, and change the play mode.

Pause and Seek Tracks

Pausing and changing the currently playing track is simple. To pause, just tap the Pause button (two vertical bars) on the bottom of the Now Playing screen. The button will toggle to the Play button. To resume, just tap the Play button.

On either side of the Play/Pause button, you'll see the Previous/Next buttons (Previous on the left, Next on the right). To move to the next track in your album, playlist, or whatever list you're currently listening to, tap the Next button. Tapping the Previous button will return the currently playing song to the beginning of the track or—if you're already at the beginning of the song—it will skip to the previous song on your list. That means that if you're in the middle of a song but you want to jump back to the previous song, just tap the Previous button twice.

Holding down the Previous/Next buttons for more than a second will rewind or fast-forward the music, respectively. At first the playback will speed up just a little (like a record being played too fast), but if you keep the button held down, you'll start quickly jumping ahead or back.

If you want to jump to a specific place in the song, tap the screen once to bring up the playback control overlay. See Figure 4-3 for a better look at the overlay. Now drag the white scroll ball to any part in the song and let go. Just clicking on an area won't work; you have to drag the playback ball. The time on the left of the scroll bar reflects how many minutes and seconds have elapsed into the song, and the time on the right reflects how much time you have left.

Adjust the Volume

The horizontal slider at the bottom of the Now Playing screen controls your volume. To adjust the volume of the track, tap the white scroll ball and drag it back and forth. Move it to the right to increase volume, left to decrease. To mute the playback, just slide it all the way to the left.

SHORTCUT *You can also adjust your iPod volume any time it's playing, no matter what application you're using on your iPhone, by using the hardware volume rocker button on the left side of the iPhone.*

FIGURE 4-3   The playback overlay allows you to control playback, seek tracks and change playback options.

Change the Play Mode

Along with just about every other music playback feature, Apple's made it very easy to get to and change the Play mode on the iPhone. Instead of requiring you to go all the way back to a settings menu, like you did on the iPod, you can change the Play mode in just two presses. First, bring up the playback control overlay by pressing on the middle of the Now Playing screen. To change repeat options, press the repeat button on the left (the loop) to cycle between Normal, Repeat All, or Repeat One. Normal will stop when you reach the end of the current album or playlist, depending on how you started the playback of this song. Repeat All will continuously cycle back to the start of the playlist when playback reaches the end. Repeat One will play back only the current song, over and over, in an endless loop. A white icon means you're on Normal mode, a blue icon is Repeat All, and a blue icon with a small 1 on it is Repeat One. Figure 4-3 shows both Repeat All and Shuffle On.

To change playback to Shuffle mode, just tap the Shuffle button on the right side of the playback control overlay. It looks like two lines intersecting, pointing to the right. If the icon is blue, it means Shuffle mode is on and your current playlist will play back in a random order. If it's white, it plays back normally.

View an Album's Tracks Quickly

If you're listening to a song in a playlist and need a fast way to see a track listing for the album this song belongs to, just hit the button on the top right of the Now Playing screen. The entire album's track listing is displayed here, in order, complete with song times (Figure 4-4). You can quickly jump to another song on that album just by tapping it here.

Rate a Song

Rating a song on the iPhone is extremely easy, requiring only two presses! From the Now Playing screen, launch the album view by hitting the square button on the top right with three horizontal lines on it. Both the album art and the icon will flip to their reverse side (Figure 4-4), with the album art replacing the small list icon on the right and the list replacing the album art in the middle. Now, choose a star rating (0-5) from the stars on the top. The easiest way to do this is to place your finger down and scroll to the number of stars you want, rather than just tapping on the desired star.

> **TIP**   *Rating a song isn't just a good way to remind yourself whether you enjoy a particular track; you can actually use smart playlists to come up with creative ways to filter your music. For more on this, see Chapter 5.*

Move Back to the Previous Screen

As we said earlier in the chapter, you can go back to the previous screen (Artists, Playlists, Albums, and so on) from the Now Playing screen by hitting the left-arrow button on the top left of Figure 4-1. This gives you an easy way to view the playlist or album you were accessing when you chose to play this song.

FIGURE 4-4   The album track view makes it easy to jump around inside an album

SHORTCUT *There's actually an even easier way to go back one screen from the Now Playing screen! All you have to do is place your fingertip on the album art and swipe quickly from left to right. The previous screen will slide from the left into view. Unfortunately, swiping to the left from the previous screen doesn't bring back the Now Playing screen, but you can hit the button on the top right or tap the currently playing song to do so.*

Browse Albums with Cover Flow

One of the most jaw-dropping features of the iPod is Cover Flow, as shown in Figure 4-5, which provides a beautiful graphical interface for browsing all of your iPod's albums by their album cover art. In Cover Flow mode, you can browse, view, and play songs from your albums.

Navigate Cover Flow

Using Cover Flow is simple—in fact, you don't have to push any buttons at all to access it. First, make sure you're running the iPod application. Then just take your iPod and turn it onto either side to take it into landscape mode. The iPod will sense that you're holding it sideways and automatically switch into Cover Flow mode. Likewise, exiting Cover Flow mode is as simple as rotating your iPhone back to portrait mode.

Once you're in Cover Flow, you can flip through your albums in a few ways. To move slowly from album-to-album, drag your finger across the screen in either direction. If you want to move through your albums more quickly, a quick flick (quickly drag your finger across the screen and release) will do the trick. Lastly, you can navigate with precision within any album currently visible on the Cover Flow screen (seven covers should always be visible unless you're at the beginning or end of your collection) by tapping that album cover.

FIGURE 4-5 Cover Flow mode is slick-looking as well as functional, allowing you to jump through your albums fast by flicking

If your albums have not been assigned album art, Cover Flow will display a generic black cover with musical notes, which isn't really much fun. However, you can add album art to your music and replace the generic placeholder using iTunes. See Chapter 6 to find out how.

Play Music in Cover Flow

Once you find an album you'd like to play and have it centered on the screen, tap the album cover (or tap the small i button on the bottom right of the screen). The album will flip over to Track view, which lists every track from that album that's been synced to your iPhone. Scroll through the tracks, find a song, and then just tap it to play. (The currently-playing track will always have a Play icon next to it.)

To flip over the track listing and return to normal Cover Flow navigation, either tap the small album thumbnail on the top right of the track view, tap the small i button on the bottom right of the screen, or just tap anywhere outside of the track view window.

You can play or pause the current track at any time in Cover Flow by tapping the Play/Pause button on the bottom left of the screen.

Your music isn't the only thing available in Cover Flow. In fact, podcasts and audiobooks are accessible through Cover Flow, as well. Since most podcasts and audiobooks have associated artwork, they're a nice addition to your Cover Flow library.

Create a Playlist on the Fly

When you're out and about with your iPhone, you don't have to settle for the already-made playlists—you can create a custom playlist on the fly as well! It's called the On-The-Go playlist, and it's the first entry under the Playlists section. You can't customize the name (it's always On-The-Go), but you can add anything to this list, play it, and save it as a new playlist the next time you sync with iTunes. Here's how you'll do it:

First, go to the Playlists screen and click On-The-Go. The Songs list, with your entire iPhone's worth of music, will slide into the display as shown in Figure 4-6. You can add songs here by clicking on the song name or clicking the + button on the right. If you accidentally added a song you don't want, don't worry. You can't remove it from this screen, but you can remove it from the playlist later.

You don't have to scroll through your entire music library to add songs. You can go to any of the views, such as Playlists, Genres, Artists, or Albums, and add songs from there. It should make it much easier to filter using one of these views instead of your master song list. You can even add entire playlists or albums by going to a playlist or album and clicking the Add All Songs option on top. After you're finished, press the Done button on the top right.

To edit your On-The-Go playlist, press the Edit button on the top right. From the edit screen, you can clear the entire playlist, which is useful, since you only get one On-The-Go playlist to use when you're on the go. You can also delete individual songs by first pressing the red - button on the left, and then pressing the Delete button on the right. Rearranging the songs is as easy as using the drag bars on the right to rearrange the music in the order you want.

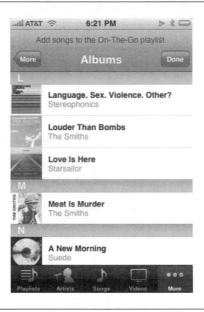

FIGURE 4-6   You can create and edit a playlist directly from your iPhone with the On-The-Go playlist.

NOTE   *The next time you sync the iPhone, your On-The-Go playlist will be cleared from your phone and converted to a standard playlist called On-The-Go in iTunes. If this isn't the first time you've synced an On-The-Go playlist, your playlist will be called On-The-Go 2, or On-The-Go 5, depending on how many times you've synced before. You can add these playlists back to your iPhone as standard playlists by choosing to sync them in the iTunes Sync Configuration screen.*

Limitations

Although the iPod in the iPhone is a pretty feature-complete implementation of the iPod, you can't quite do everything you can on a standard iPod classic. Here are the things that are missing from your iPhone's iPod.

- **No video out**   You can't hook the iPhone up to a TV like you could a iPod classic, so it's currently impossible to get video out onto a big screen.

- **No lyrics support**   There's no way to view lyrics for any of your songs, even if you've got lyrics already embedded into the track info.

- **Limited accessory support**   Although it supports a handful of iPod docks and various other accessories, the iPhone doesn't support a lot of iPod gadgets, such as the Nike+iPod sport kit.

- **Storage space**   Even though you have an 8GB or 4GB iPhone, it won't hold as many songs as your 8GB or 4GB iPod Nano. 700 Megabytes of space is taken up on your phone by the operating system right when you buy it, so you'll only be able to hold a maximum theoretical 7.3GB or 3.3GB of music. Remember, that's only if you store nothing else on your phone except music, which is something not many people will do.

- **Accessory compatibility**   Not all iPod docks and car adapters will work with the iPhone. Either look for the Made for iPhone label before you purchase a product, or do some quick googling to see if other people have had luck with the combination. You can also see Chapter 15 for more information on which accessories will work with your iPhone.

Play Podcasts and Audiobooks on Your iPhone

Of course, the iPod can do more than just play music. If you're a fan of the spoken word, your iPhone handles podcasts and audiobooks like a charm.

With the default setup, you can access your audiobooks and podcasts through the More button on the iPod home row. From this point, you can play back audiobooks and podcasts the same way you play back music: just tap the item you want to listen to and your iPod will start playing. Playing back and navigating podcasts works almost exactly the same as playing back music as described earlier, however, podcasts and audiobooks have a couple cool features that set them apart from regular music. For example:

- The iPod keeps track of the playback time on podcasts and audiobooks, so that even if you stop and move on to other music, you can pick up where you left off when you return. That means if you've listened to the first 10 minutes of a 20-minute podcast, take a break and listen to some music, and then come back to the podcast, you'll start right up at the 10-minute mark.

- To help you keep track of which podcasts you've already listened to, the iPod marks all fresh podcasts with a small blue circle on the left side of the track list. Once you start listening to a podcast, the blue circle will disappear from that track. Think of it kind of like read or unread mail in your email inbox.

- Video podcasts that you access through the Podcasts screen (rather than the Videos screen) will play back as audio-only (see the next section for more on video playback), generally with a screen capture of the video as the album art. The handy thing about this feature is that you can save battery life or multitask by listening to the audio-only version. Conversely, when you watch a video podcast, playback will stop as soon as you leave the video playback.

NOTE   *If you don't have any audiobooks or podcasts in iTunes, see Chapter 6 for more on subscribing to podcasts or getting audiobooks using iTunes.*

Play Videos on Your iPhone

Your iPod has one of the most gorgeous video screens on the portable market, so let's take advantage of it. Playing videos on your iPhone works much the same way as playing anything else, but with a few small differences. To see a list of your videos, launch the iPod and tap the Videos button on the home row. (If you don't have any videos, see Chapter 6 for more on how to get videos into iTunes.)

Navigate Videos

When you enter the Videos screen, you'll see thumbnails of all of your videos to the left next to a description of the video (descriptions include things like title, video time, or number of episodes, depending on the content). There are three categories of videos you can play with the iPod: Movies, TV Shows, and Podcasts, and they will be organized alphabetically within each category in that order, as shown in Figure 4-7.

If you've got multiple episodes of a TV show or video podcast, it will be indicated by a small gray arrow on the right side of the entry. To watch a video, just tap its listing and turn your iPod sideways into landscape mode. When a video starts playing, you'll notice there aren't any buttons or controls on the screen—just pure, unadulterated video. To bring up the video controls, tap the screen once. The video control overlay will appear. You can dismiss this screen by tapping once anywhere outside of the controls.

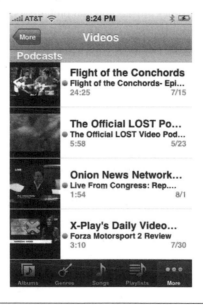

FIGURE 4-7   Navigating videos is as easy as navigating music, or anything else on your iPhone.

If the video control overlay looks familiar, it should; it's basically the same controls you see on the Now Playing screen. And like the Now Playing screen, you can play and pause by tapping the Play/Pause button; track forward or backwards by tapping the Next and Previous buttons; fast-forward or rewind by holding the Next and Previous buttons; change the volume using the volume slider (or the iPhone's hardware volume button); and jump around in the video using the progress slider at the top of the screen.

TIP   *iTunes store-purchased videos actually have chapter information embedded inside. This means that the next and previous buttons let you jump forward and backward from chapter to chapter. This makes it easy to find your way around a 2-hour movie.*

If you decide you want to stop watching the video and go back to the Videos screen, just tap the blue Done button on the top left of the video playback control.

Zoom Videos

The iPhone's screen is a peculiar size: it doesn't exactly fit widescreen movies (i.e., letterbox), but it's also not square enough to fit regular TV shaped videos. Instead, it's a compromise between the two. In an effort to compensate for this and let you decide how you want to view your videos (whether you want to take advantage of all of the iPhone's screen real estate or view the video as it was originally intended), the iPhone has a video zoom feature.

There are two ways to zoom in or out on a video:

1. Tap the video to bring up the video control overlay and then tap the button on the top right, which looks like two diagonal arrows either pointing toward or away from each other.

2. Double-tap the screen.

Delete Videos

To help you conserve space, the iPhone will ask whether you want to delete a video when you finish watching it. A handful of videos can take up a huge chunk of your 4GB or 8GB memory, so to delete the video, just press Delete. Note that this won't delete the video from your computer, so if you accidentally tapped Delete, you can re-sync it back to your iPhone the next time you sync.

You can also delete videos without watching the whole video first. Just swipe your finger from left to right across the listing of the video you want to delete. A Delete button will show up on the right side of the entry, which you can press to confirm deletion. To cancel the delete, press anywhere else on the screen.

Customize the Bottom Row

As we mentioned before, the bottom row of the iPod application lets you access your music and movies in different ways. By default, the bottom row buttons give you quick access to Playlists, Artists, Songs, and Videos. The fifth button, More, displays more views; specifically: Albums, Audiobooks, Compilations, Composers, Genres, and Podcasts (for details on each, see the section "Navigate the iPod").

FIGURE 4-8   It's a good idea to customize the bottom row so you can place your frequently used icons on the top level.

The fact is that you're limited to just four categories on the home row. But the benefit of the iPhone's all-software interface is that you can completely customize which four views you want to appear on the bottom row. To do this, tap More and then tap the Edit button on the top left of the More screen. The Configure screen (see Figure 4-8) will slide into view, listing all of your available bottom row buttons.

I really like scrolling through my music by album, for example, so I swap out the Videos button for the Albums button. To do so, just drag the button you want to add to the slot on the bottom row you want it to replace.

Maybe you like the buttons that are already in your bottom row and you just want to adjust their order; you can do that, too. This time, from the Configure screen, just drag-and-drop the four editable home row buttons to reorder them. When you're happy with your newly-customized iPod home row, tap the Done button on the top right of the Configure screen.

Buy Music with the iTunes Wi-Fi Music Store

Two months after the iPhone was released, Apple introduced the iPod Touch, and with it an application that wirelessly (over Wi-Fi) browses and downloads music directly to your iPod. They also brought that ability over to the iPhone with the iTunes Wi-Fi Music Store application. Best of all, songs you purchase wirelessly will sync back to your computer the next time your dock your iPhone.

Browse the iTunes Wi-Fi Music Store

When you start up the iTunes Wi-Fi Music Store, you'll be greeted with the store interface. On the top, there's the New Releases, What's Hot, and Genres Tabs. On the bottom, there's the Featured, Top Tens, Search, and Downloads Tabs.

- **Featured**   Selected songs and artists that Apple decided to highlight
- **Top Tens**   The bestselling songs of the moment, sorted by genre
- **Search**   Search for songs, artists, and albums here, just as you would on a computer.
- **Downloads**   View both currently downloading files and the queued download files. You can see how many downloads are pending by the red number on top of the Downloads icon.
- **New Releases**   The latest songs released on iTunes
- **What's Hot**   The popular songs on iTunes

If you find a song that you're interested in, but that you're not quite ready to buy, tap the song to hear a 30-second preview.

Buy Music with the iTunes Wi-Fi Music Store

Buying music on the iTunes Wi-Fi Music Store is easy as well. Whenever you're looking at a song—under any view—you can tap the price button on the right-hand side to bring up the Buy button. Tap the Buy button to confirm that you want to buy the song, and you'll be prompted to enter in your iTunes password. Once entered, the song will jump into your Downloads section. You can view the songs you're currently downloading by tapping the Downloads button.

Buying albums works the exact same way. Instead of tapping the price button next to an individual song, tap the price button underneath the album name. If you're sure you want to buy the album, confirm the purchase by tapping the Buy button. This will add all the songs from that album into your download queue and start downloading.

Buy Starbucks Music with the iTunes Wi-Fi Music Store

Apple also partnered with Starbucks, which enables you to access not only the iTunes Wi-Fi Music Store from Starbucks, but Starbucks music as well. When you're within range of a participating Starbucks location, you'll get free access to wirelessly browse both stores (but not web surfing and email checking) in order to purchase songs. You won't need to get a login or password from the cashier in order to use this feature.

When you load up the iTunes Wi-Fi Music Store at a Starbucks, a Starbucks icon will appear on the bottom left. Tapping this will bring you to the Starbucks interface, which has the currently playing song (the song playing in the store) on the top of the screen, as well as another section to access the last ten played tracks. You can even browse around their other sections below the Recently Played section to see the other featured music that Starbucks has.

Buying music from Starbucks works the same as buying it from the regular iTunes Wi-Fi Music Store. Tap the Price button next to a track or an album to bring up the Buy button, and tap the Buy button to purchase the song. Your iTunes account password may be required.

Tweak Your iPod Settings

There are a few tweaks that give you even more control over your iPod and can make the iPod experience even more enjoyable. To get to these, go to the Home screen, launch the Settings app, and then find and tap the iPod listing to get to the iPod Settings screen, as shown in Figure 4-9.

- **Sound Check** This option allows songs recorded at different levels to be played back at the same volume. If you have a playlist with two albums, one recorded really loudly and the other softly, you may find yourself fiddling with the volume every time the track changes. Sound Check equalizes this. To turn it on, open up iTunes preferences on your computer (Mac or PC), go to Playback, and then select Sound Check. Next, in your iPod Settings, make sure Sound Check is switched on.

- **Audiobook Speed** You can speed up audiobooks to play back faster if you want to save time, or slower if you need time to make out words more clearly.

- **EQ** The EQ customizes the sound output to accommodate a certain musical style or speaker type. For example, Small Speakers is a good option to choose if you're playing back music through the iPhone's built-in speakers. Spoken Word is a good option for audiobooks.

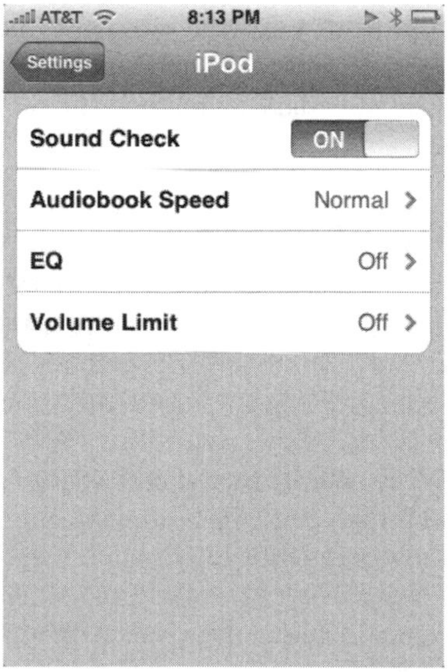

FIGURE 4-9 The iPod settings screen

- **Volume Limit**   To prevent music and videos from being accidentally played back at a really loud volume when you have your headphones on, drag the volume slider under Volume Limit. To prevent anyone else from changing this volume limit, click Lock Volume Limit and type in a four-digit code.

Use the Headphones and Other Accessories

Along with letting you control calls, the iPhone headphones actually let you control music and video playback as well. To pause a song or video, all you have to do is click the in-line button once. To resume playback, click it again. To skip to the next song, click the in-line button twice in quick succession.

> TIP
>
> *You don't have to manually pause playback every time you want to take your headphones out and put your iPhone away. The mere act of unplugging the headphones pauses playback, letting you quickly shove both iPhone and headphones in your pockets for a quick dash out the door.*

Use Your iPhone with an iPod Dock

The iPhone will work in most iPod speaker docks, even if they don't have an explicit Made for iPhone label (this applies to virtually all products that came out before the iPhone. To find out whether they work together, just plug your iPhone into the dock and start playing back a song. If the dock isn't expressly Made for iPhone, a warning window will come up asking whether you want to turn on Airplane mode in order to avoid possible interference. Turning on Airplane mode means you won't get any calls, SMS messages, or emails, so most of the time you'll want to answer no. However, answering no means you may have some static and interference on the speakers occasionally when the iPhone is communicating with the cell phone network.

> TIP
>
> *Like unplugging your headphones, unplugging the iPhone from a dock automatically pauses music and video playback. This lets you quickly take your iPhone with you when you need to leave, without forcing you to fiddle with onscreen controls.*

Further Accessorize Your iPhone

Just like with the iPod, there are a lot of third-party accessories that extend and supplement the iPhone's functionality. For example, Belkin's headphone adapter allows all types of headphones to be plugged into the iPhone's recessed headphone jack. Also, there's a Shure microphone adapter that lets any headphone plug in, but also includes an in-line microphone so you can make calls with any headset too. And of course, many iPod docks (like the iCarta Toilet Paper dock) work just fine with the iPhone. See Chapter 15 for more information on which iPod docks, car adapters, and remote control units work with the iPhone, and any gotchas you have to watch out for.

Chapter 5

Sync and Manage Your Music and Movies with iTunes

How to...

■ Familiarize yourself with iTunes

■ Add music and videos to iTunes

■ Make and manage playlists

■ Make custom ringtones for your iPhone

■ Sync music and video to your iPhone

You can take your iPhone with you anywhere, and when you do you're carrying with you the best portable music and media experience this side of your desktop computer. There's only one way you can sync music and video onto the iPhone, and that's with Apple's hugely popular digital jukebox-and-then-some application, iTunes. You may already have been using iTunes before you bought your iPhone, but we're going to show you how to use iTunes to take full advantage of your iPhone; from using the iTunes Store to buy music and movies, to ripping CDs and DVDs to your iTunes library, to creating custom dynamic playlists to store it all.

Familiarize Yourself with iTunes

You're probably already at least slightly familiar with iTunes (shown in Figure 5-1)—especially after using it to sync data between your iPhone and your computer in Chapters 1-4—but if you've never used iTunes to manage your music and videos, there are a few ins and outs you might want to familiarize yourself with in order to make syncing media to your iPhone even simpler.

The iTunes interface is made of a consistently two-paned interface. The first pane on the left is a narrow sidebar with a list of subheadings under the headings of Library, Store, Shared, Devices, and Playlists. Clicking any of those subheadings will change the content of the second pane, which is the main iTunes content window. These subheadings include:

■ **Library** You can access your Music, Movies, TV Shows, Podcasts, Audiobooks, iPod Games, and Internet Radio through the Library section of the content sidebar. If you click Music, for example, all of the music in your iTunes library appears in the main content pane. You can view much of your Library content in three modes: List, Grouped, and Cover Flow modes. List view shows your music or video in one long list that can be sorted in any number of ways by clicking on the column headers (by Name, Artist, or Album, for example). Grouped view sorts your music, podcasts, or audiobooks in lists next to their album art and displays your videos by thumbnails. If you've been using the iPod on your iPhone, you should already be familiar with the third view, Cover Flow, which displays every album in your music library by album art (or podcasts by associated images, videos by thumbnails, and so on). Clicking on an album in Cover Flow mode in iTunes displays the tracks from that album below the artwork.

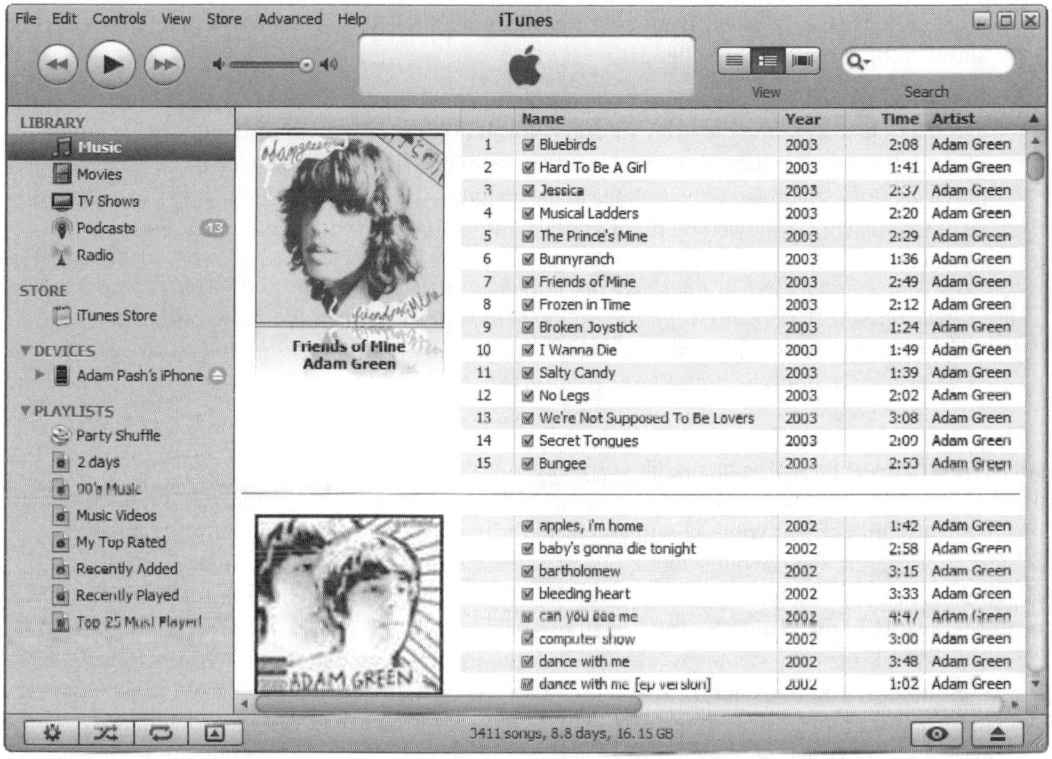

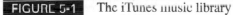

		Name	Year	Time	Artist
	1	☑ Bluebirds	2003	2:08	Adam Green
	2	☑ Hard To Be A Girl	2003	1:41	Adam Green
	3	☑ Jessica	2003	2:37	Adam Green
	4	☑ Musical Ladders	2003	2:20	Adam Green
	5	☑ The Prince's Mine	2003	2:29	Adam Green
	6	☑ Bunnyranch	2003	1:36	Adam Green
	7	☑ Friends of Mine	2003	2:49	Adam Green
	8	☑ Frozen in Time	2003	2:12	Adam Green
	9	☑ Broken Joystick	2003	1:24	Adam Green
	10	☑ I Wanna Die	2003	1:49	Adam Green
	11	☑ Salty Candy	2003	1:39	Adam Green
	12	☑ No Legs	2003	2:02	Adam Green
	13	☑ We're Not Supposed To Be Lovers	2003	3:08	Adam Green
	14	☑ Secret Tongues	2003	2:00	Adam Green
	15	☑ Bungee	2003	2:53	Adam Green
		☑ apples, i'm home	2002	1:42	Adam Green
		☑ baby's gonna die tonight	2002	2:58	Adam Green
		☑ bartholomew	2002	3:15	Adam Green
		☑ bleeding heart	2002	3:33	Adam Green
		☑ can you see me	2002	4:47	Adam Green
		☑ computer show	2002	3:00	Adam Green
		☑ dance with me	2002	3:48	Adam Green
		☑ dance with me [ep version]	2002	1:02	Adam Green

3411 songs, 8.8 days, 16.15 GB

FIGURE 5-1   The iTunes music library

- **Store**   There's only one item under the store heading, and that's the iTunes Store. Clicking it will open the iTunes Store (naturally), from which you can buy music, movies, TV shows, and other premium content. The iTunes Store launches much like a website in the main content pane, so once it's open, you can interact with the contents of the store like it's a web page.

- **Shared**   iTunes lets you share your library on your local network with other iTunes users so you can stream media to and from other computers. If iTunes detects a shared library on your network, that shared library will automatically be listed under the Shared section with a descriptive name (like Jason's Disco-filled Library). Click on a shared library to view all of that user's shared media. From that point, playing a song from another user's shared library works the same as playing a song from your own library.

■ **Devices**   You may have noticed that any time you plug in your iPhone, it shows up in a list under Devices. Apart from your iPhone, only docked iPods and inserted CDs will show up under the Devices header.

■ **Playlists**   All this media wouldn't be worth much without a simple way to organize it, and that's just what the Playlists section is for. It holds the Party Shuffle playlist, a number of default smart playlists, along with every custom playlist you create (see more on creating playlists, both smart and regular, later in the chapter). The Party Shuffle playlist will always sit at the top spot, followed by all of your smart playlists and then regular playlists.

NOTE   *The Shared and Devices headings are only visible under specific conditions, so don't be alarmed if they're missing! Shared items appear only when there are other shared iTunes libraries available on your network. Devices only appears if you've inserted a CD or you've docked your iPhone or an iPod.*

At the top right of the iTunes window is the iTunes search box. This text box searches the contents of whatever part of your media you're currently viewing. For example, if you're looking at your music library, you can search for any part of a song (title, artist, album, and so on) and the main content window will produce dynamic, as-you-type results for the music matching your search. On the other hand, if you're viewing the iTunes Store, the search box works more like a regular search box on a website. Type in what you're looking for, then hit enter to see results in the iTunes Store.

You can tweak the way iTunes works through the Preferences dialog box. To open the iTunes Preferences window, click Edit and then Preferences (or type CTRL-,) on Windows, or click iTunes and then Preferences (or CMD-,) on your Mac. Inside the Preferences window, you can access loads of iTunes settings, all of which fall under the categories of General, Podcasts, Playback, Sharing, iPhone, Apple TV, Store, Advanced, and Parental. We recommend going through the Preferences window one section at a time to get a better idea of how you can tweak iTunes to work exactly how you want, but we'll also discuss a few settings that we personally like to change later on in this chapter.

NOTE   *iTunes' Help section has many tips and tricks to help you get the most out of your music and videos before you get them onto the iPhone. Not only can its shortcuts save you time, but there is also information for hidden features that you may not be aware of.*

Add Music and Videos to iTunes

You can only sync media to the iPhone that you've already got in your iTunes library. That means that before you can play any media with your iPhone—whether it's music, video, podcasts, or audiobooks—you need to put that media into iTunes. Depending on how you like to acquire your digital media, there are a handful of simple ways to get music and videos into your iTunes library.

Buy Music and Videos from the iTunes Store

To find and buy media from the iTunes Store, just click on the iTunes Store link under Store in the left column of iTunes. Once in, you're greeted with the iTunes Store interface, with links on the left-hand side that take you to Music, Movies, TV Shows, Music Videos, Audiobooks, and Podcasts. The iTunes Store shown in Figure 5-2 works a lot like a traditional website, only it's embedded in iTunes instead of your web browser. You can either browse around the store with the links presented to you on the page, or if you know exactly what you want, type in the search term in the top right corner of iTunes.

After you've chosen a song, movie, or album to buy, just click on the Buy Song, Buy Movie, or Buy Album button for that selection. If you're not already logged in, iTunes will ask you for your Apple account information and log you in. Since you already attached credit card information to your account when you signed up for iTunes in order to activate your phone, iTunes will automatically charge you the appropriate amount. You can take a look at all your purchased items by clicking the Purchase link on the left side of iTunes, under Store. You can even track the download progress of currently purchased items here as well.

FIGURE 5-2   The iTunes Store

NOTE *iTunes has two methods of purchasing songs, 1-Click and Shopping Cart. If you choose the 1-Click method, your songs will automatically be purchased and downloaded as soon as you click the Buy button. If you use the Shopping Cart method, all your purchases will be added to a cart first for you to view and approve before any money is transferred.*

Import Your CDs into iTunes

Unless you were born in the twenty-first century (or the first century, A.i. [after iPod]), chances are you own a few CDs. Since you've already spent your hard-earned money on this music, there's no reason why you should have to buy it all over again just to get the songs into iTunes. That's why Apple made it simple to rip a CD to your library, as shown in Figure 5-3. To do this, follow these steps:

1. Launch iTunes and insert the CD you want to rip. Wait a few seconds for iTunes to recognize that you've inserted a CD and then retrieve the album's information from

FIGURE 5-3   Importing a CD into iTunes

Gracenote CDDB (an online database containing album information like track titles, artists, and album names). If your CD is recognized (most are), all of the CD's track information will show up in iTunes.

2. Depending on your settings, once iTunes retrieves the album information you may be prompted to import the CD into your iTunes library. If you want to import the entire album, go ahead and say yes. If not, you can choose which songs you don't want to import by unchecking the boxes next to them. When you're ready to import, click the button on the bottom right of iTunes that says Import CD to start importing the album.

3. In the iTunes display, you'll see the song that is currently being imported along with the time remaining. When a song has finished importing, you'll see a green checkmark icon next to it. Just wait for all of your songs to import and you've done it: That album now lives as digital music files in iTunes.

Download and Import Music into iTunes

The iTunes Music Store isn't the only way you can get music into iTunes, and by extension, onto your iPhone. There are many other subscription music services you may already be subscribed to, like Rhapsody, Napster, and Zune Marketplace, which let you buy or rent tracks. But the songs that come from these stores use a Digital Rights Management (DRM) scheme that is incompatible with iTunes and the iPhone. In other words, these songs are protected from being played in software and hardware music players that don't support their particular standard (just like non-iPod music players can't play most music from the iTunes Music Store). However, the online digital music store eMusic sells DRM-free MP3s, and there are many websites where you can download free and legal MP3s that don't contain DRM and can be imported into the iPhone easily.

Did you know?

MP3 Is a Widely Used Format for Digital Music

By default, iTunes rips songs to AAC format, and although AAC is a very high-quality format, it isn't as widely-supported as the ubiquitous MP3 format, which enjoys support from virtually every digital music player known to man, including your iPhone. To ensure greater portability of your music (and prevent you from feeling locked into one product just because you've ripped all your music in one format), we suggest ripping your CDs as MP3s. To do so, go to the Preferences menu and click the tab labeled Advanced. Next click the Importing tab. Select MP3 Encoder from the Import Using Dropdown menu and Higher Quality (192 kbps) from the Setting dropdown.

Import MP3s

Once you've downloaded MP3s onto your computer, it's easy to import them into iTunes. First make a new playlist by going to the File menu and clicking New Playlist and naming it anything you like. (You don't have to make a new playlist, but we find that it helps to keep your newly imported music in one place so you can easily organize it afterwards.) Select that playlist in iTunes, then drag your MP3s from your hard drive into the right-hand pane. iTunes will start importing your music and populating the playlist with songs. After it's done, you're free to play back the songs or sync them to your iPhone just like all the rest of your library.

Import WMAs

Importing unprotected Windows Media Audio (WMA) files is just like importing MP3 files, but requires one additional step. With MP3s, iTunes will import only a pointer to the file in order to find the song when you need it. This way there aren't multiple unnecessary copies of the song floating around your hard drive when you only need one. With WMA files, iTunes will actually transcode the songs and change the format from WMA to something it can understand—namely, to whatever default audio encoder you've set in the iTunes Preferences (see the Did You Know sidebar earlier in this chapter for more information). It's not necessary to know the difference between WMAs, MP3s, and AACs, but you should know that when you import WMAs, your original files are untouched and a new file is created. If you don't have any other use for your WMAs, you may want to delete them or archive them somewhere else to save space.

Organize Your Songs' Meta Information

When you buy songs from iTunes, the music files you download already have data embedded in them telling you who the artist is, the track name, and the CD it belongs to. That may not be the case for MP3s you download off the Internet. What's this data (also known as metadata or ID3 tags) for? Many things, such as making it easy for you to identify a song, organize your music, and even make smart playlists. To add or edit this data, first select a song, right-click on it, and then select Get Info. A new window will appear (Figure 5-4) with several tabs for adding metadata. Here's a rundown of what each of them means:

- **Summary** A general overview that gives you a read-only, non-modifiable synopsis of the file. Here you can see what type of file it is, the bit-rate it was encoded at, how many times it's been played, and most importantly, where it is in on your computer (or on the network).

- **Info** The area where you'll do most of your modifications. You can change all the song identification information here, and iTunes will auto-complete most of the fields for you with entries you've previously entered for other songs.

- **Sorting** If you've entered in data for your songs in the Info tab, you can change how the songs are sorted in the Sorting tab. For example, if there is more than one composer for a song, you can make iTunes sort by only one them when sorting by composer. Or, you can put down something completely different to sort by under composers.

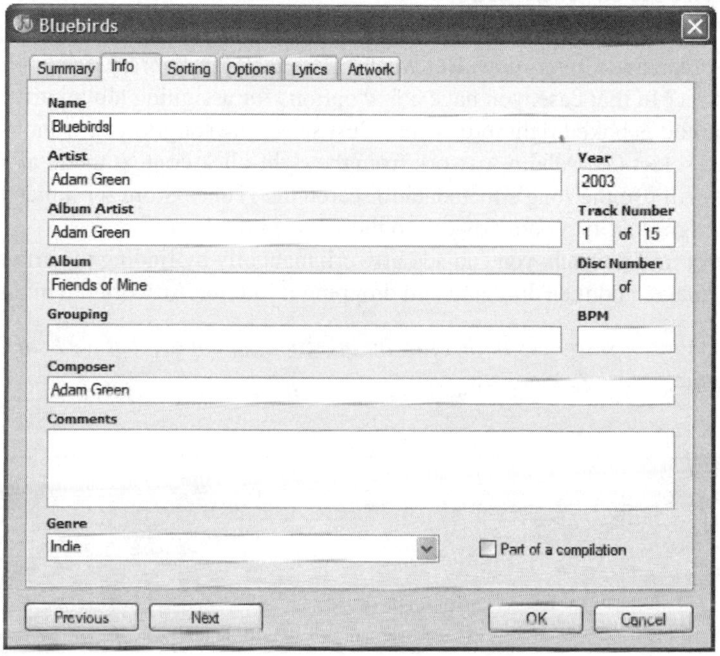

FIGURE 5-4   The Info metadata screen

- **Options**   These are mostly playback options, such as volume and equalizer adjustment. You can also manually tell iTunes to remember the position you left off playing a track.

- **Lyrics**   This is where you copy and paste lyrics for a song. If a song has lyrics embedded, you'll be able to view them during playback in iTunes.

- **Artwork**   The Album cover or album artwork can be added or deleted here (*and in the Info tab*). The album art shows up on your iPhone when playing tracks and browsing in Cover Flow mode.

SHORTCUT   *You can modify metadata for multiple songs at the same time by highlighting them, right-clicking on them, and then clicking Get Info. After you get to the Info screen, modifying everything else here is the same as modifying a single song. Just be aware that changing song titles will modify them for all the tracks you select. You'll probably want to stick to changing stuff like album name, genre, and other fields that are constant across the entire album.*

Add Album Artwork to Your Music

The iPhone takes full advantage of tracks that have been assigned album artwork, both through the Now Playing screen and Cover Flow. But what if a track in your library doesn't have album artwork assigned to it? In that case, you have a few options for assigning album artwork.

The easiest method is baked right into iTunes. Just select the song(s) you want to add album artwork to and then select Get Album Artwork from the right-click context menu as shown in Figure 5-5. iTunes will use the song's metadata to search the iTunes Store for a match, then automatically add high-quality album artwork to the selected track(s).

If iTunes doesn't find a match, you can add artwork manually by finding the artwork yourself online, saving the image, and then dragging and dropping it into the Artwork tab in that file's info.

TIP *There are a lot of resources online for finding good album art, but we heartily recommend.* http://www.cdcovers.cc/.

FIGURE 5-5   Adding an album cover to your songs makes Cover Flow view that much more appealing.

Make Video Content for Your iPhone

You don't have to buy videos from the iTunes Store to get good video content onto your iPhone. In fact, you can actually make your own iPhone-compatible videos out of DVDs or other videos you already have on your computer. All it takes are the right tools.

Transcode Videos into iPhone-Compatible Format

The iPhone can only play videos encoded in one of two video formats: H.264 and MPEG-4. These files can end in .m4v, .mp4, and .mov file extensions. Some .mov files can be converted for your iPhone directly in iTunes by right-clicking the video and then selecting Convert Selection for iPod. However, not all of your movies will work using this method. There was a time you'd need to be somewhat of a video guru in order to convert incompatible videos to the proper formats, but nowadays there are several programs that make it easy to convert videos specifically for playing on the iPhone.

Convert Videos for Your iPhone Online with Zamzar (Windows/Mac)   If you've got a high speed Internet connection and a video file you'd like to make compatible with your iPhone, the easiest method for converting it is with the Zamzar website. To use it, point your desktop web browser to http://zamzar.com/

Once you're there, the steps for converting your video are spelled out for you:

1. Browse your computer for the file that you want to convert. You can even convert a YouTube video for your iPhone by clicking the URL link given above.
2. Choose iPhone from the dropdown menu under Video Formats.
3. Enter your email address. Zamzar works by first converting the video to the appropriate format on their servers, and then sending you a link to download the iPhone formatted video when it's ready.
4. Click the Convert button and wait for your browser to finish uploading the video file.

That's all there is to it. As I said, when your video has been converted to the appropriate format, you'll receive an email with a link to download the file. Remember that Zamzar has a 100MB limit on videos, so if you have a larger video file you'd like to convert—or you'd prefer converting the videos yourself—see one of the following sections on converting videos to iPhone-compatible formats using desktop applications.

Convert Videos for Your iPhone with iSquint (Mac)   You can convert virtually any video format to an iPhone-compatible format on your Mac using a freeware program called iSquint. First, go download iSquint here:

http://www.isquint.org/.

After you install iSquint, launch the application. Now just drag and drop the video file you want to convert into iSquint, select the radio button next to Convert for my iPod, and then check the Add to iTunes and H.264 Encoding checkboxes. Click the Start button. iSquint will convert the video (as shown in Figure 5-6) and automatically add it to iTunes, where it will be ready for syncing the next time you dock your iPhone. Feel free to adjust the quality settings slider in iSquint to your taste, remembering that the higher quality the video, the more space it will take up.

If you're a big fan of YouTube but you don't want to rely on streaming the video from the Internet every time you want to watch it on your iPhone, there are a couple of great Mac applications that make doing this easy:

- **TubeTV (freeware)** `http://www.chimoosoft.com/products/tubetv/`
- **PodTube (shareware)** `http://djodjodesign.free.fr/podtube.html`

Convert Videos for Your iPhone with Videora (Windows)   Converting video to an iPhone-friendly format on Windows is a breeze, too. There are a lot of different programs available for Windows—both free and shareware—that can handle this job, but the software I'm going to use in this section is called Videora iPhone Converter, and you can download it here: `http://www.videora.com/en-us/Converter/iPhone/`

If you see more than one Windows download, be sure to grab the one labeled Windows GUI. After you install Videora, here's how it works:

1. Launch Videora iPhone Converter, and then click the tab at the top labeled Convert.

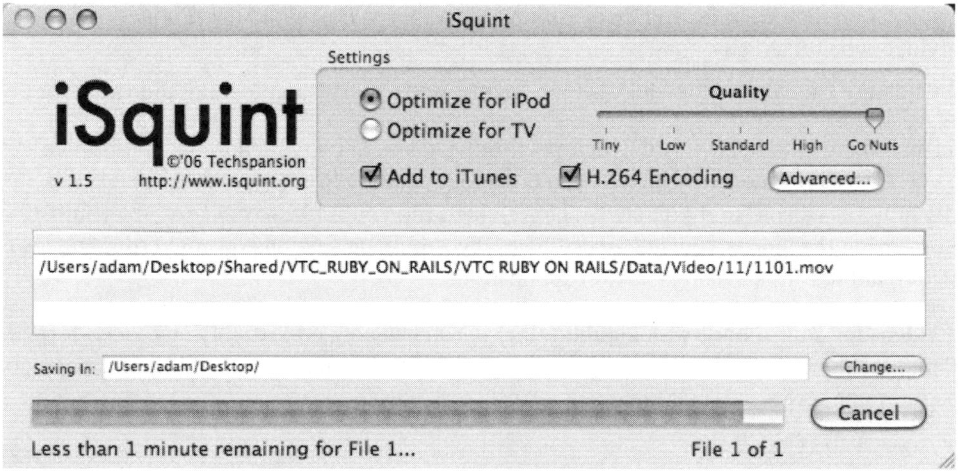

FIGURE 5-6   iSquint converting video

2. At the bottom of the window, you'll see a button that says Select File. Click that button and navigate through your Windows folders until you find the video you want to convert for your iPhone.

3. Now you can tweak the video settings. You should probably keep most of the items set to their defaults, but feel free to play around—especially with video quality—to find what works best for you.

4. Now click the Start Converting button on the bottom right of the Videora window. Your file will start converting to an iPhone-friendly format. You can see the estimated time the transcode will take and follow the progress bar as seen in Figure 5-7. Often, transcoding this way can take nearly as much time as the video is long, so make sure you've got some time.

5. When Videora has completed transcoding the video, click the Library tab. You should see your new video listed. Select it and click the Add to iTunes button on the bottom right of the window. The video should automatically be added to your iTunes library, and is now ready to sync to your iPhone.

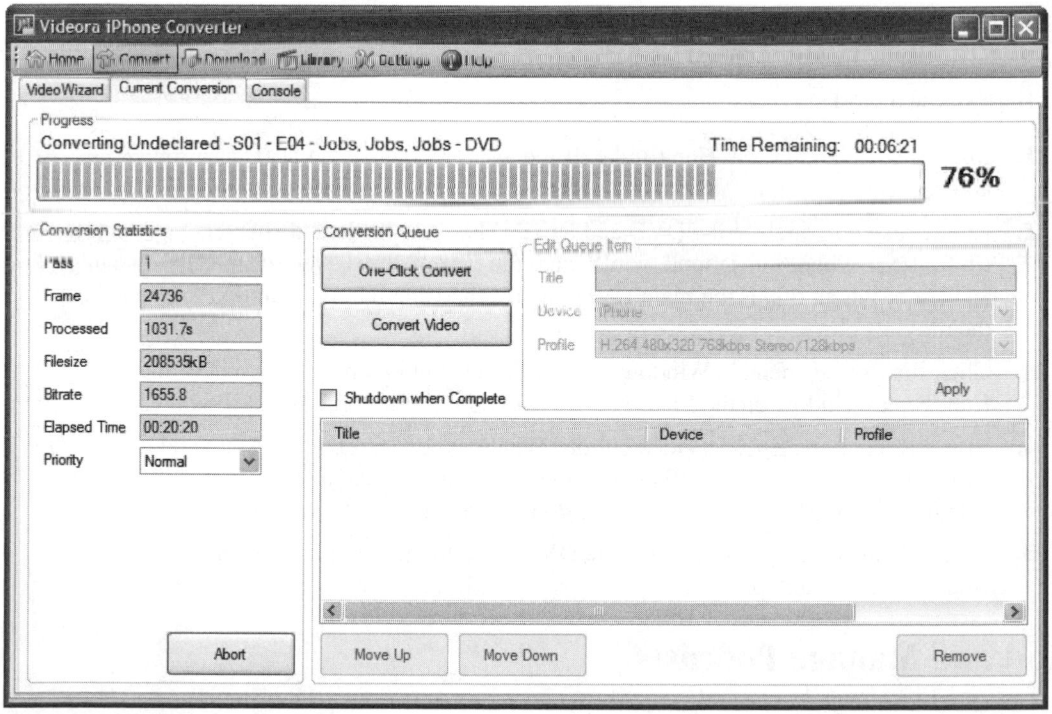

FIGURE 5-7   Videora converting video for your iPhone

TIP *You can make Videora automatically add all converted videos to iTunes by first clicking the Settings tab and then ticking the checkbox labeled Add Converted Videos to iTunes Library.*

Videora can also download and convert YouTube videos for iPhone consumption if you don't want to rely on an EDGE or Wi-Fi connection every time you want to watch your favorite YouTube video. Go to the Download tab in Videora, browse YouTube for the video, and click the Download button (it looks like a green arrow pointing at a hard drive). iPod Video Converter will take care of the rest.

TIP *If you download a lot of video off the Internet, another free program called iPodifier can actually monitor a folder and automatically convert all new videos to an iPhone-friendly format and add the new file to iTunes.*

Rip DVDs into iPhone Format with HandBrake (Windows/Mac)

Sure you can buy movies from the iTunes Store ready for iPhone consumption, but if you already own the DVD, you don't want to waste your money on the same movie a second time. Instead, you can rip the DVD to a video file on your computer, move it into iTunes, and then sync it to your iPhone. The program we'll use to do this is called HandBrake, and it's available for free on both Windows and Mac. First, download HandBrake here and install it:
`http://handbrake.m0k.org/`

Here's how it works:

1. Insert a DVD and launch HandBrake. If it doesn't recognize the DVD as a source automatically, you may have to click Browse and direct HandBrake to your DVD drive.

2. HandBrake will analyze the DVD and let you choose the title and chapters you want to rip for your iPhone (in general, you'll want the first title and every chapter). You can get an idea of which title is the main DVD title by choosing the title duration that matches the movie's playtime.

3. Click the Presets menu in Windows, or the Presets button on the top right of the HandBrake window on the Mac. You'll see several presets; choose an iPod preset.

4. Now just click the Encode Video button (Windows) or Start button (Mac) and sit back while HandBrake rips the DVD to one big file. This can take a while, so you won't be able to rip a DVD on your way out the door to the airport. Make sure you plan ahead.

5. When HandBrake finishes ripping the DVD, drag the file into iTunes for syncing whenever you want to.

Find and Manage Podcasts

Podcasts are user-created radio and video shows you can easily download using iTunes. These (mostly) free programs are created by professionals and amateurs alike and are then released and

Video Requires Lot of Space on Your iPhone

A ripped movie can take up a lot of space on your iPhone. For example, an hour and a half movie ripped from a DVD with HandBrake will require about 1GB of space. You can easily fit a 1GB movie on the iPhone, but if you already have a lot of content synced, you may have to remove other movies or music to make room.

distributed over the Internet in the form of episodes. You can subscribe to a podcast using iTunes, so that whenever a new episode of the podcast becomes available, iTunes will automatically download it for you. It can be hard to sift through all of the available podcast content and find the gems, but the iTunes Music Store makes it simple.

Find and Subscribe to Podcasts

Open up the iTunes music store and click Podcasts on the left side under iTunes Store. This will take you to the podcast section of iTunes. You can browse this section just like the rest of the iTunes Store by clicking on categories you're interested in or performing a direct search (in the search box on the top right) to find a specific podcast. If you're new to podcasts, you can click around in the Today's Top Podcasts box and the Featured Video Podcasts box to see what others think are the best recent podcasts. Once you choose a podcast and want to subscribe to it, click the Subscribe button on their podcast page as shown in Figure 5-8. Make sure it says Free next to the podcast unless you're intending to buy a premium podcast.

Manage Podcasts

When you subscribe to a podcast, it will be added to your podcast directory and the most recent episode (along with all future episodes) will automatically be downloaded into iTunes. To play back your podcasts, click Podcasts under the Library section in the left iTunes sidebar. You'll see the podcast you just subscribed to with a gray triangle on the left. Double-clicking the entry will play the latest episode. However, if you click the gray arrow, the podcast will expand to show you all of its episodes.

> TIP
>
> *Just like on your iPhone, a blue dot next to a podcast indicates that you haven't listened to or watched any of that podcast yet.*

You can download any individual old episodes of the podcast prior to the most recent episode by clicking the Get button, or you can grab all of the old episodes by clicking Get All.

FIGURE 5-8 Subscribe to podcasts with iTunes.

Choose Which Podcasts Sync to Your iPhone

You have a lot of options for how you sync podcasts, so dock your iPhone, go to the Podcasts sync tab, and let's dive in. First, make sure to check the Sync box on top. Then, from the dropdown menu, you'll see that you have loads of options for which and how many podcasts you sync. You can sync

- All podcasts, or just the 1–10 most recently downloaded episodes, regardless of whether or not you've already listened to or viewed them
- All unplayed podcasts, or just the 1–10 most recent unplayed episodes
- All new podcasts, or just the 1–10 newest episodes

The difference between an unplayed and new podcast is pretty subtle. Basically, a podcast is no longer new after the first time you start playing it—just as an email is marked as read as soon as you open it. However, a podcast can be unplayed—but not new—if you started playing it but never finished it. It's not considered played until you listen to or watch the entire podcast all the way through to the end.

How to ...   **Manage Podcasts in iTunes**

Just as podcasts can take up a good deal of space on your iPhone, they can occupy a lot of space on your computer as well, especially when you've clicked Get All on a podcast with a big archive or you've been subscribed to a podcast for a long time. Instead of manually monitoring your disk space and deleting old podcasts, go to the Podcasts section of the iTunes Preferences and change the setting labeled Keep. You can tell iTunes to keep all episodes, all unplayed episodes, your most recent episodes, or the last 2–10 episodes. If you want to manually manage your podcasts, deleting old podcasts from iTunes that you don't want anymore is still a good idea. When you delete a podcast, iTunes will ask you to confirm that you want to remove it from your library and then whether you want to move the actual file to your Trash/Recycle bin or keep the files. If space is an issue, tell iTunes to move the file to your Trash/Recycle Bin.

Download and Create Audiobooks with iTunes

If you like listening to books on-the-go, you'll need to become familiar with how to get audiobooks into iTunes. Whether you're buying them through iTunes, Audible, or importing your own, it's a fairly simple process.

Buy Audiobooks from iTunes

Go to the iTunes Store homepage and click Audiobooks under the iTunes Store sidebar. iTunes will display a list of categories, highlighted audiobooks, and a list of the top ten audiobooks. You can navigate through the audiobook offerings this way, or if you know specifically what you're looking for, you can use the iTunes search box on the top left of the iTunes window. When you find the audiobook you want, click the Buy Book button to purchase and download the audiobook. Audiobooks aren't cheap (they can cost up to $50), so make sure you're buying the right one.

After the download is complete, you can find the book by clicking Audiobook under the Library section of the iTunes sidebar.

Buy Audiobooks from Audible.com

If the book you're looking for isn't available in the iTunes Store, check out the online audiobook website Audible.com. Audible houses an enormous library of audiobooks, so chances are if the title you're looking for is available as an audiobook, Audible has it. If you're on a Mac, audiobooks you download from Audible will be automatically added to your iTunes library. Windows users should download a program from Audible called Audible Download Manager for iTunes and iPod, which helps you push downloaded audiobooks directly into iTunes. You can find it here:

```
http://www.audible.com/software/
```

Make Your Own Audiobooks

If you've already got audiobooks that you purchased on CDs, or maybe you've got MP3s of audiobooks, you can still get them into iTunes and have them be recognized as audiobooks. It just takes a little more effort and know-how.

For audio files on your computer that are already encoded with the AAC audio encoder and have the .m4a filename, it's pretty simple. Just find the file on your hard drive and change the .m4a extension to .m4b, which is the default file extension for audiobooks in iTunes.

If you've already ripped an audiobook to MP3 format, you'll need to convert it to AAC before renaming it. You can do this directly in iTunes by setting the default encoder to AAC (though in general we recommend keeping it set to MP3 for reasons discussed earlier in this chapter) through the Advanced Importing Preferences shown in Figure 5-9, then right-clicking the song and selecting Convert Selection to AAC. This all may seem like a bit of a pain, but if you already own an audiobook in one form or another, it may be worth it to avoid spending another fifty dollars.

TIP *Windows users can download a freeware program called MP3 to iPod Audio Book Converter that will handle all of this legwork through a simple interface. You can download it at http://www.freeipodsoftware.com/.*

Make and Manage Playlists

Unless your library only contains a handful of albums and songs, you'll want to organize music and movies into playlists. This allows you to not only line up a bunch of songs for a certain occasion—say, a house party you're hosting—but it also helps you organize your music so that you can be very selective about what you sync to your iPhone. There are two types of playlists: standard playlists and smart playlists.

Build a Playlist

There are three ways to create a regular playlist:

- Click File, and then New Playlist.
- Highlight more than one file in your current view (any view is fine, even of another playlist), click File, and then New Playlist from Selection. You can also just drag the highlighted files into the left column and onto the word Playlists.
- Click the + button on the bottom left of your iTunes window.

Once you've created a playlist using any of these methods, type a name for it. Now you'll want to start putting media inside! You can add media by dragging anything from your iTunes library or from other playlists into the one you've just created.

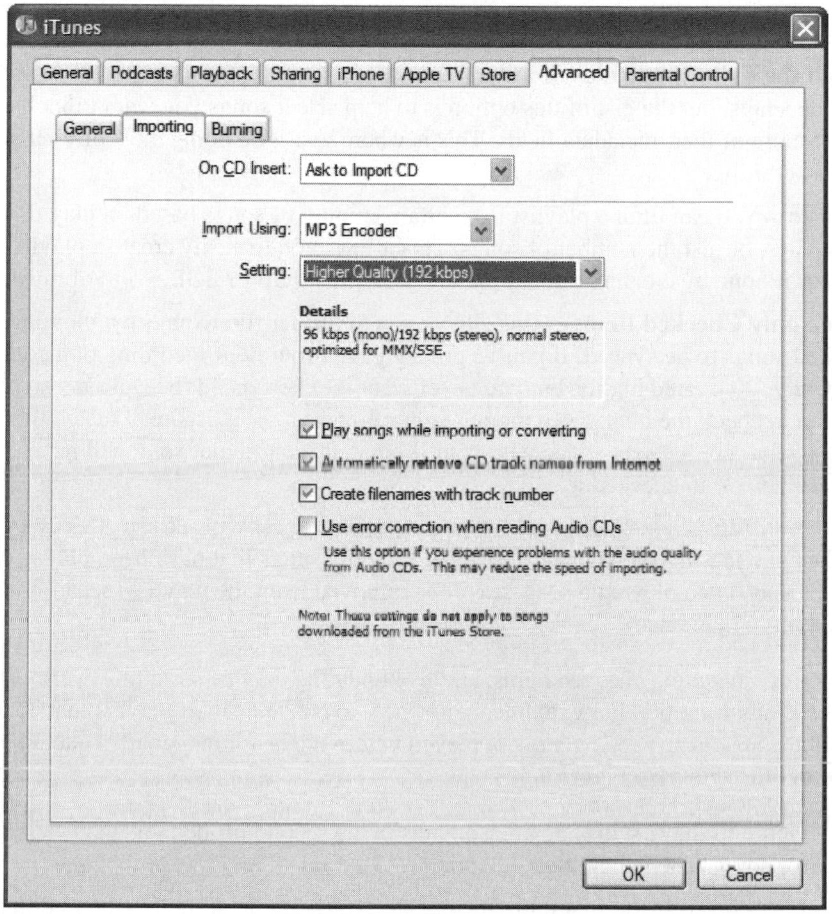

FIGURE 5-9   The iTunes importing preference screen

Create a Dynamic Smart Playlist

Smart playlists are where iTunes shines as a music management application. If you've been diligently rating songs and making sure all your music has the right metadata, all that work is about to pay off. With smart playlists, you can create playlists that contain only your favorite songs (songs with four or five stars), songs that were made in the '90s, songs that haven't been played in the last year, songs you've played less than five times, songs you've skipped more than five times, or pretty much anything at all. It's up to you and your creativity to think of ways you can group certain songs together while excluding others. Here's how you start.

To build a smart playlist, first click File, then New Smart Playlist.... Now, you'll have four top-level options to choose from.

- **Match the Following Rule**   You can actually create multiple rules to include and exclude songs, but the gist of this option is to help select songs you want to include by one or more of their metadata fields. This is where you'll be doing most of your smart playlist crafting.

- **Limit to**   You can limit a playlist to a certain amount of songs based on play time, size of the files, or just the number of songs. This allows you to easily create a playlist to sync on your iPhone by creating a smart playlist with only 4GB or 8GB worth of music.

- **Match only Checked Items**   This allows you to further filter songs by allowing only checked songs to be synced. If you've got a gigantic four hour recording of a concert that you you've rated highly, but you never want it to be synced (because it's so huge), you can uncheck the item. Even though your other smart playlists may match this into playlists that you've set to sync with your iPhone, this particular song will never sync because you've unchecked it.

- **Live Updating**   Selecting this option means your playlist will refresh after every song finishes playing. If you have a playlist that has only songs that have been played once, as soon as you finish playing a song, it will be removed from the playlist (because it's been played more than once).

While limiting, matching checked items, and live updating may be straightforward options, matching rules is anything but. For example, here's how to create a smart playlist that contains the highest rated songs in any rock genre not played within the last three months, excluding the band Wolfmother (as shown in Figure 5-10):

1. Select Genre in the first dropdown, Contains in the second dropdown, and Rock in the third dropdown. Then click the + button.

2. Select Last Played in the first dropdown and Is Not In the Last in the second dropdown. Type **3** into the third box, and select Months in the fourth dropdown. Then click the + button.

3. Select My Rating in the first dropdown, Is Greater Than in the second dropdown, and select 3 stars in the third box. Then click the + button.

4. Select Artist in the first dropdown, is not in the second dropdown, and type **Wolfmother** in the last box.

The first line takes in all the songs in your library that have the word Rock in the genre field. This means you have songs with plain-old Rock, Southern Rock, Hard Rock and even This is Kinda Rock, because they all have the word Rock in the genre section. The second line filters out songs that have been played in the last three months—by specifying that you only want songs

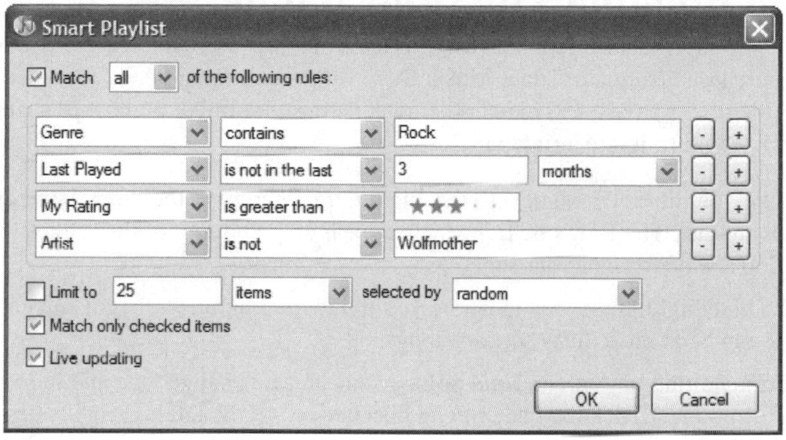

FIGURE 5-10   Creating smart playlists allows you to organize your library in a way normal playlists can't.

that haven't been. The third line says you only want songs that you've rated with four or five stars, since you specified you want songs with greater than three stars. The fourth line, which narrows down the artist, ensures that you won't have any Wolfmother songs in this playlist even if you've categorized them under the Rock genre, rated their tracks four or five stars, and haven't listened to them in the last three months.

This example is just a starting point for all your smart playlists, and you can come up with much more creative lists based on other fields you've used and data iTunes has collected. Whenever you listen to music, iTunes records whether you've skipped the song or played it all the way to the end, and even how many times you've listened to this total. Using these fields lets you further narrow down songs to the ones you enjoy the most.

TIP   *The website* http://smartplaylists.com *has a lot of tips for creating and customizing your smart playlists.*

Customize Your Playlist View

After creating a playlist, you can adjust the way they appear in iTunes. To change which columns appear, right-click on any column header and left-click on any column heading type. A check next to it means it will show up; no check means it won't. After you've selected columns, you can left click and drag them around to reorder them in the top row. To sort by one of the columns, just click on it and the column header will darken. Click again to reverse the sort order.

Make Custom Ringtones for Your iPhone

Shortly after the iPhone's release, Apple updated iTunes to allow users to create ringtones from music they've purchased from the iTunes Music Store for an additional $0.99, provided the track is eligible (eligible tracks have a bell icon in the track listing). If you've purchased a ringtone-eligible song, you can turn it into a ringtone:

1. Either click on the Bell icon next to the eligible track, or go to the Store menu and select Create Ringtone. The Ringtone Editor will appear at the bottom of the iTunes window, displaying a waveform of your song.

2. Drag the blue highlighted area to where you'd like the ringtone to begin and end. Your ringtone can be at most thirty seconds long.

3. Aside from editing the start and end points, you can also change fade and loop settings for your ringtone. Check the Fade In/Out checkboxes on the left and right sides of the highlighted portions of the song to toggle a volume fade. When your ringtone ends, it will loop back to the beginning. You can set the time between loops from the Looping dropdown menu.

4. While you're editing your ringtone to perfection, click the Preview button to hear what your finished ringtone will sound like with the current settings. If you don't like it, just keep tinkering until you're satisfied. When you are satisfied, click the Buy button to purchase the ringtone. iTunes will create the ringtone and automatically add it to the Ringtones section of your Library.

To sync the ringtone, dock your iPhone and go to the Ringtones tab. From here you can choose to sync either All Ringtones or Selected Ringtones the same way you sync music. Since ringtones are rather small, it won't take up much space if you decide to sync all ringtones. However, if you've got a lot of ringtones, you might prefer syncing only a few so that it's easy to find and assign custom ringtones on your iPhone.

Sync Music and Video to Your iPhone

We covered the basics of syncing music and video in Chapter 2, and honestly there's not all that much to it beyond the basics! Read on to get a couple of tips and tricks we haven't shown you yet. And remember, only music and video files that the iPhone and iTunes can support will be synced to your phone. Double-check the sections on converting music and videos to formats your iPhone can understand if the movies or songs you're trying to sync aren't making it to your iPhone.

Sync Music to Your iPhone

To sync music, just select your iPhone in iTunes, click the Music tab, and then check the box next to Sync Music. Then either choose All Songs and Playlists, if your library is small enough to fit onto the iPhone, or Selected Playlists if you only want a few playlists. If you've been creating smart playlists designed to get the most music onto your iPhone, now's the time to choose those. Check the playlists you want to sync (as shown in Figure 5-11).

If you select more songs than your iPhone can hold, iTunes will prompt you with a warning that will ask whether you want iTunes to delete photo albums and pictures to make room. If you select no, iTunes will tell you how much space it needs on the iPhone, how much free space is available, and then ask if you want to turn off Podcast syncing. If you select no again, you'll give iTunes no choice and it will refuse to sync your songs to the iPhone until you de-select a few playlists.

Checking the Include Music Video option allows you to sync music videos as well, which come bundled with some songs and are available for purchase individually on the iTunes Music Store.

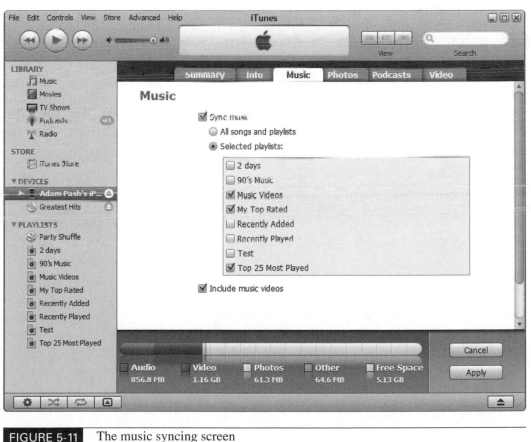

FIGURE 5-11   The music syncing screen

Sync Podcasts to Your iPhone

Syncing podcasts is just like syncing music. First, select your iPhone, then the Podcasts tab, and then the checkbox next to Sync. Now you have the option of syncing all podcasts, unplayed podcasts, or new podcasts (and also 1, 3, 5, or 10 of their most recent episodes). After selecting this, you have the option of applying those rules to all your podcasts or only to selected podcasts. As a reminder, the blue dot next to each podcast means there are new episodes in a podcast.

Sync Video to Your iPhone

Under the Video tab, you can choose to sync TV Shows or Movies. Syncing Movies is straightforward; just click Sync Movies and then pick the ones you want to sync. TV Shows have the option, like podcasts, of syncing all or unwatched episodes (the option for 1, 3, 5, or 10 episodes exists as well), before you choose to sync all your TV shows or just selected TV Shows or Playlists.

Now that you've mastered your iPhone's phone and iPod features, it's time to dive into the iPhone's breakthrough Internet features, starting with email.

Part III

Access Email and the
Internet on Your iPhone

Chapter 6

Set Up, Send, Receive, and Manage Email and SMS

How to...

- Set up mail
- Navigate and read email
- Send email
- Manage your email
- Send email attachments
- Tweak mail settings
- Navigate and read SMS
- Send SMS messages
- Manage SMS messages

One feature that all smartphones have in common is the ability to send and receive email. The iPhone is no exception. Apple's revolutionary phone has features like push email, which means messages come straight to you as soon as people send them without having to check every five minutes, not to mention the ability to open PDF, Word, and Excel attachments. It can even check multiple email accounts, as shown in Figure 6-1. Best of all, every message is displayed just like it appears on your desktop, in full, rich, HTML glory. You're not missing out on anything when you read your email on your iPhone.

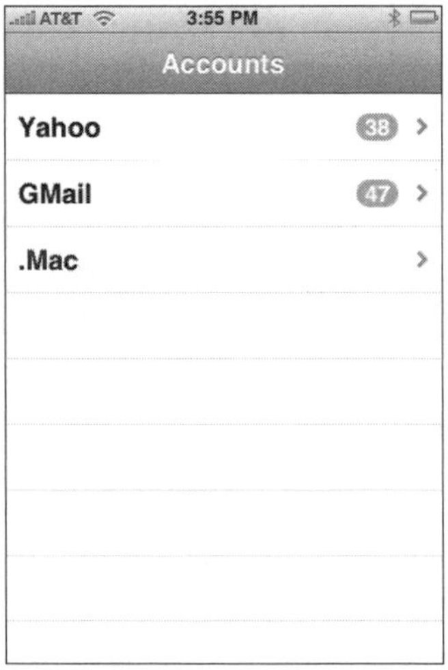

FIGURE 6-1 Mail can check multiple accounts simultaneously.

Set Up Your Mail

There are two ways to configure your iPhone to send and receive mail. The first involves importing pre-existing mail settings from your computer, which is especially convenient if you're already using the same account on your desktop. The second allows you to set up an account right on your iPhone, which works particularly well if you use webmail services like Yahoo Mail or Gmail.

Import Settings from Your Desktop

Importing settings from your desktop's email client is the easiest way to get your current accounts onto the iPhone, as long as you're using Mail.app or Entourage on the Mac, or Outlook, Outlook Express, or Windows Mail on Windows. To do this, dock your iPhone, click the Info tab in the iPhone section of iTunes, and make sure the check box next to Sync Selected Mail Accounts is checked as shown in Figure 6-2. Now you can select which accounts you want to sync; this is useful if you want your iPhone to only check a specific email account (for example, your personal email and not your work email). Once you click Sync and move the account data to your iPhone, it will be able to access your email just like your desktop does.

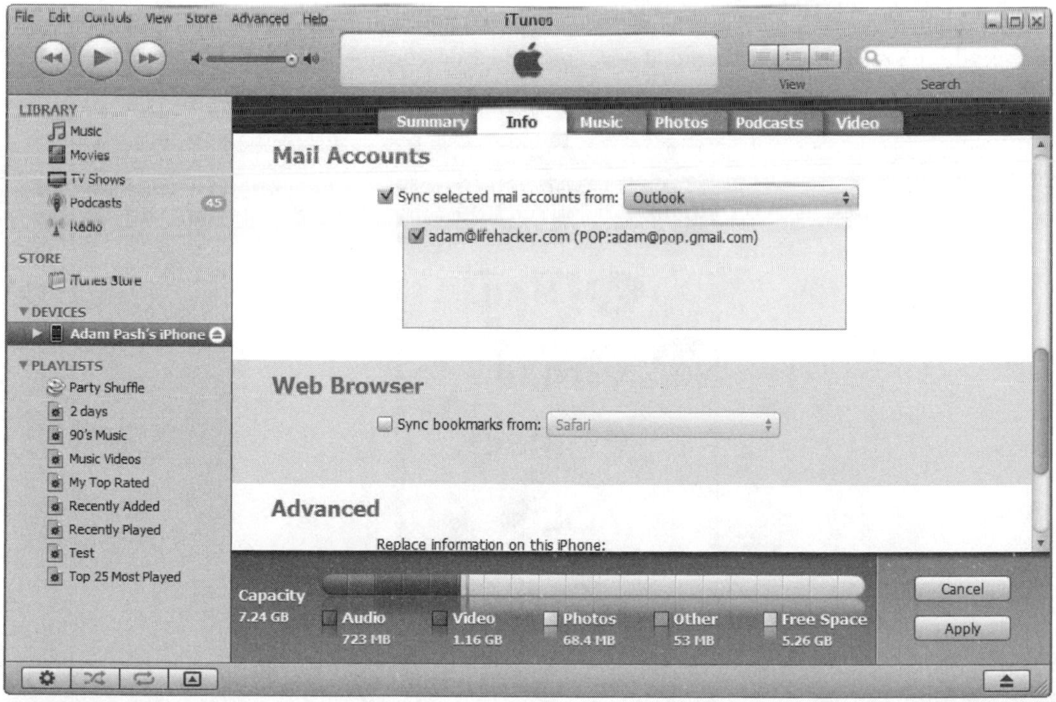

FIGURE 6-2   Import email settings from your desktop email client with iTunes.

Set Up Mail on Your iPhone

If you aren't importing your email settings from a desktop email application, you'll find that setting up your email to work with popular webmail services like Yahoo Mail, Gmail, .Mac, and AOL is almost as simple as logging into your webmail. If you don't use one of these webmail applications, or you use an office email server like Exchange, setting up your iPhone mail will take a few more steps.

To set up a new email account, go to the Home screen, tap Settings, and then tap Mail to access your Mail settings. You'll see the screen in Figure 6-3. At the top of the screen, under Accounts, tap Add Account. From here you can choose to set up a Yahoo Mail, Gmail, .Mac, AOL, or other email account.

Set Up Mail with Popular Webmail Clients

Setting up any of the four popular webmail applications works exactly the same way. Just tap the type of email you use (Yahoo Mail, Gmail, .Mac, or AOL), then enter your name, email address, the password for that account, and a description of the account. The name you enter into the Name field will show up in the From field when you send email from this account. Whatever you enter into the Description field will be the name of the account in the list of accounts under the Mail application. If you plan to access multiple email accounts of the same service, make sure you use different names in the description.

When you're finished, tap Save. Your iPhone will verify your account information to make sure everything's working, and then that account will automatically be added to Mail–ready for use.

FIGURE 6-3 The iPhone can make setting up popular webmail accounts easy.

Set Up Mail with Other Webmail and Office Mail Servers

Setting up Mail to work with other email servers works much the same way as setting up email with your regular desktop email clients. In the Mail section under the Settings application, tap Add Account, and then tap Other. An Account Setup screen will slide into view with three tabs: IMAP, POP, and Exchange. You need to know the same basic information to set up a new account no matter which of the three you're using. If you don't have this info on hand, consult your web host's help page.

First, enter the name you want to display in the From field when you send an email. Enter the email address you're setting up in the Address field and the name of the email account in the Description field just as you want it to appear in Mail application. Then you'll need to enter information for this account's incoming mail server, including Host Name, User Name, and Password, followed by the outgoing mail server information, which requires a Host Name, but for which a User Name and Password are optional.

If you don't know all of this information off the top of your head, including whether you're accessing your email via an IMAP, POP, or Exchange server, you should contact your IT Administrator for help

Some webmail applications offer specific instructions for setting up an account on your iPhone. For example, Google has instructions for setting up a hosted Google Apps email account which can be found at:

`http://tinyurl.com/2jx8tq`

TIP

Some workplaces may require you to establish a Virtual Private Network (VPN) connection before you can download your email. See Chapter 12 for more instructions on how to set up a VPN connection from the iPhone.

Did you know?

The iPhone Has Some Microsoft Exchange Support

Microsoft Exchange is the email system that most corporations and organizations use. The iPhone can support Exchange mail, but only if the Exchange server has IMAP email turned on. This is not a feature normally activated for everyday operation, so to get the iPhone to work with Exchange you may have to contact your IT Administrator to have them turn on IMAP mail. There may be some security concerns, so your IT department may not want to enable IMAP mail. In this case, your only choice is to wait for possible native Exchange support from Apple, or wait for third-party add-ons, which allow you to enable the iPhone to connect to Exchange without having to turn on IMAP.

Navigate and Read Email

Now that your email is set up, we'll discuss how to download, navigate, and read your email. We'll also discuss how to make sure your desktop and your iPhone email can co-exist, minimizing potential conflicts between the two.

Download New Email

Before you can read new mail, you have to download it. With the exception of Yahoo Mail, which is automatically delivered (it's push email), you have to check your account to get new messages. Here's how you do it.

1. Open the Mail application.

That's it! The email application will automatically start downloading new messages, as indicated by the Activity Spinner on the very top bar of your phone (to the left of the current time). If you're inside an account, you can also see activity by the bottom status bar text changing to Checking for Mail... and the progress spinner to the left of it, just like it shows in Figure 6-4. After Mail finishes checking for new email, the status bar will display the last date and time this email account was checked, which should be right now if you just finished checking email.

You can manually check for new email by tapping the Refresh button on the bottom left (which looks like an circular arrow pointing at its tail) from any folder inside an account.

You can also set Mail to automatically check messages. To do so, open the Settings application from the Home screen, go to Mail, and scroll down to the Auto-Check option. You can tap this to change your auto-checking to check every 15, 30, or 60 minutes, or you can leave it on manual if you want to only get mail when you manually check.

FIGURE 6-4   Mail can check for new email, either automatically or manually.

> **NOTE**   *If you're out on the road and have the auto-check option enabled, you may miss an incoming call when your phone is checking mail over the EDGE data network. This is due to an iPhone limitation which only lets you receive calls when your EDGE connection is not in use. Actively downloading a few messages (or one large message) will tie up your phone. It won't normally cause a problem, but if you're waiting for an important call we recommend turning off auto-check.*

Navigate Emails with Mail

Reading messages is just as easy as downloading them. To start, go to the Inbox of any account. Just drag your finger to swipe and scroll through your list slowly, or flick to move through your list fast. Scrolling through your messages is the same as scrolling through any list on the iPhone. Once you've picked a message, tap anywhere on that entry and the message will slide in from the right.

In the message itself, you'll notice a bunch of details. Here's what the top bar means, starting from the left of Figure 6-5.

- **Back Arrow**   This arrow should say something like Inbox (49), which means you can tap this to go back to the Inbox (or whatever screen you just came from). The 49 tells you how many new messages exist in that mailbox.

- **Message Number**   The middle of the upper bar should say something like 1 of 50, meaning you're on the first message of the 50 messages in your inbox. Increasing the number of messages downloaded to your iPhone will increase the second number, and progressing through your messages will increase the first one.

- **Up/Down Buttons**   These buttons let you cycle to the next and previous messages without having to go back to the list view and manually tapping another entry. This is useful for going through your messages one-by-one, quickly.

Reading email on the iPhone looks just like email on your desktop.

The info fields within each message tell you who sent the message and who the message is addressed to:

- **From** This is the person who sent you the message. Tapping on this field will bring up an info screen displaying more details about the sender. If this person is already a contact, this will pull up the contact screen. That means you can do anything you can do from the contact screen, like call the contact, map their address, or send a new text message (all of which are handy if you want to reply to an email without using email). If the sender isn't already a contact, you'll get a screen that lets you email this person back, create a new contact, or add this email address to an existing contact.

- **Details/Hide** The Details/Hide toggle lets you show or dismiss the To and Cc fields. You may want to hide this most of the time if you're the only recipient in your email, but displaying details can be useful to see who else received this message.

- **To/Cc** When you display details, you get to see who this particular email is sent or cc'ed to. Tapping on your own name (assuming you've assigned your email accounts to your contact information) will bring up your own contact info screen. If you have multiple email addresses assigned to yourself, you can tell which one the email was sent to by looking at which one of your email addresses is blue.

- **Mark as Unread** Tap to mark this message as unread. Again, Mark as Unread is only available when you display details.

The bottom bar lets you perform actions on the message. These actions include

- **Refresh** The circular refresh button on the bottom left checks for new mail no matter where you see it in the Mail application.

- **Folder** Tapping this button brings up a list of mailboxes that you can move this message to. You can move it to one of the folders that you save your messages in, or you can even move it into the trash.

- **Trash** Pressing the Trash button deletes the message by moving it into the trash. You'll even get a neat animation of the message shrinking into the open trash can.

- **Reply/Forward** The arrow pointing to the left brings up the Reply/Forward overlay. Here, you can reply, reply to all, or forward the message. Reply just starts a new message with the sender in the To field; Reply all will send the reply to everyone in the To and Cc fields; and Forward will forward this message to another email address.

- **Compose** Tap this button to compose a completely new message. The new message actually has nothing to do with the message you're currently viewing—it's just an easy way to start a new message without having to go into the Inbox.

Reading a message is easy as well, thanks to the iPhone's gesture system. To scroll through the message, swipe it, like you would a list. You can also flick through the message if it's very long. You'll notice that the contents of the message may be very small, especially if there's an

Mail Hooks into Other Applications

Like many of your iPhone's applications, Mail can recognize the phone numbers, web addresses, and even YouTube and Google Maps URLs within your emails and route them to the appropriate application. For example, if someone sends you a message that includes a phone number, you can tap it to call the number. Even more impressive, if someone sends you a link to YouTube or Google Maps, the iPhone will open the YouTube or Google Maps application to open the video or address in their respective iPhone application.

image inside. To zoom in and get a better look, take your fingers and perform the spread action. It's the same action you've been doing in all the other applications. To zoom out, just pinch. You can also click links in your email as well, which will open up Safari and take you to the web page.

View Mail Attachments

The iPhone may not have a standalone viewer for PDF, Word, and Excel documents, but you can actually read all of them inside the Mail program. If you receive one of these file types in an email, you'll see a little icon in your message (see Figure 6-6) prompting you to tap to download

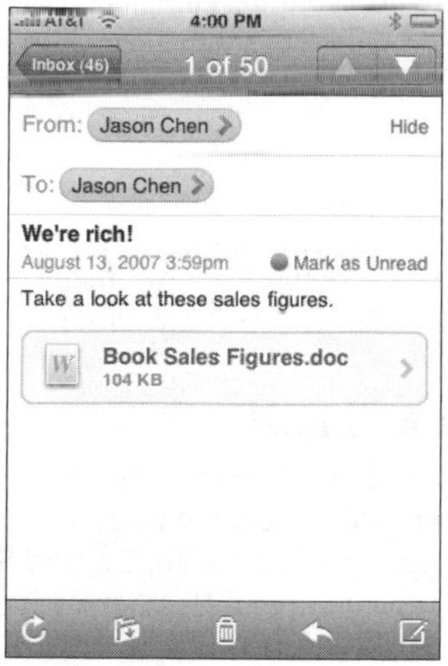

FIGURE 6-6   You can view PDF, Word, and Excel attachments in Mail.

and view. Tapping on the message will start downloading the attachment, and when it's done, a new viewer screen will show up. These documents will display much like they display on your computer, but they are read-only, meaning you can view, but not edit, their contents.

You can use gestures such as scrolling and pinching when viewing these attachments as well. And when you leave the attachment, the Mail application actually saves a copy inside the internal memory so you won't have to download the file *again* when you want to go back to it.

Make Your iPhone and Desktop Mail Co-exist

If you're checking email on both your iPhone and your desktop mail client, you could run into the problem where a message shows up only on your iPhone and not your desktop or vice versa. To avoid this problem, you want to make sure your iPhone always leaves a copy of the email on the server when it's accessed. Here's what you do:

1. Open up the Settings application from the Home screen.

2. Tap Email

3. Choose an email account.

4. Scroll down to the bottom and tap Advanced.

5. Tap the Delete From Server option at the bottom of the screen and make sure it says Never.

By doing this, you can make sure that reading your email on the iPhone won't affect your desktop email. You have to do the same thing on your desktop as well. Find your account information on your email client there and then set the option to either never delete messages from the server, or delete messages when they're moved from your Inbox. The second way ensures that you can still have two clients (your desktop and your iPhone) receive messages, but won't have to download old messages again when you've already removed them from the Inbox of your desktop.

Send Email

Sending email is simple as well. You can compose a new email from scratch, reply to email you've received, or forward email just like you can on your desktop.

Compose and Send a New Email

To compose a completely new email, click the Compose button on the bottom right of any mail screen, as long as you've drilled-down into an account (see Figure 6-7). This will bring up the new email screen. Just like regular email, you've got To, Cc, and Subject fields, and then the email body. Just tap any of the fields to enter them. Here's how they work:

■ **To**   Enter the email address of the contact you'd like to enter in the To field. If you've added email addresses to your contacts, you can access them in a couple of ways. First, you can start typing in the name of a contact. Mail will search both the contacts to whom

FIGURE 6-7   The Compose Email screen

you've assigned email addresses along with any contacts from whom you've received email in the past (yes, Mail even remembers email addresses from people you haven't assigned as contacts). Second, you can tap the blue + icon on the right of the To field to bring up a list of your contacts. Just tap the contact you want to email and their email address will automatically be added to the email you're composing. (If that contact has been assigned multiple email addresses, you will have to choose which one to email after you tap the contact.) Finally, if you want to send an email to someone whose email address isn't in your iPhone, you can type out the whole address manually (note that the keyboard even has the @ sign on the bottom row for easy access).

- **Cc**   If you want to Cc a contact (send a carbon copy of an email), enter their address in the Cc field using one of the methods for adding a contact to the To field described previously.

- **Subject and Body**   This isn't the first time you've sent an email, so this part is pretty self-explanatory. Just type out the subject of your email in the Subject field, the content of the email in the body, and you're ready to send.

To send an email once you've finished composing it, simply tap the Send button at the top right of the Compose screen. Mail will send your email (you can watch the send progress bar at the bottom of the screen) and play a whoosh sound (the same sound Mail.app uses on the Mac) to confirm that it was sent. If for some reason you aren't connected to Wi-Fi and you don't have a signal on the EDGE network, Mail will alert you that it could not send the email and file it in the Outbox to send next time you have an Internet connection.

FIGURE 6-8   Reply to or Forward any email with Mail

Reply to or Forward an Email

You can reply to or forward any email you're reading by tapping the Reply/Forward arrow icon at the bottom of the email (on the right next to the Compose button). A Reply/Forward dialog like Figure 6-8 will slide onto the screen with up to three buttons: Reply, Reply All (only available if your email had more than one recipient, or if your email address isn't in the To or Cc fields), and Forward.

Tapping Reply will compose a new email with the sender of the email you're replying to in the To field, the same subject filled in with Re: prepended to the original subject, and the body filled in with the text of the original email. At this point, it works exactly the same as composing an email. Write your reply, edit any fields you want, and tap Send when you're finished. To reply to the sender along with every recipient of an email, tap the Reply All button and then follow the same steps discussed previously.

If you want to forward an email to another contact, tap the Forward button. The subject will be automatically filled in with Fwd: prepended to the original subject, and the body of the email will hold the body of the original email. All you need to do is enter contacts you want to forward the email to, add or edit any other field you want, and then press Send.

Manage Your Email

Although the iPhone already trims your email by allowing at most 200 messages in your inbox, it's still tricky to keep it readable and manageable. By both deleting old messages and filing messages you want to keep, you can maintain a usable inbox without much hassle.

Delete an Email

There are three ways to delete a message from your inbox. To delete from the list view, just swipe your finger from left to right on an entry and a Delete button will show up. Tapping Delete will then delete your message by moving it into the Trash folder. Alternately, you can click the Edit button on the top right and an icon will show on the left side of every message. Tap this, then the Delete button to delete.

You can also delete an email by viewing a message and then pressing the Trash button on the bottom bar. This will accomplish the same thing as the swipe method; namely, moving your message into the Trash. There's no easy way to delete multiple messages at once, so you will have to repeat either of these two methods a few times to clear your inbox of unwanted mail.

After you've deleted a message, there are actually two more things you can do with it. To permanently delete a message, go to the Trash folder and delete it again with any of the three delete methods. This will remove the message from your iPhone permanently. To undelete a message, open up that message in the trash and hit the Folder button. This will bring up a list of mailboxes that you can move the message to. Depositing this message anywhere other than the Trash will undelete it.

File and Organize Email

Because the iPhone will only keep a maximum of 200 messages in your inbox, you will have to move your messages into different folders if you want to save them. However, this only works if you are using Yahoo Mail or IMAP mail, which let you create folders on the server so you can view them on the iPhone. Here's how you move a message.

First, open a message. Now click the Folders button (second one from the left on the bottom). This will give you a list of folders you can drop this message into. To file an email, just tap the folder you want to move the message to. Unfortunately you can't create folders in this screen, so you will have to use your desktop email client to create folders beforehand.

How to ...   Send an Email Multiple Times

You can send an email multiple times without retyping it using using the drafts folder. After you send a message, find that message in the Sent folder and move it into the Drafts folder. Next, open it up and make any changes you need to, such as changing the recipient's email address and changing names in the email. When finished, just tap Send to send the message again. Or, you can send the message again to the same person by not changing anything and tapping Send immediately.

Send Email Attachments

Although you can't manually add attachments to a message when you're composing an email, you can still actually send photos, notes, web pages, and YouTube links to your friends. Here's what you do:

■ **Notes**   Open a note and click the Mail button (second from the left on the bottom bar). This will create a new email with the content of the note copied into the body of the email.

■ **Photos**   Open a photo and click the Send button (the first button on the left on the bottom bar). Then choose the second option, Email Photo. A new email message will be created and you'll see an animation of the picture being placed into the body of the email.

■ **Web Pages**   Open the address bar and click the Share button (top left button). This will create a new message with the URL inside the body.

■ **YouTube**   Open a video's info screen (tap the blue arrow to the right of any video), and press the Share button. A short message that says "Check out this video on YouTube," along with the URL, will be entered into the body of a new message.

Tweak Mail Settings

If you're not happy with the default Mail settings, you can change them to fit your needs. First, we'll touch on accounts. By going into each account, you can change your displayed name, the outgoing server address, or even disable the account entirely. Here are some of the more advanced features:

■ **Outgoing Server**   You can change the outgoing server of an account to the outgoing server of another, different account if you want to make it seem like you're sending messages from the other account. This could be useful in situations like Hosted Gmail, or where you're forwarding messages from one account to another and trying to make it seem like messages are coming from the first.

■ **Removing Deleted Messages**   Under Advanced, you can set messages to never delete, or delete after a day, a week, or a month. This frees up space on your iPhone, especially if you get a lot of messages with large attachments.

■ **Deleting Messages From the Server**   Another Advanced option, this can be set to Never, After Seven Days, or After You Remove the Message From the Inbox to remove email from your email server.

■ **Mailbox Behavior**   Again under Advanced, for certain mail accounts (like .Mac), you can assign the location to store drafts or sent messages. You can choose to store them either on your iPhone or on the server.

It's best not to fiddle with your mail account's settings unless you or your network administrator have a reason to, but you should feel free to change other mail settings to customize your experience however you like. Here's what each option in Figure 6-9 does.

- **Auto-Check**   Change the interval for your iPhone to automatically check your accounts to see if there are any new messages.

- **Show**   This shows 25, 50, 75, 100, or 200 of the most recent messages in your Inbox.

- **Preview**   Changing this option will change the amount of lines displayed from each message in your Inbox list view. Setting it higher will allow you to read some emails without even opening them up, but it also makes scrolling through large lists take slightly longer.

- **Minimum Font Size**   If the default font size for messages is too small, you can increase it here to make text easier to read.

- **Show To/Cc Label**   Turning this on will show a To or Cc icon next to messages that are actually addressed to you. This helps if you're on a lot of mailing lists, or if you get bulk email, by letting you discern important messages right away.

- **Always Bcc Myself**   This lets you send a Bcc of your messages to yourself whenever you send mail. Bcc stands for blind carbon copy, which means the person you're sending the message to will have no idea you're sending a copy to yourself.

- **Signature**   By default, your signature is "sent from my iPhone", and will be attached at the bottom of every message you send. Feel free to change this to anything that suits you.

- **Default Account**   Choose the default account you want your messages to send from. This is used when you click the Share button from Photos and YouTube, for example.

The mail settings screen

Navigate and Read SMS Messages

The iPhone handles SMS messages in a unique fashion that you probably haven't seen on your old mobile phone. Rather than clogging your SMS inbox with individual messages, the iPhone threads text messages, as in Figure 6-10, into a conversation that looks and behaves much like instant messaging chat applications (specifically, it looks exactly like Mac OS X's iChat). This chat-like interface leads to a much cleaner, much more useful SMS inbox.

As a result, navigating SMS messages is very much like navigating email messages. To start, tap the SMS icon from the Home screen. If you've received SMS messages already, this screen will have a list of every contact that you've communicated with over SMS. Note that these are conversations with contacts and not individual messages. To see individual messages, you'll have to dive one level deeper into each contact's screen.

Send SMS Messages

You can send an SMS message to a contact in a couple of different ways: by starting a new SMS conversation thread, or by continuing a current SMS conversation.

To start a new SMS conversation, tap the new message icon at the top right of the main Text Messages screen; a New Message window will slide into view (as shown in Figure 6-11). Just like Mail, you can fill the To field either by typing the name of the contact until you see the contact's name in the dynamic search results, or you can tap the blue + icon to find the contact in your Contacts list. Or, if this isn't one of your contacts, you can type in their phone number using the number pad. After you've added your recipient, just type your message and press Send.

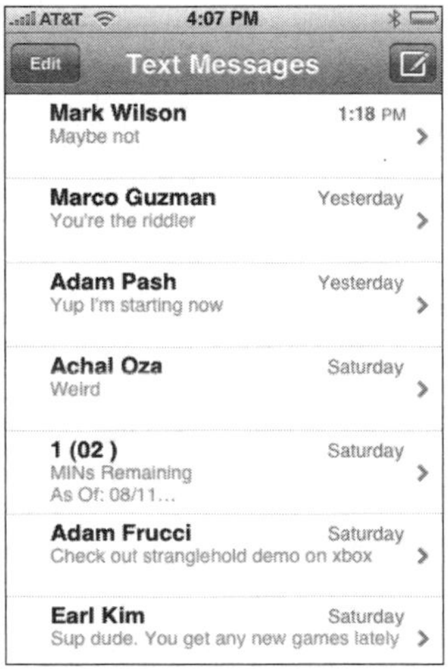

FIGURE 6-10   The SMS list

FIGURE 6-11   Composing a new SMS message. Your messages are on the right, in green, and the other party's messages are on the left, in gray.

TIP
You can start a new SMS thread with a contact from their contact pane in the Phone app as well. Just click the Text Message button and the SMS window will come up.

You can reply directly to a current SMS conversation without starting a new thread by replying to an SMS message in your Text Messages inbox. To do so, tap a current conversation, then tap the text box at the bottom of the screen. Then just type your reply and press Send.

NOTE
Unfortunately, the iPhone can only send SMS messages to one recipient at a time.

Manage SMS Messages

Like Mail, there are a couple of ways you can delete a message from your Text Messages screen. The quickest and easiest way to delete an SMS message is using the swipe method. Swipe your finger from left to right across the message you want to delete, then tap the red Delete button that appears next to the message. Alternately, if you tap the Edit button at the top left of the Text Messages screen, each message will get a red – icon next to it. Tap the – icon next to any message you want to delete, and then press the red Delete button.

If you don't want to delete a contact from the Text Messages screen, but you do want to clear the contents of a thread, tap the contact name to view the thread and then press the Clear button on the top right of the screen. A confirmation dialog will slide onto the screen. Tap Clear Conversation. The Clear Conversation option is a bit of a strange one. Rather than deleting the conversation, it clears the contents of the thread and moves the empty conversation to the bottom of your Text Messages window.

SMS Limitations

Although the SMS application is a pleasure to use, there are some limitations that you should be aware of so you don't think you're missing out on a feature because you're not sure where to find it. These limitations are present at the time of writing, but can be (and might have already been) fixed by Apple in a software update.

■ **No MMS/Picture Messages** Even though the iPhone has a camera, you can't send MMS or picture messages to other people. If they send one to you, you'll get a regular text message (SMS) with a web address and login info to visit to view that picture. Some times, the login won't work. And it's not a clickable link either, so you will either have to write down the info to enter into Safari, or wait until you're home and view the picture on your computer.

■ **No Character Counter** SMS messages have a 160-character limit before the message is broken into two separate ones, but the iPhone doesn't have a character counter. This makes it hard to tell how many characters you have left in this message.

■ **No Multi-Recipient Messages** You can only send messages to one person at a time, thanks to the iChat conversation approach Apple took in structuring the SMS application. This means you have to send multiple messages manually when you have to send a message to many people. And without the copy and paste feature, you'll actually have to type the message multiple times too.

■ **No Instant Messaging** The SMS application may look like iChat on the Mac, but there's no IM features anywhere. Since the default AT&T iPhone plan only comes with 200 messages, you should be careful not to run over your limit by thinking this is more IM than SMS.

Now that you've mastered the desktop-class email client, let's move on to Safari—the iPhone's desktop=class web browser—in Chapter 7.

Chapter 7

Browse the Internet with Safari

How to...

- Navigate the Web with Safari
- Read RSS feeds
- Sync bookmarks with your desktop
- Take advantage of iPhone-specific web applications
- Access Safari from other applications and vice versa
- Learn Safari's limitations
- Tweak Safari settings
- Avoid crashing Safari

The iPhone is a breakthrough Internet communicator, and nowhere is that more apparent than in its built-in web browser, Safari. Safari brings you the Internet the way you've always known it, the same way your desktop computer displays it—the way it's supposed to be. If you've ever tried browsing the web from another mobile device, you know just how groundbreaking Safari is. Open the Home screen, fire up Safari, and let's get browsing!

Navigate the Web with Safari

You'll notice right away that Safari contains a lot of the same components as a desktop web browser, as you can see in Figure 7-1. Aside from a few special behaviors, it works exactly like a desktop web browser.

FIGURE 7-1   The Safari screen

Visit a Website by URL

To visit a website when you know its URL, tap the address bar at the top of Safari. The iPhone keyboard will slide onto the screen so you can enter in the URL of any website. You'll notice a few small changes to the iPhone keyboard. In place of the space bar, you've now got a period (.), slash (/), and .com button (see Figure 7-2). Why? Because you won't ever need to type a space when you're typing a web address, but you will regularly need to type those characters. In fact, the .com button, which will end most of your web addresses, is an incredible time saver that you will almost certainly grow to love.

For example, let's check out the New York Times homepage at nytimes.com. Type in **nytimes**, tap the .com button, and then just tap the blue Go button. If you're connected to a Wi-Fi network, the site will quickly load the New York Times homepage in all its full screen, desktop web browser-like glory. If you're running off the comparatively slow EDGE network, you might want to get comfortable—maybe do some bird watching—while you wait for the page to load.

Navigate Safari with Gestures

It's great to see a full website rendered in a mobile browser, but the fact is, unless you've got some sort of super-human vision, you'll hardly be able to read a lick of the text on most sites without doing a bit of zooming. Like the rest of the iPhone's applications, there are all kinds of gestures that make browsing the Web with Safari simple and intuitive:

- **Swipe**   Web page content can be scrolled in every direction by dragging your finger across the screen. However, since Safari zooms to sections of a web page, and you

| FIGURE 7-2 | The Safari address bar and keyboard |

regularly want to scroll these sections, a vertical or horizontal swipe will quickly lock into a vertical or horizontal-only swipe if the iPhone thinks that's what you're doing. Unless you swipe diagonally from the start, that swipe will lock into a vertical or horizontal scroll.

- **Tap**   Any time you see a link you want to follow, just tap it the same way you'd click a link on your desktop.

- **Double-tap**   When you see a section of a website you want to take a closer look at, whether it's text or an image, just double-tap that area on your screen. Safari will recognize that section of the web page and zoom in perfectly to fit it to your screen. To drill down farther into another part of the section you're zoomed into, just double-tap a different part of the screen. Safari will continue to re-center, zooming in or out, on new sections each time you double-tap a section, provided you don't try zooming on the same section twice in a row. Double-tapping the same section a second time concurrently will zoom all the way out, back to the full screen view.

- **Tap-and-Hold**   Before you follow just any link on a web page, sometimes you want to know where the link is taking you. To find out on your iPhone, just tap and hold the link for just a second. A gray text box will pop up displaying the link text and the web address it's linked to. To open the page, just pull your finger off the link. If you've decided you don't want to go where the link is taking you, move your finger slightly in any direction before pulling it off the link.

- **Pinch/Spread**   To take more granular control over how Safari zooms content on a web page, you can use your old friends pinch and spread. Pinching the screen will zoom out, while spreading two fingers apart on the screen will zoom into the page. In most cases, the double-tap method will be more efficient, but if you're not happy with the results of a double-tap, pinching and spreading the content is a good alternative

- **Flick**   If you're viewing a long web page, the flick is the quickest way to get from top to bottom or anywhere in between. Quickly drag your finger across the screen and then let go.

- **Two-finger Swipe**   A relatively little-known and hardly ever used navigation feature of Safari is the two-finger swipe. Occasionally, a website will have content inside the browser window that has its own scrollbar inside a small frame. A regular swipe won't scroll that content, but a two-finger swipe will.

SHORTCUT   *If you've finished reading a long page of content and you want to get back to the top of the page, you could zoom out and flick your way up, but there's a much quicker and easier way. Just tap the info strip at the very top of your iPhone—the one with your cell phone signal, clock, and battery meter—and Safari will quickly scroll all the way back to the top just like when you hit the Home key on your desktop.*

Navigate Safari with Buttons

Safari on the iPhone is just a lightweight version of the same Safari browser that ships with all Macs and is also available on Windows. It also uses many of the same navigational buttons and conventions as the regular Safari.

When you're viewing a web page, the very top of the browser will display the title of that page. Then below it, starting at the left, you have various buttons, including the

- ■ **Add Bookmark Button**   This button does exactly what it sounds like— it adds a website as a bookmark. We'll discuss bookmarks in more detail later on in the chapter.

- ■ **Address Bar**   This displays your current URL and is where you tap if you want to enter a new web address or search Google. When a page is loading, the Address bar will show the progress of the web page with a blue meter running over top of the address. This can help you know when you need to move on from a slow connection (for example, twenty seconds of waiting has only loaded 25 percent of the page).

- ■ **Refresh/Stop Button**   This button changes depending on the state of the browser. If you're loading a page, the Stop button is visible (it looks like an X). When a page has finished loading, the Refresh button (a circular arrow pointing at its tail) shows instead.

The bottom of the application has another bar with four buttons. Again, starting from the left, they are the

- ■ **Back Button**   This moves your browser to the page you visited before your current page.

- ■ **Forward Button**   This moves you ahead a page, but only works if you've used the Back button first.

- ■ **Bookmark Button**   This button looks like an open book, and gives you access to frequently used web pages or even just pages you want to remember without memorizing a long URL. See later sections for more on using bookmarks.

- ■ **Pages Button**   Safari lets you keep multiple pages open at one time, and this button gives you access to your different pages and allows you to open a new page. See more on viewing multiple sites with pages later on.

Navigate Safari in Landscape Mode

If you turn your iPhone to either side, Safari shifts into landscape mode just like in Figure 7-3. This gives you a wider browsing view that you might find more suitable for some web pages. Not only does the wide landscape view increase the size of the text of any given zoom, but the keyboard is much bigger in landscape mode as well. All the keys are wider, which could help if you're still not quite 100% confident in your iPhone typing.

FIGURE 7-3   Safari in landscape mode

Safari is the only application that allows you to type into the keyboard in widescreen landscape mode.

Search the Web

If you're like most people, you spend a significant portion of your browsing time looking up information on search engines—specifically Google. Rather than wasting your time going to the Google homepage every time you want to do a web search, Safari comes with a Google search box included. In fact, you probably noticed the search box the first time you typed in a URL. Just tap the Address bar like you're going to enter in a new web address. Below the Address bar, you'll notice a rounded text box with a magnifying glass search icon. Tap that text box (you'll notice the space bar returns to your keyboard), type your search query, and tap the blue Google button.

Did you know?

You Can Change Your Default Search Engine

Safari's default search engine is Google, but you can switch your search engine to Yahoo if you prefer. Go to the Home screen and launch the Settings application, then navigate to Safari and tap the Search Engine box. Then just tap your preferred engine.

Use and Manage Bookmarks

The iPhone's keyboard is a lovely piece of engineering, but that doesn't mean you want to enter in long web addresses with it every time you want to visit a new web page. This is especially true considering the predictive text feature is of no use to you here, since websites don't follow normal grammatical rules. Instead, you can create bookmarks (the same way you do on your desktop) that provide you with quick and easy access to any website.

Add a Bookmark

To bookmark the page you're currently viewing in Safari, tap the Bookmark button (+) in the top left of Safari, and the Add Bookmark screen will slide into view (see Figure 7-4). You can edit the title given to the bookmark if want something shorter than or different from what's already assigned, which defaults to the web page's full title. Bookmarks can be filed into any folder you choose. When you're happy with the bookmark's title and folder location, tap the blue Save button on the top right of the screen (or tap Cancel if you changed your mind).

NOTE   *You can also sync your bookmarks to and from Safari on your desktop. That means that rather than creating bookmarks one-by-one on your iPhone, you might find it much easier to create bookmarks with Safari on your desktop or use your existing desktop bookmarks. We'll cover syncing bookmarks with your desktop in more detail later in this chapter.*

View a Site from Your Bookmarks

Now that you've created a few bookmarks, we'll show you how to view a site from your bookmarks. Tap the Bookmarks button on the bottom of Safari to bring up all of your Bookmarks. To open

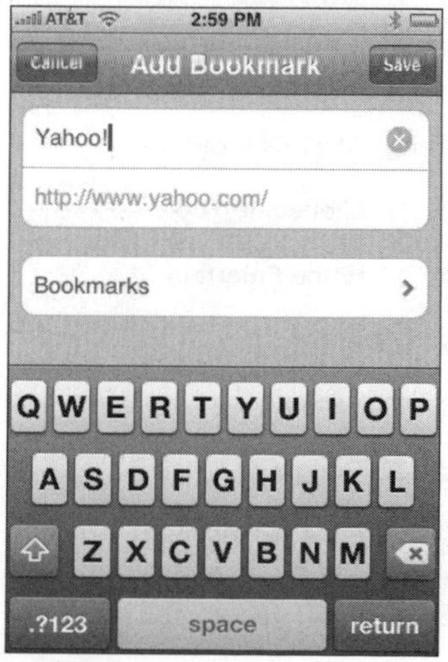

FIGURE 7-4   The Add Bookmark screen

a bookmark, simply tap the bookmark title. If you've created folders, you'll notice that all your folders have gray arrows next to them. You can also drill down into folders to find and select more bookmarks. Just like the iPhone's iPod application, when you drill into a folder you'll see a new arrow button on the top left of the screen that indicates the folder above the one you're in. Tap this button to return to the folder you came from.

As soon as you find the bookmark you're looking for, just tap it and Safari will open that web page. If you don't find what you're looking for, you can go back to the main Safari screen at any time by tapping the blue Done button.

Edit and Organize Your Bookmarks

If you don't take charge of your bookmarks early on, it can be easy to let your bookmarks folder get disorganized and out of control. However, the iPhone makes it really easy to delete, rename, reorder, and file your bookmarks, so no matter what state your bookmarks folder is in, getting it organized is simple. To get started, open the Bookmarks screen and tap the Edit button on the bottom left of the screen. All of the bookmark content will become editable, as shown in Figure 7-5.

To delete a bookmark or folder, just tap the red – icon, and then tap the big red Delete button to confirm that you want to get rid of a bookmark.

You can edit any bookmarks or folders that have a gray arrow on the right when you're in Edit mode. Tap the item you want to edit. An Edit Bookmarks or Edit Folder screen will slide into view. From here you can rename the bookmark or folder, change the URL associated with a bookmark, or refile the bookmark or folder into another folder.

You can add a new folder by tapping the New Folder button on the bottom right of the screen, naming the folder, and then choosing which parent folder you want to file it into. Finally,

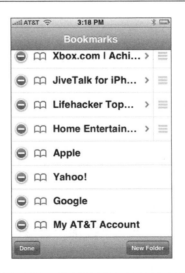

FIGURE 7-5 The Edit Bookmarks screen

you can reorder any folders and bookmarks within a folder in Edit mode by using the drag bars on the far right. When you're finished editing and organizing your bookmarks, tap the blue Done button on the bottom left of the screen.

Find a Site You've Visited in Your History

Safari keeps track of the websites you've visited in the History folder, which is always at the top of the Bookmarks page. Your browser history is organized into folders by day, so if you want to find a website you were viewing recently and you can remember what day it was, with a little searching you may be in luck. If you don't like that a web page has been tracked by your history, you can remove it by tapping the Clear button on the bottom left of the History screen. Just keep in mind that you can't remove an individual website from your history; tapping the Clear button will clear your entire browser history.

View Multiple Websites on Separate Pages

Safari on the iPhone lets you have multiple web pages open at the same time, just like on a desktop web browser. By default, you're only browsing on one page, but whenever you click a link from an email, an SMS message, or one of the iPhone's other applications, a new page will open up automatically. To create a new page by yourself, just click the pages button on the bottom right. It looks like two squares next to each other. When you click this, your current page zooms out and you can click the New Page button on the bottom left to create a new page to browse on as shown in Figure 7-6.

To scroll between pages, tap the pages button, swipe the screen left or right to browse your open pages, and then tap to pick the one you want. The white dots below each page let you know

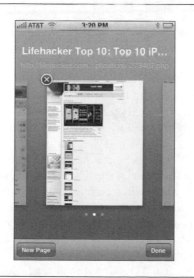

 Screenshot of the pages button pressed, browsing between pages

which page number it is. Once you've created a couple of new pages, you might find that you want to get rid of some of them. To do so, tap the pages button again, and then tap on the red X on the top left corner of each page.

Opening up a lot of pages can make the iPhone noticeably slower, especially when you're opening content-rich pages with a lot of dynamic content. To prevent this, try to close pages you're no longer using.

Watch Video and Listen to MP3s

Safari has its limitations when it comes to playing media in your browser (see the section on limitations later in this chapter), but it can play some video and audio in the browser; namely MP3s and some specially-formatted .MOV video files.

If you click a link to any MP3, Safari will download and stream that MP3 in a special media window in your browser. Likewise, if you play a compatible .MOV file, Safari will download and play the video in landscape mode. MP3s are available all over the Internet, but right now the best place to find videos you can play using Safari is the Apple Trailers site:

```
http://apple.com/trailers/
```

If streaming video is your cup of tea, you'll really want to take advantage of the YouTube application, which we'll cover in more detail in Chapter 11.

How to ...   Read RSS feeds

In case you aren't familiar with RSS feeds, they're stripped-down versions of websites that you can view with an RSS reader to quickly see when new content is created on the site. RSS feeds on the iPhone are handled through Apple's Mac reader website, but that fact should be totally transparent to you. By using RSS, you can have all your websites in one place—your RSS reader—and can tell which sites have been updated without actually having to go to each one.

To open an RSS feed, just find a website that has an RSS feed (Gizmodo.com and Lifehacker.com, for example), and open that site's RSS feed with Safari. The browser will forward you to reader.mac.com, which will then render the new entries in the Mac Reader style (See Figure 7-7). This makes it easy to get individual entries (from news sites, for example) without a lot of extra content, which helps you browse that much more quickly when you're out on the road with your EDGE connection.

Once your feed is loaded, you can bookmark this page just like any other web page by clicking the + button on the top left and creating a bookmark.

FIGURE 7-7   Sample RSS screen

Sync Bookmarks with Your Desktop

To make sure your bookmarks are always up to date, you can sync them between the Safari on your iPhone and the Safari on your desktop. It's very easy to do when your iPhone is connected. Just click on your iPhone on the left hand side, click the Info tab, scroll down to Web Browser, and then check the box next to Sync Safari Bookmarks. That's it! Every time you sync your iPhone, the bookmarks you created on your computer will make their way onto your phone, and vice versa.

Take Advantage of iPhone-Specific Web Applications

When the iPhone was first released, Apple did not provide software developers with the ability to develop applications designed to run natively on the iPhone. Although the efforts of many benevolent developers have already made third-party applications on the iPhone a reality (see the Spotlight section for more), Apple has encouraged developers to make iPhone applications using the Web and Safari. There are a handful of really good web applications built specifically for the iPhone that you might want to take advantage of. The list of iPhone web apps is constantly growing, so rather than try to provide you with an exhaustive list, we're just going to highlight a few of our favorites.

■ **MockDock/Mojits/Appleopolis**   These web applications mimic your iPhone Home screen and let you customize the buttons for launching other iPhone-specific web applications. These are especially good pages to get started with since they aggregate iPhone web applications by category and popularity. You can edit your start page to display any number of iPhone web applications in the same way as the iPhone Home screen (as shown in Figure 7-8). Launching a web application from one of these start pages will open the web page in a new window, so your start page is always available to access more of your favorites.

```
http://mockdock.com/
http://www.mojits.com/
http://appleopolis.com/
```

- **OneTrip**   You can build and save a shopping list quickly and easily by category with OneTrip, one of the first (and still one of the best) iPhone web applications available.

```
http://onetrip.org/onetrip/
```

- **Beejive and FlickIM Instant Messaging**   Many disappointed iPhone owners feel lost with out instant messaging on their new phones. Several web applications answered the call for Safari-based IM, but the two we like best are Beejive and FlickIM. Both can connect to multiple chat programs and handle multiple chats at once.

```
http://iphone.beejive.com/  and  http://flickim.com/
```

- **Showtimes**   Browse movies in your area by zip code. Showtimes takes full advantage of Safari's integration with other iPhone applications (see the next section) by providing links for phone numbers and addresses of movie theaters, meaning when you find a

FIGURE 7-8   MockDock lets you customize icons and acts as a useful start page.

movie you want to see, you can call the theater for more information, or, view the theater in Google Maps by simply tapping a link in Safari.

```
http://tinyurl.com/2mugck
```

■   **Bejeweled**   Pass the time anywhere with this popular puzzle game from the comfort of your Safari browser.

```
http://static.popcap.com/iphone/
```

In addition to iPhone web applications, you can power up Safari with *bookmarklets*, which contain small snippets of Javascript (a web programming language) and can be added to Safari as bookmarks. Bookmarklets can help you search a page for text, look up a word in an online dictionary, research a topic on Wikipedia, and more, without ever requiring you to visit a web page first. To use most bookmarklets, you just tap the associated bookmark, type a little text in the pop-up, and then hit OK. Bookmarklets provide a quick, simple way to access information without loading a web page to do so first. To get started, check out this excellent list of iPhone bookmarklets.

```
http://tinyurl.com/2y4aqf
```

Access Safari from Other Applications and Vice Versa

Thanks to the iPhone's tight integration across applications, you can open up Safari links from many places. For example, if your friend emails you a link, clicking on it will create a new page in Safari and load the right page automatically. You can also load links from the SMS application if the URL is formatted correctly, or you can load local city info from the weather application by clicking the Y! button on the lower left. You can even open URLs in Safari from Google Maps and the Stocks app.

You can also load other applications from Safari as well. If you see a phone number on a web page, clicking it will bring up a prompt asking you whether you want to call the number. Clicking on an email address will open up the email application and compose a new message to the person. Likewise, clicking on an address will load Google Maps with that address pinpointed.

If you find a cool web page you want someone else to see, click the address bar and then the Share button. This will bring up an email window so you can send the link off to your friends.

Learn Safari's Limitations

Although Safari is a desktop-class browser with plugin support, there are a few things it can't do. It doesn't have Flash support, which means you can't go to youtube.com and view video there. (The video in the YouTube app is specially encoded for the iPhone to get around this problem.) The iPhone also doesn't currently support Java, so Yahoo Games and other Java webapps won't work. And other than some Quicktime movies, streaming video such as Windows Media or Real Video won't work either.

Tweak Safari Settings

Just like in a regular desktop browser, there are some settings in Safari you can tweak to enhance or speed up your browsing session. Here's a quick look at what the options in Figure 7-9 are and what they do.

- **Search Engine**   You can switch your search engine from the default Google to Yahoo if you like.

- **JavaScript**   Many websites, including sites that host the web applications for your iPhone we covered a little earlier in the chapter, use JavaScript. Disabling this will speed up browsing slightly, but make some pages behave oddly and other pages completely unreadable. We recommend leaving this on unless you have a reason to turn it off.

- **Plug-Ins**   This allows you to play back Quicktime movies and various audio files inside your browser. You should leave this on unless a specific movie or audio file is crashing Safari, which will happen very rarely.

- **Block Pop-ups**   This prevents web pages from opening up new windows uninvited, which are usually pop-up ads that you're familiar with on the desktop. We suggest you leave this on.

- **Accept Cookies**   Cookies are little pieces of data that websites use as storage bins for information. This info can be your login (to automatically log you in to a site when you visit), so we recommend leaving it set to From Visited. This lets sites you're actually viewing leave cookies, but blocks cookies from ad sites that you're not directly visiting.

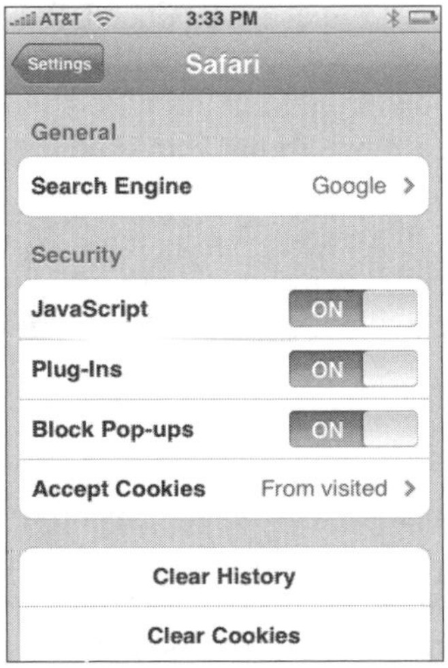

FIGURE 7-9   The Safari Settings screen

- **Clear History**   If you're like Adam and you're ashamed of the sites you've been browsing, click Clear History. This will prevent any wandering eyes from accidentally seeing your surfing habits. The downside is that you won't be able to go into your history to find a page you viewed a few days ago but forgot to bookmark.

- **Clear Cookies**   Not a huge deal if you've been accepting cookies by default, but if you want to clear your login info from certain websites, you can do so here.

- **Clear Cache**   The iPhone stores web page data, such as images, in its internal memory in order to speed up subsequent visits to the same website. If you're running low on space, you can clear the cache here to free up some more room to take pictures or receive emails.

Avoid Crashing Safari

If you've browsed the web at all on your desktop, you'll be familiar with the fact that browsers can crash. It's the combination of infinitely variable websites with infinitely variable inputs from you that make it tough to crash-proof browsers. The Safari on your iPhone is no exception. Here are some tips to make your browser more stable.

- **Avoid Opening Too Many Pages**   Although the iPhone lets you open many pages at once, try to keep your pages down the minimum amount you can use to browse comfortably. If you open up too many, not only does Safari slow down, it's much more likely to crash as well, kicking you back to the Home screen in the process.

- **Avoid Pages with Too Much Rich Content**   Safari supports JavaScript, and in turn, rich web applications, but you want to avoid web applications that aren't specifically designed or optimized for the iPhone. Visiting sites with a lot of JavaScript and huge images make it more likely for your browser to crash.

You now know everything you need to know in order to browse the Web from your iPhone with the same agility as you browse sites on your desktop. In Chapter 8, we'll show you how Apple brought the same agility to your appointment book with Calendar.

Part IV

Stay Informed and Organized with Your iPhone

Chapter 8

Manage and Sync Appointments with the Calendar

How to...

- Manage your schedule with Calendar
- Use your desktop calendar to manage your schedule
- Sync the Calendar with your computer

Your days of carrying around a memo planner or unusable mobile calendar are over. With Calendar, you can add, edit, and sync events between your iPhone and desktop calendar application—whether it's Outlook on Windows or iCal and Entourage on Mac. With the iPhone in your pocket, you can see your daily and monthly appointments at a glance (Figure 8-1). You'll never be late again.

FIGURE 8-1   The Month View shows an overview of your month's appointments.

Manage Your Schedule with Calendar

The first thing you need to do in order to start scheduling is to start the Calendar application. Just go to the Home screen and tap the Calendar button to get started.

Navigate the Calendar

The first thing you'll notice when you're in the Calendar app is that there are three views you can choose from: List, Day, and Month. To move between these three views, just tap one of the three view buttons on the top of the screen, and the Calendar will display your events in that view. Here's what each view has to offer. (Figure 8-1 shows the Month view and Figure 8-2 shows the Day view.)

- ■ **List View**   This displays all of your appointments in a text list by day, time, and date. This view extends for two years.

- ■ **Day View**   This is an hour-by-hour display of your day's appointments. You can scroll through from 12 AM oneday to 12 AM the next day. Appointments appear as colored

FIGURE 8-2   Day View gives you a close up of what you've got planned for the day.

bubbles that span the length of the appointment and contain the appointment title and location. Any all-day events appear at the top of the Day view.

■ **Month View**   The Month view gives you a nice view of your events for the month in a traditional month-long calendar format. You can view events one day at a time in the list at the bottom of Month view.

One constant in all these views is that you can tap the Today button to refocus your view on the current day. This shortcut is particularly handy when you've been checking appointments for some time in the future and you want to quickly jump back to today's events. However, navigating days in each view manually is simple as well.

■ **List View**   The Swipe and Flick options you've used to navigate lists throughout the iPhone are intact in List view. Swiping helps when you're trying to find an event in the next few days, but if you're trying to see if you're free in a month, a quick flick works better. As you scroll up, the gray bar with the date will move up to replace the previous date, and everything between two gray bars represents all the events belonging to the date above. When you find an event you want to view, just tap anywhere on the event to view the event info.

■ **Day View**   You can view all the events on one particular day (12AM to 12AM). Swiping and flicking works here, but there isn't much reason to use a flick unless you're trying to get to the top or bottom of a day fast. When you see an event, just tap it to bring up the event detail pane. You can move forward or backward a day by tapping the right and left arrows on the top bar, next to the date.

■ **Month View**   View the entire calendar at a glance and focus in on a specific day to see what your schedule for the day looks like. You can tell which days you've scheduled events on by looking for a small dot on the bottom of that day. When you tap a day, the bottom of the screen displays a miniature List View, letting you swipe up and down to choose an event. Tap on an event to see the Event Details pane.

Inside the event info pane (shown in Figure 8-3), you can view details such as the name of the event, its location, and most importantly, the date and time of the event. We'll go over how you edit these fields a bit later in the chapter.

Add Events to Your Calendar

To add a new event to your calendar, tap the + button on the top right of either the List, Day, or Month view. If you're in List view, the event will have a default date of whatever day is at the very top of your list. If you're on Day or Month view, the default date will be the currently selected day. Once inside the Add Event screen as shown in Figure 8-4, you've got a bunch of options. Here's what they all mean.

■ **Title**   The name of this event. This can be something along the lines of "Meet Adam at the movies," or "Get toe reattached."

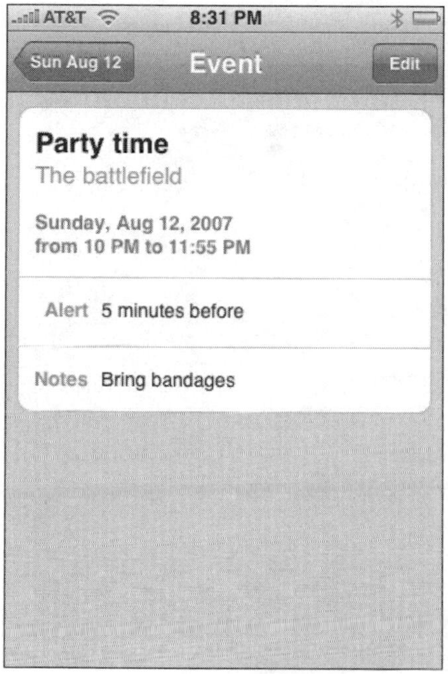

FIGURE 8-3   The Event info screen displays all the details for your event.

- **Location (Optional)**   This is a note to yourself describing where this event is held, such as Home, Work, or Hospital.

- **Start & End**   The date and time the event starts or ends. You can choose any day and any time in five-minute increments. Today will be displayed as Today in the spin-wheel, and you can even choose to have an event span multiple days.

- **All-Day (Optional)**   Toggle this to On to denote that your event, such as a vacation or jury duty, will take up an entire day. You can also create multiple all-day events.

- **Repeat (Optional)**   If you want to make this event repeat automatically in the future, you have the option of choosing between every day, every week, every two weeks, every month, or every year. There are actually more advanced options for repeating events, such as repeating an event every week only on Tuesdays and Thursdays, but those are only accessible from the calendar on the computer.

- **End Repeat (Optional)**   Set the date when your event stops repeating. An example of this would be to end your monthly orthodontist appointment in two years when your braces come off.

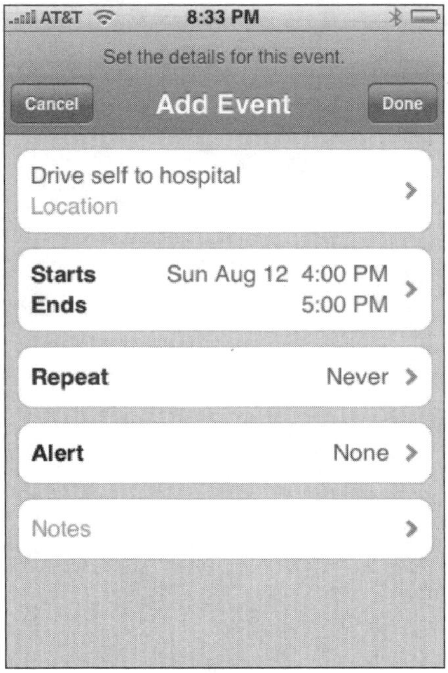

FIGURE 8-4 Add new events to your calendar on the iPhone.

- **Alert (Optional)** You can have the iPhone display an alert (or two) on or before the event is due, complete with vibration and audio. The second alert selector only appears after you've set a first alert.

- **Notes (Optional)** Write down some notes related to the event, such as the address of the event's location, numbers of people you need to call when you get there, or the URL of the restaurant.

The only thing new in the Calendar app is the way you select a time and date. The dials work exactly the same as a real, physical dial. Take your finger, place it on the dial, and scroll up or down to adjust the entry. Like browsing lists, you can flick up and down fast to jump to a time or date further away. All the other options here should be fairly straightforward, but some, such as special repetition, are only available if you create an event on the computer and sync it to the iPhone.

Edit and Delete Events from Your Calendar

Editing events is as easy as creating them. From any view (List, Day, or Month) tap an event. When the Event Info pane slides in, tap the Edit button on the top right. This brings up a screen that is exactly like the Add Event screen, which you should be familiar with if you created this event on the iPhone. Just tap any field to modify it, and when you're done, tap Done.

To delete an event, bring up the edit screen like you did previously. Now, scroll to the very bottom and tap the Delete Event button. If this is a repeating event, the iPhone will ask if you only want to delete this, or if you want to delete all future events. If this is a single-time event, just tap Delete Event.

Use Your Desktop Calendar to Manage Your Schedule

Although you'll be making and viewing events on your iPhone calendar, most of your scheduling will probably take place on your computer. It is, after all, where you do most of your work during the day. Here's how you create a new event on iCal, Entourage, or Outlook so you can sync them to your iPhone.

Schedule Events with iCal

Here's how you schedule events with iCal:

1. Create a new event by clicking File, and then New Event, or by pressing COMMAND + N on your keyboard.

2. Enter in the event name and location.

3. Choose whether this event is an all day event by checking All-Day.

4. Choose a time for this event to start and end. This can be a multi-day event if the end date is later than the start day.

5. Choose repeat options. These are the same as on the iPhone, except for the addition of a Custom Repeat option.

6. Choose attendees. When you start typing, iCal will automatically grab contacts from your Address Book to auto-complete your entry.

7. Choose a calendar to put this event into. You can't tell which calendar these events belong to on your iPhone, but it's useful for organization on your desktop.

8. Choose an alarm. The alarm time will carry over onto the iPhone.

9. Type in some notes to yourself.

That's it! You're done. If you're interested in creating custom repeat options, here's what you do. In the repeat step, select Custom from the dropdown. Now if you select Daily, you can choose to repeat it every x number of days. If you select Weekly or Monthly, you can choose which days of the week or month to repeat. If you choose yearly, you can choose which month and which day of the month to repeat. These will carry over to the iPhone, but you can't actually create an event like this on the iPhone itself. You can only create them on the computer and sync them over.

Schedule Events with Entourage

Here's how you schedule events with Entourage.

1. Either click File, New, and then Calendar Event, or click the New button and then click Calendar Event. Alternately, if you're in Calendar view, just click the New button.

2. Fill in the subject and location fields with the title of your appointment and its location.

3. Choose the start and end dates and times.

4. Check whether you want this to be an all day event

5. Change recurrence options (same as repeat on the iPhone). You can create slightly more advanced recurrence options here than you can on the iPhone. They will carry over.

6. Choose a reminder time (this is the same as Alert on the iPhone).

7. Enter in travel time. This doesn't carry over to the iPhone.

8. Enter in some notes for this event.

9. Click Save.

After entering in your information, you have to make sure your Entourage calendar is being synced with iCal. iTunes can only sync data between the iPhone and iCal, so you have to use iCal as a proxy. Go to your Entourage preferences, then click Sync Services. Look to see that the checkbox next to Synchronize Events and Tasks with iCal and .Mac is checked.

Schedule Events with Outlook

Here's how you schedule events with Outlook:

1. Create a new appointment in Outlook by switching to Calendar view and then clicking File, New, and Appointment. You can also do this by clicking the New button on the Outlook toolbar, or by pressing the CTRL + N keyboard shortcut.

2. Fill in the Subject and Location fields with your appointment title and, obviously enough, your location.

3. Use the Start Time and End Time dropdown menus to choose both the start and end dates and times of your appointment. If the appointment will last all day, check the box next to All Day Event.

4. If it's a recurring event, click the Recurrence button and choose the recurrence pattern of the appointment. You can schedule repeating events on your iPhone, but Outlook's recurrence settings allow you to set up more advanced recurrence schemes, like the second Saturday of every month, so it's good to set up repeating events here.

5. Choose a reminder time from the Reminder dropdown menu to get an alert 15 minutes to 2 weeks ahead of the appointment. This will show up as the alert time on the iPhone.

6. Enter in any notes you have for the event. Like most of the rest of the appointment fields, your notes will sync to the iPhone.

7. When you're finished, click Save and Close.

Sync the Calendar with Your Computer

Next to music and videos, syncing your schedule with your computer is probably the best reason for docking your iPhone every day. It's important to make sure your appointments are matched up on both your phone and your computer to avoid scheduling conflicts. Syncing your calendars requires the same process for iCal or Outlook. Here's what you do, starting from the screen shown in Figure 8-5.

1. Connect your iPhone to your computer, open iTunes, and then click on your iPhone in the sidebar.

2. Open the Info tab.

3. Check the box next to Sync Calendars From and choose Outlook in the Calendars section on Windows, or Sync iCal Calendars on Mac.

4. **Mac only:** Choose to either sync all calendars or only selected calendars. If you choose to sync selected calendars, tick the checkboxes next to the calendars you want to sync.

5. **Mac only:** Choose a default calendar you want the events created on your iPhone to be synced to.

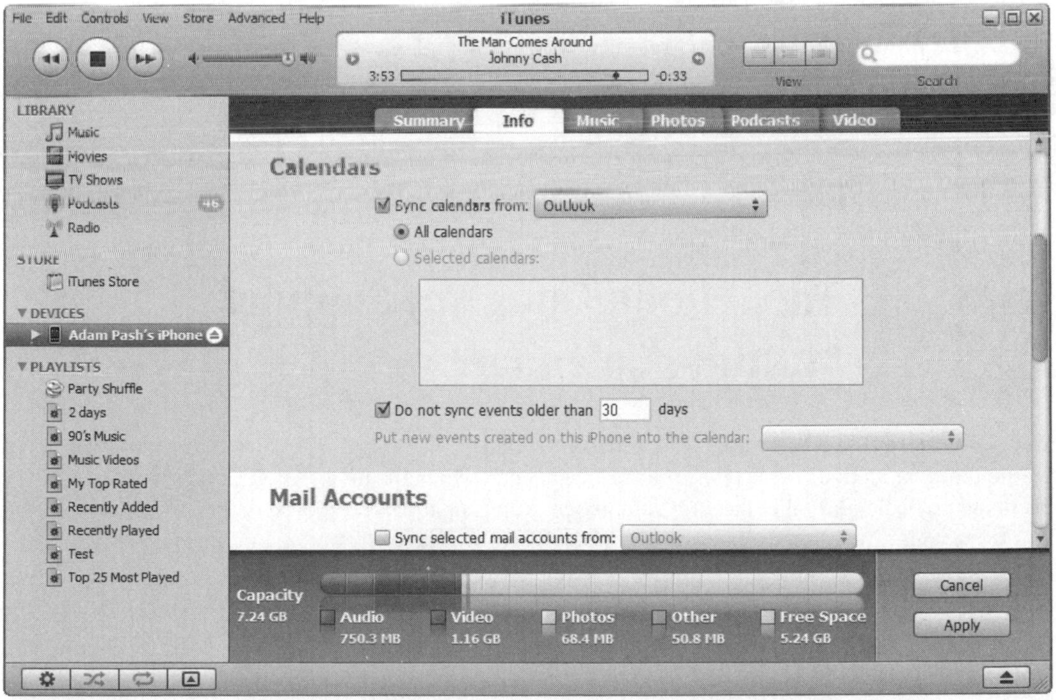

FIGURE 8-5   The Calendar sync screen

6. Decide how many days worth of past appointments you need synced to your iPhone. If you want to sync all events, no matter how old, uncheck the box next to Do Not Sync Events Older Than *x* Days. If you can't think of a good reason why you need to access your old appointments past a certain number of days, tick the checkbox and then how many days of past appointments you want to sync (the default is 30).

7. Click Sync to finish.

After it's done syncing, the calendars on the iPhone and on your computer will be exactly the same.

TIP   *If you're having trouble syncing your iPhone with Outlook or Outlook Express on a Windows-based computer, Apple has a support page to address some potential issues. Follow the steps listed on the following page to work around any problems you may have.* `http://docs.info.apple.com/article.html?artnum=305845`

Resolve Sync Conflicts

If you change the details of an appointment on both your computer and your iPhone between syncs so that the two appointments contain conflicting information, iTunes will catch the conflict and ask you to resolve the conflict now or later. To resolve the conflict, click Now to take a look at the two events. The red text highlights where the two events conflict, as shown in Figure 8-6. Pick the event info that's more accurate and then click Done.

You'll be prompted to resync the calendars now or later. Unless you have a reason to keep one of the conflicts around for a little while longer—maybe to write down the information so you don't lose it—go ahead and click Sync Now.

Did you know?   # The iPhone Does Not Support Multiple Calendars

Both Outlook and iCal support multiple calendars to help you separate your tasks. Your iPhone, on the other hand, does not support multiple calendars, which means you don't get to assign events to any calendar other than the default one. You can, however, choose one calendar that you want your iPhone-created events to sync to. The Calendar Sync option in iTunes lets you choose any existing calendar in *Outlook* or iCal. (The option currently appears grayed out for Outlook syncs, which indicates that iTunes may support calendar specification for Outlook in the future. See Figure 8-5.) Whenever you create an event on the iPhone, your event will be deposited into your selected calendar after syncing with your computer.

FIGURE 8-6 If an appointment contains conflicting information, the Conflict Resolver will alert you and help you fix the conflict.

TIP *If you're experiencing sync issues related to time zone conflicts, you can go into the iPhone settings and adjust time zone support. This is under Settings, then General, then Date & Time. Below the Calendar section, you can either turn off Time Zone Support to have all your events take the time zone of whatever zone you're currently in, or manually adjust the time zone yourself by selecting a city.*

Sync Your Appointments with Google Calendar

As of this writing, the iPhone does not support syncing your calendar with any web-based calendar application, such as the increasingly popular Google Calendar. However, there are several tools available that provide a bidirectional sync between Google Calendar and Outlook (Windows) or iCal (Mac). This means Google Calendar and your local calendar will always have the same appointments as long as you run the sync. That also means that whether you update your calendar online, on your computer, or on your iPhone, you can be sure you have the most up-to-date appointments across the board. We recommend the following:

■ **SyncMyCal (Outlook)** This automatically keeps your Google Calendar and Outlook calendar in complete sync. After you purchase and install the SyncMyCal plugin, your calendars sync back and forth without any effort on your part. SyncMyCal has a free trial version, but a fully–licensed copy will set you back $25.

`http://www.syncmycal.com/home.htm`

■ **Spanning Sync (iCal)**   For Google Calendar and iCal syncing, Spanning Sync is the best option for Mac users. You can download a 15-day trial version to see how it works for you. If you like it, a one-year subscription costs $25; and if you really like it, you can pay a one-time fee of $65 for a lifetime subscription.

`http://spanningsync.com/`

On the other hand, if you're cheap like I am and/or you have some technical knowledge and like rolling up your sleeves and getting to work on your computer, you can sync Google Calendar with iCal using a free, open source application called GCalDaemon. It takes a little work to get set up, but if you're up for it, you can find step-by-step instructions here:

`http://tinyurl.com/336kln`

Now that you've mastered your schedule, we'll dive into using your iPhone's built-in Camera and Photos applications to create and share memories on-the-go in the next chapter.

 How to ...   **Manage Your To-Do Lists**

Although both iCal and Outlook have built-in to-do lists that let you manage items you need to get done but that aren't necessarily tied to appointments or events on a calendar, your iPhone's calendar does not support to-do lists as of this writing. To remedy this problem, we turn to web-based to-do list managers that provide both a desktop and iPhone-optimized interface for adding to, managing, and editing items on your to-do list. There are many available, but we like

■ Remember the Milk

`http://rememberthemilk.com`

■ Ta-da Lists

`http://tadalist.com/`

■ Nozbe

`http://nozbe.com/`

If you don't like the idea of an online to-do list, you could just create a manual—though not terribly robust—list on your iPhone using the Notes application.

Chapter 9

Take Pictures and View Photos on Your iPhone

How to...

- Take pictures with the iPhone's camera
- View and manage photos with the Photos applications
- Share photos and customize your iPhone with photos
- Sync Photos to and from your computer
- Tweak the photos settings

The iPhone's large 3.5-inch screen is great for viewing videos in the iPod app, as you saw in Chapter 4. Naturally, this same giant screen makes viewing pictures on-the-go a pleasure as well. Imagine taking your entire vacation photo album with you wherever you go, or even using them as wallpapers or contact photos. Not only that, but you can use the iPhone's 2-megapixel camera to shoot great looking 1600×1200 resolution images and share them with your friends over email. In this chapter, we'll show you how to do all of this and more.

Take Pictures with the iPhone's Camera

Let's start by taking some pictures. From the Home screen, tap the Camera application. The Camera app will start up, and the closed iris will open up to reveal a full-motion video display of what the camera lens sees. To take a picture, just tap the camera button—that's the button on the bottom of Figure 9-1. You can either take a picture in vertical portrait mode or horizontal landscape mode by just tilting the iPhone in either direction. When you turn the camera, the little camera in the shutter button turns as well to indicate that the camera has changed orientation.

Once you hit the shutter, the iris will close and the iPhone will make a shutter noise, saving the taken picture to your iPhone's internal storage. You can also hold the shutter down until you're ready to take a picture. This helps you time the picture correctly, especially if you're holding the camera out to take a shot of yourself. To view pictures you've taken, tap the pictures button on the bottom left. This will bring up the Camera Roll, which is the folder on your iPhone that holds all the pictures you've shot with the iPhone. To get back to the camera from the Camera Roll, tap the pictures button again.

TIP

If you work at a job where privacy and security are a top priority, you may not be allowed to carry any phone that has a camera. But that doesn't mean you have to throw your electronic baby out with the bathwater. You can enjoy all of the iPhone's other fabulous functions by simply having the camera removed from your phone by a company called iResQ for $100.
`http://www.iresq.com/iphone/`

FIGURE 9-1   Shooting a picture requires just two steps, pointing the camera and tapping the shutter button.

How to ...   **Take Great Pictures with the iPhone**

The iPhone camera may be convenient, but it's not perfect in all conditions. To make the camera super simple to use, Apple excluded features like flash, shutter, and exposure; settings that you can adjust in other cameraphones to make your pictures as polished as possible. You can help compensate for the lack of end-user adjustment settings by taking photos in conditions optimum for the iPhone's camera. First and foremost, you'll have great results when taking pictures in daylight (or situations where there's enough light) and when the subject is still. At nighttime, in the dark, pictures become fuzzy, grainy, and sometimes blurry. You should avoid these situations whenever possible.

View and Manage Photos with the Photos Application

Now that you know how to take photos and to view them, let's move on to viewing pictures you've synced to the iPhone from your computer.

View and Navigate Photos

To get started, go to the Home screen and launch the Photos application. You'll see the Photo Albums screen, from which you can access the Camera Roll (this holds all your iPhone camera pictures) and every album you've synced to the iPhone (we'll go over how to sync albums later in this chapter). Your photo albums are laid out in a list, with a small thumbnail of the first image inside to the left of the album name, just like in Figure 9-2.

Tap the album you want to view to open it up. The top of this screen displays the title of the photo album (for example, Summer Vacation '07), and the black arrow button to the left of the title will take you back to the main Photo Albums screen.

FIGURE 9-2   The album list view

To view a photo by itself, first head inside an album. This is the view that holds square thumbnail images of every picture. You can scroll the thumbnails by swiping or flicking the screen, and view any image in the album by tapping the image thumbnail. As you can see in Figure 9-3, these thumbnails are large enough to make out details, but small enough so you can see a bunch of them at once.

Once you're viewing an image, you'll see a top bar that displays the photo's number along with the total number of photos in the gallery (such as 6 of 23). On the left of the top bar, you'll see a black arrow button displaying the album name. You can go back to the thumbnail view of your photos at any time by tapping this button.

While you're still viewing an image, the bottom bar allows you to navigate an album using the onscreen overlay, as seen in Figure 9-4. The left and right arrows allow you to progress forward or backward in the album, the Play button starts a slideshow, and the Action button on the far left of the bottom overlay lets you do things with the photo you're currently viewing, like email the photo, use it as wallpaper, assign it to a contact, or upload it to a web gallery. We'll discuss the Action button in detail later on in this chapter.

 Get a quick look at the contents of an album with the thumbnails.

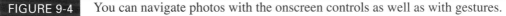

FIGURE 9-4   You can navigate photos with the onscreen controls as well as with gestures.

You can rotate the iPhone any time you're viewing a picture to change between landscape and portrait mode. In fact, you can rotate the phone a full 360 degrees to view the photo in every orientation possible. Changing the view is especially handy for getting a better look at pictures. Pictures taken in a landscape orientation fill up the screen better in Landscape mode, while the opposite is true with pictures taken in a portrait orientation.

If you view a picture for a moment without touching the screen, the navigation overlay will fade away so that all you see is your photo. You can bring the overlay back at any time by tapping the screen. In general, though, you'll want to view your photos without the distracting overlay. You can do this while still navigating your photos by using gestures.

Browse Photos with Gestures

When you're browsing photos on your iPhone, half of the fun is taking advantage of the phone's multi-touch gestures to browse and zoom in on content. Here's how they work:

- **Swipe/Flick**   When you're viewing an album with multiple photos, you can move from one photo to the next by swiping or flicking your screen from the direction you want to advance. For example, if you want to view the next photo to the right in an album, just flick the screen from right to left like you're flipping the page of a real photo album. If you've zoomed in on a photo, swiping and flicking the screen lets you move around on the picture you're currently looking at. If you're zoomed in and you want to move to the next photo, either zoom out first or give the screen two strong swipes.

- ■ **Pinch/Spread**   Zoom in and out on a photo by spreading apart (zoom in) or pinching (zoom out) two fingers on the screen.

- ■ **Double-Tap**   You can quickly zoom into an image by double-tapping the screen. Unlike the spread method, double-tapping doesn't allow you to choose how far you zoom in. If you've already magnified a picture, whether using the spread or double-tap method, a second double-tap will zoom out to fit the full image on the screen.

View an Album as a Slideshow

Viewing slideshows on the iPhone's gorgeous screen offers a great way to enjoy photos away from your home computer without lugging around an actual photo album. To start a slideshow, choose an album from the main Photo Albums list and then tap the play button on the bottom of the individual photo album screen.

If you're already viewing an image inside an album, tap the screen to bring up the overlay and then tap the play button in the center to start the slideshow from the picture you're viewing.

NOTE   *You can tweak the way that slideshows play back on the iPhone—including slide duration, transition effects, repeat, and shuffle—by tweaking the Photos Settings. We'll discuss these settings more at the end of this chapter.*

To stop a slideshow at any time, just tap the screen.

Delete Photos

If you've taken a picture that you don't particularly like, deleting it is a simple process. When viewing a photo in your Camera Roll, you'll notice a small trash can icon on the bottom right of the overlay. Just tap the icon to delete the photo. Unless you've synced this picture to your computer already, you'll be losing it forever. Make sure you want to delete this picture before you confirm.

Did you know?

Watch a Musical Slideshow

Not only can you enjoy slideshows on your iPhone, you can actually enjoy them with a soundtrack! Just start up your iPod application, pick a song, and then start playing it. Now hit the Home button, open the Photo application, and fire up the slideshow. Your songs will keep on playing as you delight in your stored memories.

Keep in mind, though, that you can't delete any photos from albums that you've synced to your iPhone. You can only delete photos inside the Camera Roll.

Share Photos and Customize Your iPhone with Photos

Besides just looking at photos—which is fun in its own right—you can do all kinds of different things with them. To start, first browse to a picture, then press the Action button on the bottom left to bring up the four options (or three, if you don't have iPhoto '08 and a .Mac account) that you see in Figure 9-5.

Set a Photo as Your Wallpaper

To set a photo as your wallpaper (meaning that it displays in the background when your screen's locked or when someone without a contact picture calls you), tap the first option: Use As Wallpaper.

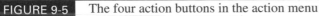
FIGURE 9-5   The four action buttons in the action menu

A dialog box will come up allowing you to move and scale the picture (with gestures) to best fit the wallpaper to the window. This means you can center the shot on something you like or zoom in to the most interesting part. See Figure 9-6 for how this overlay looks. Once you're done, tap Set Wallpaper to confirm. If you've changed your mind and don't want this photo as your wallpaper, tap Cancel.

Email Your Photos

To email a photo to a friend, tap the second option in the Action button menu: Email Photo. You'll see an animation of your photo transitioning into a new email message, which you can then fill out and send off to a contact, as shown in Figure 9-7. For more information on how email works, see Chapter 6.

NOTE *Emailing pictures to someone will downscale the resolution from its default resolution to a low 640 × 480 pixels. It's a fine way to show someone a picture you took quickly, but if you want full resolution photos, you'll still have to sync your iPhone to your computer.*

   Set and customize any photo as your wallpaper.

FIGURE 9-7   Share any photo with friends via email.

Did you know?

You Can Email Pictures to Online Photo Galleries

You can also email pictures to Flickr and other online photo sharing services. However, you have to enable email uploading on these sites first. When you do, they will give you an email address that you can send your pictures to in order to have them show up in your web gallery. We recommend creating a new contact or adding this to your own personal contact with the correct label. This method is only good for sharing pictures on the go when you don't have a computer, because photos sent over email will be scaled down to 640 × 480 resolution.

Hack Your iPhone

In the rest of this book, we've covered how to use your iPhone as Apple intended. In this special Spotlight section, we'll discuss how to install third party applications on your iPhone and unlock your iPhone for use with non-AT&T carriers.

Apple did two controversial things when they released the iPhone. First, rather than provide software developers with a development framework for making their own native software for the iPhone, they told them to make their iPhone applications on the web for Safari (a decidedly less exciting—not to mention less powerful—platform). As a result these developers couldn't take advantage of the brilliant, beautiful, and fast operating system Apple developed for the iPhone—which is itself a modified version of the OS X operating system all Macs use. Second, they released the iPhone exclusively through AT&T, meaning that anyone who wanted to buy an iPhone would also be required to lock himself into a two-year contract with AT&T. And even if the contract was up, you still couldn't use your phone with T-Mobile or an overseas carrier.

NOTE

The state of iPhone hacks is always subject to change, often because Apple releases software updates that add official features but disable third party applications as a side effect. After a software update, iPhone hackers work to figure out how to break back into the phone, and as a result, not every hack discussed in this section will always work at any specific time. We'll keep you updated with the latest state of iPhone hacks—including which hacks still apply to the latest iPhone firmware—at http://htdeiphone.wordpress.com.

For some, these limitations are trivial. For others, they make the difference between buying an iPhone and doing without.

In this Spotlight section, we'll discuss how to hack your iPhone to install third-party applications, as well as highlight several of our favorites. Then we'll introduce you to a few methods people have employed to free their iPhones from the shackles of AT&T.

CAUTION

Currently, these third-party iPhone hacks will void your iPhone's warranty, and in the case of the SIM unlock, it could even brick your iPhone. While the third-party applications in particular are generally a safe bet, you should proceed with these iPhone hacks at your own risk.

Hack Your iPhone

Until Apple opens up the iPhone to third-party software development, you actually need to run a program on your computer that—in essence—hacks into the iPhone's software innards and opens it

NOTE

It's very easy to unlock and install applications onto your iPhone, but it's also very probable that Apple will open the iPhone to third-party development sometime in the future so that you can install new apps without any hacking whatsoever. However, Apple will likely charge money for new programs—just as they did when they added support for ringtones—so these third-party hacks may still prove useful.

up so you can install other applications. This process has been termed a jailbreak by iPhone hackers.

These same iPhone hackers were developing applications to help automate the jailbreak process for regular users only a few short weeks after the iPhone was released. A few weeks after that, the applications became more polished and started incorporating more features, such as ways to add custom ringtones from your music library, or install new applications written especially for the iPhone. After only a couple of months, installing innovative third-party applications onto the iPhone was within any iPhone owner's grasp.

In this section, we'll show you how to jailbreak your iPhone, install third-party applications and games, and customize your iPhone with your own ringtones.

NOTE

Before you proceed, you should be aware that you're undertaking these iPhone hacks at your own (albeit slight) risk. Unlike the rest of the tips and tricks in this book, hacking your iPhone *could* possibly lead to problems. In almost all instances you should be able to fix the problems you encounter—if any—by a simple iPhone restore (which we detail in Chapter 16), but be aware that a risk does exist.

Hack Your iPhone with iBrickr (Windows)

As of this writing, the easiest way to open up your iPhone to applications and customization (jailbreaking) on Windows is with iBrickr by Nate True. With iBrickr, you'll not only be able to jailbreak the phone, but you can also use it to transfer files to and from your iPhone, add custom ringtones, change iPhone audio alerts, and install applications. iBrickr is located here:

```
http://cre.ations.net/creation/ibrickr
```

The first thing you'll want to do is download the newest version of iBrickr. The program comes in a .zip file, which you'll need to extract into its own folder on your hard drive before starting. We chose C:\ibrickr, but you can choose anything you like.

After you've extracted the iBrickr files, open the file named ibrickr.exe. This will show a screen similar to Figure S-1, telling you that you have to free your iPhone before you can do anything on it. If all you want to do is add custom ringtones, you can do that without freeing your iPhone. Freeing your iPhone involves several steps, some of which may change as newer versions of iBrickr are released. First and foremost, follow the instructions in the program and make sure you don't skip any steps. The second most important thing is to be patient. Some steps require modifying files on the iPhone and restarting it, and may take a few minutes depending on your phone. As of this writing, you can use iBrickr as described next.

To start off, connect your iPhone to your computer. iBrickr will tell you that you need to start iTunes and initiate a Restore, as shown in Figure S-2.

Figure S-1. The first thing you'll do with iBrickr is free your iPhone.

Figure S-2. Before you can free your phone, you have to download the firmware from Apple.

You won't actually restore your phone—you only want the firmware file that your phone downloads from Apple. So after your download starts (it will show as downloading in the downloads section of iTunes), unplug your iPhone. When the download finishes, iTunes will warn you that it's unable to find your iPhone. That's fine! Just close the warning, and then close iTunes. Plug your phone back in and return to iBrickr.

Once you click the Check again button, iBrickr will start modifying your phone. If iTunes is running, ignore it. In fact, you can shut it down altogether if you want. The iBrickr jailbreak won't affect any of your phone's normal functions. Calls, emails and Internet browsing will all still work the same.

There's no status bar or indicator section on the iBrickr screen to let you know that it's copying and editing some files on your iPhone, but rest assured that it's opening up the iPhone file system so that you can put files onto it and run customized applications. It's not abnormal for this process to take as long as 10 minutes, so this is the part where you have to be patient. Don't disconnect or shut down iBrickr for at least 10 minutes, as shown in Figure S-3. If more than 15 minutes has passed, close iBrickr, restart your phone, and start the process over again. If for some reason your iPhone is in an unrecoverable state, start iTunes and initiate a restore before you try again.

When the hacking's complete, you'll be met with a Success! message. Pat yourself on the back, wait for the iPhone to restart, and click the Sweet! button. You may need to unplug and plug in your iPhone again after it restarts, because Windows has some quirky

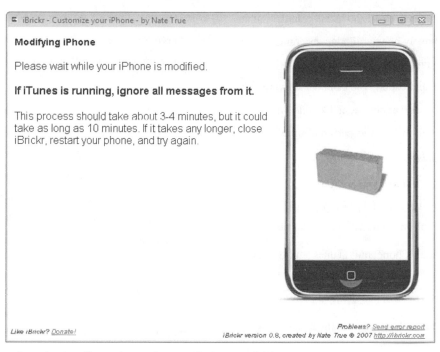

Figure S-3. Be patient when installing, as it can take up to 10 minutes to finish.

USB detection for a device that's already plugged in. You may also need to restart iBrickr if it doesn't recognize that you've plugged in your iPhone again.

When that's done, you've successfully performed a jailbreak on your iPhone! You'll be sent back to the main iBrickr screen, where you'll have four options: Ringtones, Sounds, Applications, and Files. Ringtones lets you upload custom ringtones to your phone, Sounds changes your iPhone alert noises, Applications lets you install custom apps, and Files lets you browse, upload, and download files on your iPhone. We'll cover these four options later on in this chapter.

Hack Your iPhone with AppTapp Installer or iFuntastic (Mac)

If you're looking to open up your iPhone to third-party software and you're on a Mac, you've got two choices: iFuntastic and AppTapp Installer. iFuntastic is a multi-purpose application that not only performs the iPhone jailbreak, but also lets you add custom ringtones, browse your iPhone's folders, and perform other customizations. However, we recommend using AppTapp Installer for its extreme ease of use. After it jailbreaks your phone, AppTapp Installer installs just one app, called Installer.app. Once installed, Installer. app can download, install, update, and manage applications directly from your iPhone, meaning that you won't even need to dock the iPhone to install applications. As we've stated, we recommend using AppTapp, but we'll describe both next.

Hack Your iPhone with AppTapp Installer (Mac)

AppTapp Installer opens up your iPhone for third-party software installations and then installs just one application directly on your iPhone. That application,

5

Installer.app, can download and install countless other applications directly on your iPhone, meaning that after you install it, you'll never need to dock your iPhone to install another application. You can do it all wirelessly.

As always, new applications like this may change greatly in just a short period of time. But, as of this writing, here's how it works:

1. Go to the Installer.app homepage and download the latest version of AppTapp Installer:

   http://iphone.nullriver.com/beta/

2. Dock your iPhone, quit iTunes, and then run AppTapp Installer on your Mac. Read the Welcome screen, and then hit Continue.

3. AppTapp will ask you for the latest firmware version you've installed on your iPhone. If you don't know what this is, open the iPhone Summary panel in iTunes and look for the number behind Software Version

(see Figure S-4). Be sure to quit iTunes before proceeding. Select the proper firmware version number and click Continue.

4. AppTapp will now copy files to your iPhone and install the application. Your iPhone will go into Recovery mode during this process, so don't be alarmed. AppTapp should be finished in a few minutes. You don't have to do anything at all. After AppTapp tells you that it's finished, go to your iPhone Home screen. You should now see a fresh new icon; that's Installer.app (see Figure S-5).

See the section on installing Third-Party Apps with Installer.app to install more applications using this method.

Hack Your iPhone with iFuntastic (Mac)

Using iFuntastic, you can add customized ringtones, install applications, and browse files on your iPhone.

Figure S-4. AppTapp will ask you for the latest firmware installed on your iPhone.

Figure S-5. Your Home screen has a new icon: Installer.app.

Unfortunately iFuntastic does not—as of this writing—have a centralized web site. So, in order to download iFuntastic for your Mac, head over to Google and search for iFuntastic. Chances are one of the top search results should point to the latest iFuntastic download.

After you've downloaded and installed iFuntastic, it's time to jailbreak your iPhone—a process iFuntastic is calling "unshackling." Since this software is developing at a very rapid rate, we can't exactly give you detailed step-by-step instructions for unshackling your phone with iFuntastic. Instead, follow along with iFuntastic's onscreen instructions, which do a great job walking you through the process with very detailed directions. Right now the process goes something like this:

1. Plug in your iPhone and run iFuntastic. Since this is the first time you've run iFuntastic, you need to jailbreak your iPhone, so click the Unshackle button like the one you see in Figure S-6.

2. iFuntastic will ask you to restore your iPhone to a fresh state using iTunes so that it can access your iPhone in a virgin state. The restore process can take several minutes, so be patient. iFuntastic does a good job of walking you through this, so just follow the onscreen directions.

3. After you've gone through the restore, you may need to force your iPhone into Recovery mode to complete the jailbreak. If prompted by iFuntastic, restart and force your iPhone

Figure S-6. iFuntastic lets you unshackle your phone, which is the same as jailbreaking.

into Recovery mode by holding the On/Off and Home buttons simultaneously for around 25 seconds, until the yellow triangular warning symbol comes up.

4. Once you let iFuntastic know you're in Recovery mode, it will begin writing files to your iPhone. You may see lines of code fly by on your iPhone screen; if you do, don't worry—it's just iFuntastic working its mojo. When it's finished (iFuntastic will let you know when that is), you're almost there.

5. You may have to restart the iPhone one more time before you're done, but when you do you'll notice the unshackle ball and chain icon turn into the peace-loving unshackled button. You're iPhone is now ready to handle third-party software, custom ringtones, and more.

As I said, the process may change in time, as iFuntastic is developing and changing very rapidly, but it's likely that the steps will remain somewhat similar. Even if it does change, the results are still the same—your iPhone is now able to run third-party software.

Install Third-Party Applications on Your iPhone

Once you've gone through the jailbreak process with your iPhone, you're ready to install third-party applications. Programmers have already designed applications for the iPhone ranging from games and eBook readers, to voice recorders and file browsers, so you're bound to find something useful. There are currently a few different ways to install applications on the iPhone, and, like the hacks shown

previously, these tools will change somewhat over time. We'll walk you through installing applications using iBrickr (Windows), iFuntastic (Mac), and Installer.app. Installer.app, our favorite installer of the bunch, is actually an iPhone application that helps you download, install, and manage iPhone applications directly from your iPhone.

> **NOTE**
>
> Each of the tools described installs and tracks your applications using a slightly different system, so if you install a lot of applications using different tools, you'll have a hard time keeping everything organized. Our favorite application installer is Installer.app, so if you wanted to use that, you'd need to install it once using iBrickr (Windows) or AppTapp Installer (Mac). Whatever route you choose, just be sure you stick with that route for the sake of consistency and stability. If you decide you want to use a different method, all you'll need to do is restore your iPhone to factory settings (see Chapter 16 for details) and start over again.

Install Third-Party Apps with iBrickr (Windows)

The application you used to open up your iPhone to third-party software can—among other customizations we'll describe next—install software on your iPhone as well. Here's how:

1. Dock your iPhone to your computer and run the iBrickr application.

2. From the iBrickr home page, click the Applications link to open iBrickr's application manager.

3. Click the Browse applications button. You should now see a list of applications as shown in Figure S-7, all of which can be installed to your iPhone. For your first installation, we recommend installing the Installer application, a program that actually allows you to install or uninstall applications from your iPhone without even docking to a computer. To install it in iBrickr, just click the Installer link.

4. iBrickr will automatically download and install the application to your phone. After the installation is complete, iBrickr may perform a soft reset on your phone, meaning only that the phone will go to the locked screen. Press the On/Off button, unlock your phone, and you should notice a new application icon on your Home screen.

If this is the first time you're installing an application, iBrickr will want to install the PXL daemon. Accept the dialogue and iBrickr will start. Now you'll have to restart your iPhone twice in order to get all the programs on it in the right places. iBrickr is placing a daemon onto your iPhone, which is a program that runs all the time in the background, undetected. This program lets you install third-party, user-made applications easily. So, follow the onscreen instructions in iBrickr and then restart your iPhone. When it's finished installing, click the Continue button. You'll wait for iBrickr to finish processing, after which it will ask you to restart your iPhone again. When that step is done, click the button that says Check for PXL. [PXL is the application we mentioned before that lets you install applications easily.]

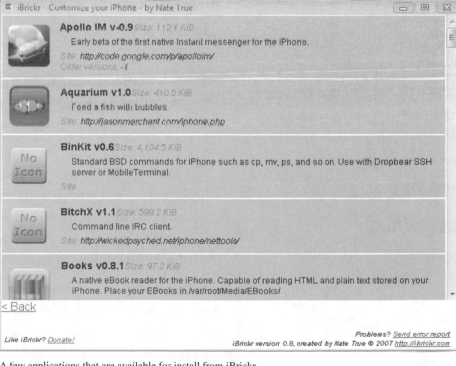

Figure S-7. A few applications that are available for install from iBrickr.

That's all there is to it! If you liked that method and you don't see yourself having a need to install any applications from your iPhone, feel free to do all of your application installations through iBrickr. However, now that you've installed Installer.app, you can now manage all of your application downloads using that application directly on your iPhone. We'll discuss how to use it in more detail later on.

Uninstall Third-Party Apps with iBrickr

It's easy to get rid of applications you've installed with iBrickr as well. Here's what you do:

1. Dock your iPhone to your computer and run the iBrickr application.

2. From the iBrickr home page, click the Applications link to open iBrickr's application manager.

3. You will see a list of applications already installed onto your iPhone in an iPhone-like interface. Find the application you want to install and click the – button. Then, confirm that you want to uninstall that application.

4. iBrickr will delete the application and soft-restart the iPhone, which means you'll be directed back to the standby screen.

Install Third-Party Apps with iFuntastic (Mac)

Once you've opened up your phone to third-party applications with iFuntastic, here's how you actually install them using iFuntastic. We recommend that you install applications with Installer.app on the iPhone, but if you prefer the iFuntastic interface, it will do the job, too.

To install applications with iFuntastic, you first have to manually find these applications and download them from the Internet. There are a couple repositories for iPhone applications around the Net, but if you're using iFuntastic to install applications, the easiest way to find apps is to go to that application's homepage on the Internet. Google will come in handy at this point.

> **TIP**
>
> You can get more complete application listings if you install applications with Installer.app on the iPhone, which manages updating the apps as well. In all, installing apps with iFuntastic is the least user-friendly option, which is why we recommend using Installer.app instead.

Once you've downloaded an iPhone application to your computer, here's how you install it with iFuntastic:

1. Dock your iPhone with your computer and run iFuntastic.

2. Click the Home Screen tab. You'll see the current layout of your iPhone's Home screen and a list of applications currently installed.

3. To install the application you just downloaded, just drag the application file (it should look something like ApolloIM) from Finder into the application list in iFuntastic. You won't be able to see the .app in the filename because OS X hides that extension for applications.

After you drop the new application into iFuntastic, you should hear a confirmation sound to indicate that the installation was successful. You should now see the new app in the application list. Now you can either drag the app to the iPhone Home screen replication in iFuntastic if you're using it to arrange your Home screen, or, if you're using one of the application launchers we'll mention later on, it should automatically show up there.

Install and Manage Third-Party Apps with Installer.app (iPhone)

After you've installed Installer.app to your iPhone using one of the previous methods, you'll be able to add tons of applications to the iPhone directly from this application without plugging in your iPhone. That's because Installer.app will list, download, install, uninstall, and even update applications for you from on online repository of iPhone applications.

You should see an icon for Installer.app on your Home screen like in Figure S-3 (if you don't, you haven't installed it yet—use one of the previous methods to do so). Tap it to launch Installer.app and let's get started.

Install an Application with Installer.app

Whenever you run Installer.app, it will go online to retrieve an updated list of the latest and greatest iPhone applications. You'll notice that the list—which looks like Figure S-8 and is organized by application type—is rather small at first. That's

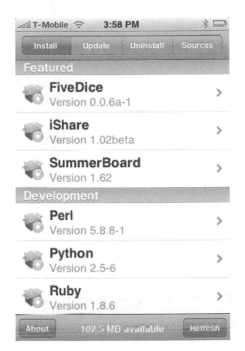

Figure S-8. Installing applications directly from your iPhone is easy with Installer.app.

because it's only listing applications hosted at Nullriver, the company that created the Installer.app.

The first thing you'll probably want to install with Installer.app is the Community Sources package, which you'll see near the top of the list of applications in the Install tab. The Community Sources package will add several other applications resources to Installer.app, meaning that after it's installed, you should see a lot more applications from several locations in your install list. Here's how installing an application or package with Installer.app works:

1. Tap the application you want to install (Installer.app calls them packages). A details screen will slide into view displaying the application's name, version number, size, and description (among other assorted details that are probably less interesting to you).

2. Tap the Install button at the top right of the Application Details screen. Installer.app will ask you to confirm that you want to install the package. To cancel, tap No. To continue with the download and installation, tap Yes.

3. Installer.app will download the application over WiFi or EDGE, and then take care of all of the application installation. When it's done, just hit the Home button and your iPhone will automatically soft-restart itself, sending you back to the Standby screen. That's it! Your new application is installed!

TIP

To read more details on an application before you install it, tap the More Info... button at the bottom right of the details screen. Installer.app will launch that application's homepage in Safari. Not all applications will display the More Info button—only those apps that have a homepage.

At the standby screen, unlock your iPhone and you'll be back at the Home screen. If the package you installed to your iPhone is an actual launchable program (some aren't, like Nullriver's ringtone package), you'll notice that you've got a new application icon next to Installer.app—this is your new application.

Since the iPhone only has four open slots on the Home screen before you start installing third-party apps, your open row can fill up rather quickly. Don't worry, though, because iPhone hackers are already two steps ahead of you. Several applications have been released that allow you to customize what application buttons appear on the Home screen,

and several more are available that act as a launch pad for all of your installed third-party apps. We'll discuss a few of our favorite application launchers next.

Update an Application with Installer.app

The great part about Installer.app is that—aside from its super-simple installation process—it actually helps you keep all of your applications up-to-date with the latest versions. Assuming you've already installed a few applications, here's how it works:

1. Launch Installer.app. After it finishes refreshing its sources, go to the Update tab on the top row of buttons. If the Update list is empty, you're already running the latest version of all of your installed software. If one of your installed applications is in the list, it means that a newer version is available. In fact, Installer.app will automatically take you to the Update tab after if finishes refreshing the application list if one of your installed applications has been updated.

2. Assuming you did have an application or two in the Update list, tap the one of the applications you want to update. Just like when you installed the application, the application's details will slide onto the screen.

3. Tap the Update button on the top right. Just like when you first installed the app, Installer.app will download the application over WiFi or EDGE and seamlessly update the existing application.

That's all there is to it! Keeping up to date with all of the applications on your computer should be this easy!

Uninstall an Application with Installer.app

Just as on your desktop, you may sometimes install an application that you decide you don't want anymore. Like installing and updating applications with Installer.app, uninstalling applications is extremely simple:

1. Launch Installer.app and then tap the Uninstall tab on the top row of buttons.

2. Find and tap the application that you want to uninstall. The details screen will slide into view.

3. Tap the Uninstall button at the top right of the screen. Installer.app will ask you to confirm that you want to uninstall this package. Tap Yes to confirm or No if you've changed your mind.

It's that simple. Installer.app will swiftly remove the application from your iPhone.

TIP

Whenever you install an application with Installer.app, you'll no longer see it listed in the Install tab—after all, why would you need to install it a second time? Instead, the application now appears in the Uninstall tab. Likewise, once you *uninstall* an application, it disappears from the uninstall tab and reappears in the Install tab so that should you change your mind and want to re-install it, it'll be there waiting.

Customize Your iPhone

Now that you've unlocked your iPhone to third-party applications and have learned to install new apps, your iPhone has been opened up to a whole new world of customization. In the following sections, we'll detail different ways you can add your own ringtones for free, customize the layout of your Home screen, access all of your installed applications using different application launchers, and theme your Home screen and system sounds.

Add Custom Ringtones

The iPhone launched without the ability to add custom ringtones to your Phone contacts. In early September, Apple integrated ringtones into the iTunes music store, but for a price of $0.99 per ringtone, and with only 500,000 eligible songs in the store.

However, by using iBrickr (Windows) and iFuntastic (Mac), you can add any song on your computer to the ringtones section of your iPhone without having to pay any extra cash. Alternatively, if you don't feel like plugging in every time you want to set up a new ringtone, the iPhone application SendSong can add any song you've synced to your iPhone directly to your ringtones without requiring you to dock your iPhone at all.

Once you add a custom ringtone using any of these methods, you can set it as your main ring in the Sounds section of the Settings application, or as a custom ringtone for any of your contacts.

Add Custom Ringtones with iBrickr (Windows)

Here's how to add custom ringtones to your iPhone with iBrickr:

1. Connect your iPhone, start iBrickr, and then open the Ringtones section.

2. Click the big fat Upload Ringtone button, as shown in Figure S-9.

3. Find a sound or music file on your computer that you want to use as a ringtone. If necessary, iBrickr will automatically change the file into a format the iPhone can understand.

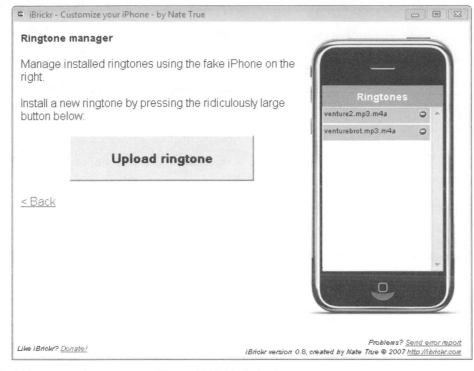

Figure S-9. Adding custom ringtones to your iPhone with iBrickr is simple.

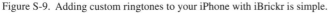

You're done! The ringtone will show up on the right-hand side, listed under the fake iPhone. To delete a ringtone, click the – icon on the fake iPhone next to the ringtone you want to delete, and then confirm that you really want to delete the ringtone.

Add Custom Ringtones with iFuntastic (Mac)

Adding custom ringtones to your iPhone with iFuntastic is very simple:

1. Dock your iPhone and launch iFuntastic.

2. Click the Ringtones button in iFuntastic to open the Ringtones folder on your iPhone.

3. Drag and drop any song from your iTunes library or from Finder to the list of ringtones in iFuntastic. If your iPhone can play the song in the iPod application, it can play it as a ringtone. iFuntastic will automatically add the ringtone to your iPhone, ready to use.

Add Custom Ringtones with SendSong (iPhone)

If you don't feel like you should have to dock your iPhone to your computer every time you want to add a new custom ringtone from your iTunes library, then SendSong is for you. SendSong is a third-party iPhone application that allows you to send any song loaded on your iPhone directly to your ringtones list. (Aside from the ringtone functionality, it also lets you email any song synced to your iPhone using Mail, but we'll focus on the ringtones for now). Here's how to do it:

1. Make sure you've installed SendSong on your iPhone using your favorite method of

installing applications (it's easily available for both Installer.app and iBrickr). Then launch SendSong.

2. When SendSong loads, you'll see a long list of every song you've synced to your iPhone sorted alphabetically by artist and album. Unfortunately you can only see the song title, so picking the song you want to add to your ringtones isn't as easy as it could be (this may be improved in future releases). Scroll the list until you find the song you're looking for and then tap it.

3. A list of song actions will slide onto the screen, like you see in Figure S-10. From here you can play the song to make sure you've picked the right one, stop playback, send the song to email, or send it to your ringtones. We're doing ringtones now, so tap the Send to Ringtones button.

Figure S-10. Tap Send to Ringtones to add the selected song to your list of iPhone ringtones.

You'll hear a confirmation sound to indicate that your ringtone was successfully added. To make sure, go to the Home screen and launch the Settings application. Now tap Sounds and then Ringtone. Your new ringtone should now be in the list of available ringtones.

> **TIP**
>
> You can remove custom ringtones you've added with SendSong by launching the SendSong application and then tapping the Edit button at the top right of the screen. You'll see a list of all of the music you added to your ringtones through SendSong. To delete one, tap the – button and then confirm your decision by tapping the Delete button.

Customize Your Home Screen

As soon as you start installing your own applications, you'll notice that you run into a small problem very quickly: There are only four open slots on the bottom row, so unless you plan on only using four third-party apps, you're going to have to find a way to manage all of your applications. There are a number of solutions to help you overcome this problem, from rearranging the Home screen, to installing third-party launcher and dock applications that help you aggregate all of your installed applications.

> **NOTE**
>
> If you're using Windows, or you've installed the SummerBoard application launcher, we recommend using rSBT to rearrange your Home screen. Check out more details in the Recommended Apps for the iphone section coming up.

Customize Your Home Screen Layout with iFuntastic (Mac)

iFuntastic lets you reorganize the icons on your iPhone's home screen, including the icons belonging to applications that actually came bundled with the iPhone. To do this, dock your iPhone, shut down iTunes, and start up iFuntastic. Once iFuntastic is started, click the Home Screen button on the left column. This will load up the options for your Home screen customization session.

So what can you do here? iFuntastic lets you manage four Home screens, worth of 20 icons each, for a total of 64 applications that you can launch from your phone (assuming you reserve four slots on each page for the Page Switcher icons). We'll assume you've already added applications to iFuntastic using the method described previously; this will give you a big list of possible apps on the left that you can drag onto the phone. Now all you have to do is pick an icon and drag it onto one of the 20 possible slots on each page, and then click Update iPhone on the bottom to transfer these settings onto the iPhone. There are a few extras on the top right of the app you can customize as well. Here's what they do:

- **Show Grid**   This shows outlines around the 20 icon slots so you can easily drop applications onto the right place.

- **Reset Home Screen**   This clears all the icon rearrangement changes you've made on the iPhone. It essentially clears everything off the Home screen, so if you don't put applications back on and then click Update iPhone, you'll end up with a blank iPhone.

- **Color**   This is a solid color background for the iPhone screen.

- **Image**   This is a background image for the iPhone screen.

- **Bottom Bar**   This gives you the option of whether or not you want that carbon fiber background strip on the bottom of the iPhone (this is the strip that holds Phone,. Email, Safari and iPod by default).

- **Show Names/Show Icons**   You can actually toggle the Home screens to display only icons, only names, or nothing at all. We're not sure why you would want to show nothing at all, except possibly as a neat gimmick to launch programs from a completely blank screen.

- **No Rotation/Counterclockwise/ Clockwise**   This is another gimmicky option that lets you use your home screen in horizontal mode, either to the left or right.

The downside to rearranging your Home screen with iFuntastic is that some of the program names will be changed (Safari becomes MobileSafari, Clock becomes MobileTimer) because iFuntastic uses the names of the programs instead of their proper names. There's no way to fix this at the time of this writing, but there may be a solution in the future.

Customize Your Home Screen Theme with SummerBoard (iPhone)

The SummerBoard application lets you customize your Home screen using one of a number of different installable themes. After you install SummerBoard, you can grab and install new Home screen themes using Installer.app. Then just launch the SummerBoard Preferences application to browse the various theming options. To try out a new theme, tap that theme's entry. When you go back to the Home screen, the new SummerBoard theme will update your wallpaper, clock, and even some of your application icons to match the new theme.

Change Your iPhone System Sounds with iBrickr (Windows)

You can change the system sounds on your iPhone— like the sound that plays when you get a new email or SMS message—using iBrickr. To do so, just dock your iPhone, launch iBrickr, and go to the Sounds screen. Click the sound effect you want to change, point iBrickr to the sound file on your desktop, and iBrickr will swap that sound for that alert.

Customize the Carrier Logo with iFuntastic

To customize your carrier logo with iFuntastic, click the Carrier Logo button on the left. The carrier logo is the AT&T logo that you see on the top left. iFuntastic comes with a couple built in, such as the iFuntastic logo and iPhone, but you can easily make your own. The only limit is that you have to make images that are 65 × 20 pixels maximum, and you should probably make one that looks good on a white background, as well as one that looks good on a black background (to swap between when the iPhone changes backgrounds).

> **NOTE**
>
> You can also customize your carrier logo and make several other small interface tweaks with the Customize iPhone application—which you can install using Installer.app.

Choose a logo by clicking the + icon and then clicking Update iPhone. Your iPhone will install the new logo, but you have to manually restart the phone for it to show up.

Browse Files on Your iPhone

Most of the time you probably won't need access to your iPhone's file system, but there are times when it can come in handy. For example, if you install the very cool NES application, you'll need to move ROMs—that is, games—to your iPhone before you can get your retro gaming fix. Currently you can do so with iBrickr (Windows) and iFuntastic (Mac).

Browse files on Your iPhone with iBrickr (Windows)

Not only can you browse files on your iPhone with iBrickr, you can upload and download files as well. Although it's not as easy as treating your iPhone as an external hard drive that you can drag and drop files onto with Windows Explorer, it's still good enough to move files to and from your phone. To start, connect your iPhone, open iBrickr and go to the Files section. The fake iPhone on the right shows a directory listing of your files, which you can browse similarly to the way you browse files on your computer. Click on a folder to access the folder, and click on a file to access the file.

When accessing a file, you can either download or delete it. To upload a file, click the upload file(s) button and then choose the files you want to upload to the phone. You can also create a folder by clicking the create folder button.

Browse Files on Your iPhone with iFuntastic (Mac)

Click the File Manager button on the left. Now you can drag and drop files onto your iPhone directly, from anywhere on your computer. Browse the folder structure with the folder system in iFuntastic, and click Update iPhone when you're done. You can both upload and download files from the iPhone using this method. It's a bit unwieldy to use your iPhone as a portable storage device with iFuntastic, but there are instances when you may need to put files onto the iPhone.

Take the NES Emulator application, for example. You'll have to manually upload NES game images to a certain directory in order for the game to work correctly. Or, if you install the third-party screenshot application that takes a screenshot of whatever's on your iPhone, you'll have to browse to the correct file with iFuntastic to get the images off your iPhone and onto your computer.

Find Recommended Apps for the iPhone

Here are a few recommended applications for the iPhone, sorted by application type. There will be many more wonderful applications released between the time of this writing and when you actually purchase the book, but this list offers a good starting point to get you going with third-party applications.

Application Manager

- **Installer.app**   As we discussed previously, Installer.app is the simplest way

to install and manage all of your third-party iPhone applications.

`http://iphone.nullriver.com/beta/`

Application Launchers/Customization Tools

- **SummerBoard**   View and launch any and all of your iPhone applications (third-party and native) with SummerBoard (shown in Figure S-11), which makes your Home screen scrollable and lets you use your own custom wallpaper and themes.

`http://iphone.nullriver.com/beta/`

- **Dock**   Dock's main goal is to allow you to access and launch any of your installed apps without requiring you to return to the Home screen to do so.

`http://cre.ations.net/creation/dock`

Figure S-11. SummerBoard lets you scroll all of your installed applications directly on the Home screen.

- **Launcher** Tap Launcher from the Home screen to view a scrollable list of all your third-party iPhone apps.

`http://iphone.nullriver.com/beta/`

- **rSBT** If you have any inclination to rearrange your Home screen icons, rSBT is a great application to do this with. After you launch rSBT, just drag and drop the icons in any order you want. rSBT works especially well in conjunction with SummerBoard.

`http://code.google.com/p/rsbt/`

Games

- **Lights Off** The first playable, third-party game for the iPhone, Lights Off requires you to solve puzzles by recognizing patterns in lights. You've solved a board when you turn all its lights off.

`http://www.deliciousmonster.org/`

- **NES** If retro gaming is up your alley, this emulator plays Nintendo games (called ROMs) that you upload to your iPhone (shown in Figure S-12). Games should be uploaded to `/var/root/Media/ROMs/NES/`. (See the Browse Files on Your iPhone section earlier in this chapter for more on browsing files on your iPhone.)

`http://iphone.natetrue.com/nesapp/`

- **iBlackJack** This is a Blackjack card game application.

`http://code.google.com/p/iphoneblackjack/`

- **Mines** This is an iPhone-optimized version of the classic Windows game, Minesweeper.

`http://www.conceitedsoftware.com/iphone/site/packages/`

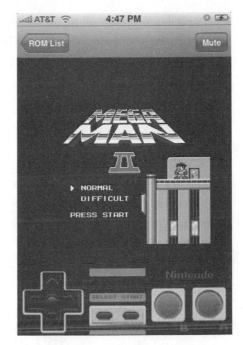

Figure S-12. Get your gaming fix with the NES application.

Ringtones

- **SendSong** Send any song you've synced to your iPhone to your ringtones, so it's ready to assign to any contact or as your default ringer. As an added perk, you can use SendSong to email any song on your iPhone using Mail.

`http://iphone.natetrue.com/`

Information/Productivity

- **Books** A simple eBook reader for reading books on your iPhone.

`http://code.google.com/p/iphoneebooks/`

- **RSS** Subscribe to and keep up with your favorite RSS news feeds on the go with this mobile RSS application.

`http://code.google.com/p/mobile-rss/`

- **SendFile**   Send files on your iPhone to your contacts via email.

  `http://iphone.natetrue.com/SendFile/`

- **iFlashCards**   Study on-the-go with flash card packs—like the GRE vocab list—you install right on your iPhone.

  `http://code.google.com/p/iflashcards/`

- **VNotes**   Record and save voice notes for yourself, and then play them back or email them (see Figure S-13).

  `http://smxy.org/iphone-apps/info/Erica.html`

- **iShare**   Upload and download files to the file sharing web site SendSpace. Requires a free registration with the SendSpace web site.

  `http://www.sendspace.com/download_ishare.html`

- **Money**   Track your transactions in a debit/credit ledger to keep an eye on your expenses.

  `http://code.google.com/p/mobilemoney/`

Figure S-13.   Record and email voice notes to yourself with VNotes.

Chat

- **Apollo**   The first native chat application for the iPhone, ApolloIM (shown in Figure S-14) is a feature-rich tool for IM that gives you the benefits of a native application—like multi-tasking and alerts—that you won't find in web-based IM applications.

  `http://code.google.com/p/apolloim/`

- **Chat**   Mobile Chat was the second app on the native iPhone IM scene, bringing with it a polished interface and a lot of promise.

  `http://blog.twenty08.com/mobilechat`

System Applications

- **BSD Subsystem**   Before you install any of the system applications coming up, you must install this one. It's not an application you'll actively use, just a package you'll need.

Figure S-14.   Chat with your instant messaging contacts with ApolloIM.

- **Finder**   An iPhone-version of the Mac's native file browser, Finder, you can use this to browse your iPhone's file system, copy and move files, and launch files and applications.

http://code.google.com/p/mobilefinder/

- **TextEdit**   Compose and edit simple text documents from your iPhone.

http://code.google.com/p/mobiletextedit/

- **Preview**   View images saved to your iPhone with this clone of Mac's Preview app.

http://code.google.com/p/mobilepreview/

- **Terminal**   Perform command line mojo from the iPhone (this is the realm of power users).

http://code.google.com/p/mobileterminal/

Miscellaneous

- **iLight**   A simple but lovable one-use application, iLight displays a bright white screen for those times you need to use your iPhone as a flashlight.

http://iphone.natetrue.com/Light

Unlock Your iPhone and Use It with Any Carrier

Although the iPhone is locked so you can only use it with AT&T, there are actually a few ways to unlock your Apple phone so that you can use it on any network. Best of all, it's perfectly legal! With the phone unlocked, you will be able to buy an iPhone and sign up for T-Mobile service as shown in Figure S-15 (T-Mobile's the only other major GSM carrier in the US). You could even take it overseas and use a European or Asian SIM card inside. There are a couple ways to do it.

Figure S-15. An iPhone unlocked for use on T-Mobile

> **CAUTION**
>
> According to Apple, unlocking your iPhone to use with non-AT&T carriers may brick your iPhone—meaning that it could make your iPhone completely unusable. Proceed at your own risk.

> **NOTE**
>
> If you're worried that unlocking your iPhone from AT&T so you can use it on T-Mobile is illegal, don't be. It's perfectly legal—at least for the next two years. The Copyright Office decided in late 2006 that it was legal for users to unlock cell phones to use on a competing network. It's very likely that the act of unlocking will remain legal at the next revision of the DMCA in 2009, but we'll have to wait and see.

Get Familiar with iPhone Unlocking Methods

The first way to unlock an iPhone is to use a forged SIM card, which lets you use a blank SIM card and a SIM writer to trick the phone into thinking that it's a proper SIM. This unlocks the phone, but has the downside of costing a hefty $96 and being fairly impractical unless you know exactly what you're doing. This does have the distinction of being the first method released to unlock the iPhone though.

You might also consider the TurboSIM method, which gives you full calling capabilities on any network, and costs around $80 including shipping. This method ships you a blank SIM that you modify using your own iPhone instead of card readers, and it's simple enough for most people to follow. The only downside is that it's not software-only.

The third method, which is probably the worst method, involves opening up your iPhone and performing complicated soldering on the electronics. Although this is free, it may cost you $399 when you accidentally break your iPhone in the process. It definitely voids the warranty. Don't consider this method unless you really know your way around a soldering iron.

The fourth method involves a paid software unlock. At the time of this writing, there are a few competing teams claiming that they've achieved a full unlock of the iPhone—and proved it as well. The benefits of this method is that it is software only, which means you won't have to worry about voiding your warranty. However, you do have to pay for the privilege, and the prices can range from $25 to $50 for other (non-iPhone) phones, depending on who is doing the unlocking.

The fifth, last, and best method is a free software unlock. The iPhone Dev Team, the team that's been working on breaking open the iPhone since its launch on June 29, has been hard at work on a software SIM unlock, and finally achieved their goal in September. There will be an easy application that you can install to unlock your iPhone, but be aware that future iPhone software updates from Apple may break the unlock. If this is the case, hackers will follow up shortly with another unlock, which you will have to apply to your iPhone again.

> **NOTE**
>
> If you really want to unlock your iPhone for use on T-Mobile or foreign GSM networks, we recommend you perform a software unlock. You can either pay someone to do it for you, which has the added bonus of being taken care of by a professional, or do it yourself with the free unlock suites. If you, or someone you know, is familiar with computers, the free unlock is perfectly safe and should be reasonably easy to do. Even if you mess up, all you have to do is perform a restore from iTunes (covered in Chapter 16), and everything on your iPhone will be back to normal.

Although it's quite easy to unlock and load programs onto your iPhone now, it's very likely that Apple will actually open up the iPhone and make it even easier to get third-party programs to run without even needing to hack at all. However, it's also likely that Apple may charge money for the privilege of installing programs—something they did when they added support for ringtones—so these third-party hacks may still prove useful.

Assign a Photo to a Contact

By assigning a photo to a contact, you'll see the assigned photo on the Contact Info pane and also whenever that contact calls. This is an easy way to eyeball your phone and know exactly who is trying to get a hold of you without having to stop and read the name. To assign the photo you're currently viewing, tap the third option in the Action button menu: Assign To Contact. This will bring up your big list of contacts for you to search through and choose. To narrow down your contacts by groups, if you've assigned groups to your contacts on your computer, tap the Groups button on the top left and then pick a group. Once you've chosen a contact, you can now move and scale the picture with gestures in order to center the view on the contact's face. When you're done, tap Set Photo. If you've changed your mind and want to pick a different picture, tap Cancel.

Upload a Photo to .Mac (Mac)

If you've own a .Mac account and you're running iLife '08, you can upload pictures from your iPhone directly to your web gallery. Web galleries are a place where you can share your iPhoto albums with your friends and family without having to send each one pictures individually. Uploading pictures from your phone directly to the web gallery lets you update your web gallery on the road without having to sync up to your computer first.

To enable this feature, you first need to make sure the web gallery is set up. In iPhoto '08, click the Web Gallery button to upload one of your albums or events to a web gallery. Now, make sure the options Allow Visitors to Upload Photos and Allow Visitors to Upload Photos by Email are checked. These need to be selected for the iPhone upload to succeed. After iPhoto is finished uploading and setting up the web gallery, we can start sending pictures from the iPhone.

To add a photo to your web gallery, tap the last option in the Action button menu: Send to Web Gallery. This will bring up a list of all your existing Web Gallery albums. If nothing shows up, it means the gallery you created in iPhoto didn't succeed, and you need to try again.

Did you know?

Contact Photos Are Bigger if Assigned from the iPhone

You can also assign a photo to your contact from your computer, and then sync the contact photo over to the iPhone. However, this results in a smaller contact picture that only shows up in the top right during a call, rather than a large picture that takes up most of the screen. The reason? There's a size limit on the pictures you can set to your contacts on the computer. You can actually use this limitation to create small pictures of certain contacts if you don't want them taking up so much real estate.

Revisit the previous steps and watch out for any error messages iPhoto may give you. Once you've picked a gallery to add this picture to, the photo slides into the body of a new email message. If you want to change the picture caption, you can do so by changing the subject line of the email. When you're done, hit Send and the photo will be uploaded to your web gallery.

Send Photos to Your Friends' Phones

Even though the iPhone doesn't support picture messaging (MMS), you can still actually send photos to your friends' phones. How? By sending messages over email and having them converted into picture messages. Each cellular provider assigns an email address to each phone number in the form of 5554445555@wireless.service.com (the domain varies by carrier, as described next). By tapping Email Photo in the in the photo's Action menu, creating an email, and sending it to this address, your email will be converted to an MMS message and delivered to your friend's phone. Instead of remembering all your friends' numbers, we suggest you create an email address under each contact with their number and appropriate email domain so you can send MMS pictures easily. Here's a list of providers and their email addresses:

- **Alltel**   5554445555@message.alltel.com
- **AT&T/Cingular**   5554445555@mms.att.net
- **Boost Mobile**   5554445555@myboostmobile.com
- **Helio**   5554445555@messaging.sprintpcs.com
- **Nextel**   5554445555@messaging.nextel.com
- **Sprint**   5554445555@messaging.sprintpcs.com
- **T-Mobile**   5554445555@tmomail.net
- **Verizon**   5554445555@vtext.com
- **Virgin Mobile**   5554445555@vmobl.com

If you don't know which cellular provider that a particular contact uses, you can actually send messages through a service called teleflip at 5554445555@teleflip.com. Teleflip will convert your message and forward it to the correct provider. They only allow 100 messages per month for free, so if you want more than that you'll have to sign up for one of their pay plans.

Sync Photos to and from Your Computer

Sure you can view photos you've taken with your iPhone's camera, but chances are you've got a lot of digital photos on your computer that you'd love to show off on your iPhone as well. With iTunes, you can set your iPhone to sync to one of several desktop photo management applications or to any folder on your computer.

Sync Photos with Your Desktop Photo Management Application

iTunes can sync photos to your iPhone using one of several different desktop photo management applications as shown in Figure 9-8. Windows users can sync photo albums with Photoshop Elements 3.0 and up and Photoshop Album 2.0 and above. Mac users can sync either iPhoto 4.0.3 and above or Aperture. Here's how:

1. Dock the iPhone, click on your iPhone in iTunes, and then go to the Photos tab of the iPhone Sync screen.

2. Check the box next to Sync Photos From, and then select whichever photo management application you use from the dropdown menu.

3. You can sync all photos by clicking the All Photos and Albums radio button. If you've got a rather large library, you probably only want to sync a few specific albums. To do so, click the button next to Selected Albums and then check the boxes next to the albums you want to sync.

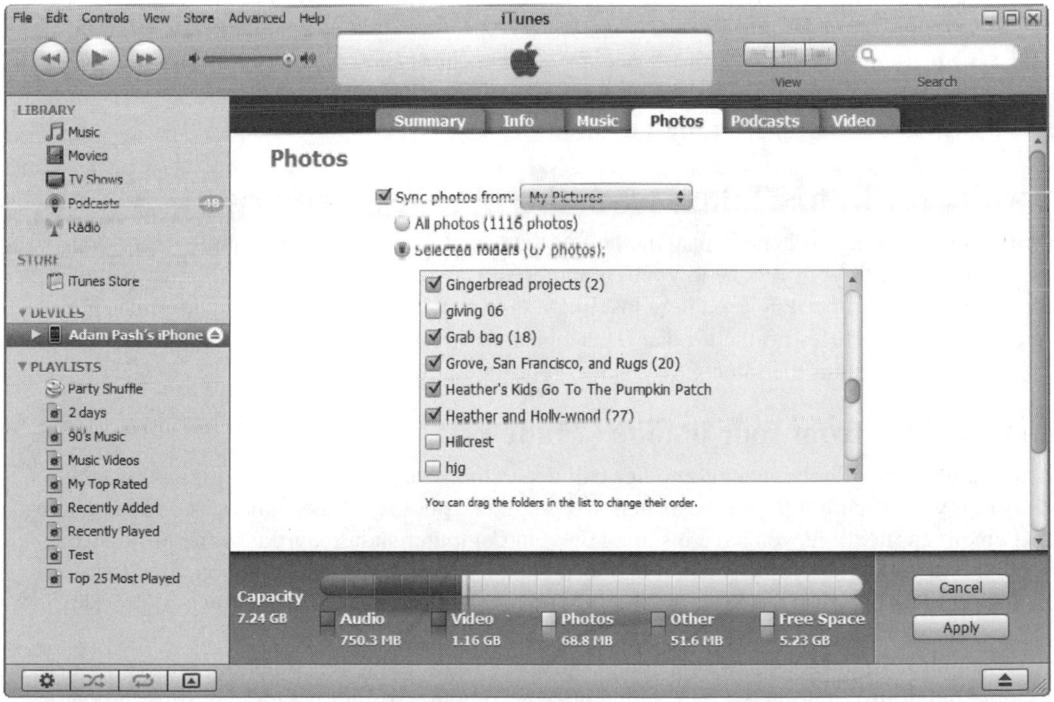

FIGURE 9-8   The Photos Sync screen

TIP
You can keep track of how many photos will end up syncing to your iPhone by looking at the number in parentheses behind either All Photos or Selected Albums. Each time you add a new selected photo, this number will update.

Sync Photos from a Folder

If you don't use one of the supported photo applications that your iPhone can sync to or you'd just prefer to manage photos yourself, you can still sync photos to your iPhone directly from a folder on your hard drive. Here's how:

1. Dock your iPhone, launch iTunes, and click the Photos section of the iPhone screen.

2. Tick the Sync photos from checkbox, then select Choose folder... from the dropdown menu.

3. From the Photos Folder Location dialog, navigate to the folder you want to sync photos with.

4. You can sync all folders and photos beneath that folder to your iPhone by clicking All Photos. You can also specify the folders you want to sync to your iPhone by clicking Selected Folders and then checking all the folders you want to sync.

TIP
When syncing photos to your iPhone, iTunes will create smaller, iPhone-optimized versions of the photos on your computer, so make sure you've got some free space on your hard drive for these extra photos. If you want to know how much space the resized photos are taking up on your computer's hard drive, just look at how much space iTunes says is devoted to photos when your iPhone is plugged in.

Download Photos Taken from the iPhone's Camera

Syncing photos to your iPhone is just one half of the deal. Chances are you want to export the photos you take with your iPhone to your computer, too. When you plug in the iPhone, your computer recognizes the iPhone camera just like it does any digital camera. In fact, iTunes plays no part in getting pictures off the iPhone. This means that you can set up your iPhone to export photos to your computer the same way you use your regular digital camera.

Import Photos from Your iPhone (Windows)

When you dock the iPhone, your computer will detect that you've plugged in a digital camera and prompt you (Figure 9-9) to take an action to get those photos off the camera. All of the photo management applications you have installed on your computer should appear in the prompt. If you see the method you prefer, select it and then click OK. If this is the action you want to take with your iPhone photos every time you plug it in, click the checkbox next to Always Use This Program for this action.

If the option you want isn't listed, click Cancel. You can set the iPhone photo import options with more detail in Windows XP by opening up My Computer, right-clicking the Apple iPhone icon, and selecting Properties. Next click the Events tab. You will see several options for what to

 FIGURE 9-9   Your computer handles the iPhone just like a camera, so you can grab photos off of it with any photo application.

do with photos when the iPhone is plugged in. You can decide to automatically start a program from the list, do nothing, continue receiving prompts every time you plug in the iPhone, or automatically import the photos to a folder.

If you're running Windows Vista, you can change the AutoPlay settings (the automatic prompt you receive when you plug in the phone) by opening the AutoPlay settings in the Control Panel or by clicking the Set AutoPlay defaults in the Control Panel link on the iPhone AutoPlay prompt. Change the default behavior using the Pictures dropdown menu.

If you choose to save the photos to a folder, you have the option to save the photos in a subfolder named by the date. You can also tell Windows to automatically delete the photos from the iPhone, which is a handy way to empty your Camera Roll whenever you sync.

Import Photos from Your iPhone (Mac)

By default, iPhoto will automatically open and prompt you to import your new photos when you connect the iPhone, as seen in Figure 9-10. To import using iPhoto, either click the Import All button or select the photos you want to import and then click Import Selected.

When you start your import, iPhoto will prompt you to keep or delete the originals on the iPhone. Since you probably don't want to keep every photo you've taken on the iPhone in your Camera Roll, I'd suggest clicking Delete Originals. Remember, the photos you import to iPhoto will be part of an iPhoto album now, so if you want to sync them to your iPhone as a photo album, you can do that just like we described previously. If for some reason you'd rather not delete the photos from the iPhone, click Keep Originals.

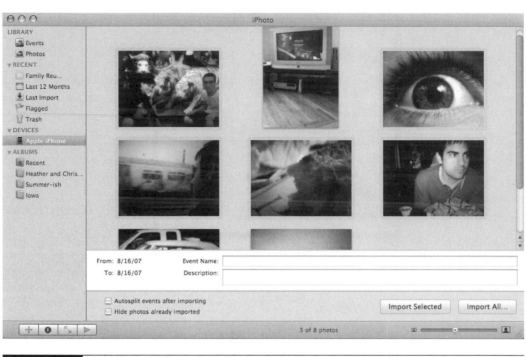

FIGURE 9-10 iPhoto can import photos you've taken from your phone.

Tweak the Photos Settings

You can adjust the way slideshows are played back inside the Photos application on the iPhone through the Settings application. Go to the Home screen, tap Settings, scroll to the bottom of the Settings screen and then tap Photos. As you can see in Figure 9-11, you have four options for adjusting slideshow settings.

- **Play Each Slide For** Whether the pictures are flying by too quickly or not quickly enough, you can adjust how long the slideshow displays one photo before advancing to the next. You can set playback times at 2, 3, 5, 10, or 20 seconds.

- **Transition** The slideshow moves between photos using one of several fun transition effects. The Cube effect rotates from one picture to the next as though your images are displayed on a rotating cube, Dissolve slowly fades from one photo to the next, Ripple uses a water-ripple effect to move between photos, and wipe across/down slides the new picture over the top of the previous one.

FIGURE 0 11   The Photos settings screen

- **Repeat**   When repeat is set to off, your slideshow will stop playing back when it reaches the last picture. Turning repeat on will keep your slideshow playing until you stop it yourself by tapping the screen, sleeping the phone, or pressing the Home button. That means that if you play a slideshow with repeat on, that slideshow will keep playing until either you stop it or your battery runs out.

- **Shuffle**   When shuffle is on, your slideshows will play back randomly rather than sequentially.

With the iPhone camera in your pocket, you can snap memories everywhere you go. In the Chapter 10 we'll show you how to use Google Maps to actually get where you're going.

Chapter 10

Use Google Maps to Get Around with Your iPhone

How to...

- Navigate the map
- Find a location
- Switch between map and satellite view
- Use Quick Lookups
- Search for businesses
- Get turn-by-turn directions
- Create a new contact from an address
- View traffic information

Although the iPhone isn't an actual GPS navigation tool, combined with Google Maps it's arguably the best non-GPS portable navigator that exists on a phone. That means if you need to get from point A to point B, even if you don't know the exact address of either, you can find them both and get turn-by-turn directions with your iPhone.

Navigate Maps

We've already covered several of the multi-touch gestures you can use to navigate your phone, but you might be interested to learn that Google Maps uses virtually all of them (except for the two-finger drag, which is currently only used in Safari). That means that if you're looking to get familiar with your iPhone's multi-touch interface without accidentally deleting something important, Google Maps is the place to do it. Here's how to navigate Google Maps with gestures:

- **Swipe** Just like everywhere else, swiping (that is, moving your finger around the screen without lifting it) will scroll the content of the map. If you want to see something that lies just outside the edge of the map you're looking at, swiping the map is a good way to get there.

- **Flick** To move more quickly to a new area on the map, try flicking the map. Flicking works well to make big jumps, but since Google Maps will need to load the images of the new area (depending on how fast your Internet connection is and how much of the map has already been downloaded) that will sometimes mean you'll be looking at gray squares instead of the map. This can make it difficult to keep track of where you are, so you'll probably want to use the flick sparingly when navigating Google Maps.

- **Tap** Unless you've already mapped an address and a red pin is visible onscreen, a single tap won't do anything. If you have looked up an address, tapping the pin will display the gray address info box. When the info box is visible, tapping it, or outside of it, will get rid of the info box; tapping the blue arrow icon will slide the address's Info pane onto the screen.

- **Double-Tap/Spread** To zoom in on the map, either double-tap the screen with one finger or spread two fingers apart on the screen. You can continue zooming in with the double-tap/spread until the map won't zoom any further. (With the double-tap, the screen will zoom slightly in and back out to indicate you've reached the limit; with the spread, the map will just stop zooming.)

- **Two-finger Tap/Pinch** You can zoom out of a map in two ways: either tap the screen once at the same time with two-fingers (Google Maps is the only iPhone app that currently uses this gesture) or use the two-finger pinch gesture.

Find a Location

There are several ways you can find a location using the Google Maps application on your iPhone; the method you use depends on the situation. Do you already know the address? Are you looking up an address of a contact? Have you already looked up this address in the past? Later on in the chapter we'll cover how to find an address using the Google Maps application by either typing in the address, accessing your contacts, or by using bookmarks. So head to your Home screen, tap the Google Maps icon to launch the Google Maps application, and let's get started.

Find a Location by Searching

If you know the exact address you want to look up, tap the search box on top of the Google Maps screen. The software keyboard will slide up from the bottom of the screen and you'll enter Search mode. Now type in the address you're looking for. When you're finished, tap the blue Search button on the bottom left of the keyboard.

TIP   *To clear a previous search without holding down on the delete button for a few seconds, tap the gray X icon on the right of the search box.*

Google Maps will find your address and drop a red pin onto the map to mark its location. The address you searched for will show up above the pin in a black box (shown in Figure 10-1). You can get rid of the black box by tapping the box or anywhere on the map; to bring it back, just tap the red pin.

If you don't know the specific address, there are other ways you can find a location on Google Maps. You can type in an intersection, which is formatted like Shattuck and University, Berkeley CA. City names and zip codes work as well, as do proper place names like Golden Gate Park or White House.

SHORTCUT   *When searching for an address, you won't always have to type in every single detail. In fact, if the Map view is already in the general region you're looking for, often all you really need to type is the street address (and not the city, state, or zip code). If there is more than one match in your region (and by region we're talking states), Google Maps will prompt you to choose from several matches.*

 An address located in Google Maps

Find a Location by Bookmarks

If you know you're going to need to look up an address several times, you might find it useful to bookmark it for quick access. Doing this is easy.

Adding Bookmarks

After you look up an address, you'll see a red pin with a black box above it, marking your address (see Figure 10-1). Inside the black display box is a blue circle with a white arrow inside. Tap the blue arrow to see the Info screen associated with that address. From this screen, you can do all sorts of useful Google Maps things, but right now all we're concerned with is the Add to Bookmarks button. To add the current address as a bookmark, just tap the Add to Bookmarks button.

Now you can give a name to your bookmark to make it easier to find. For example, I've bookmarked my home address in Google Maps and called it simply, Home.

Find a Bookmarked Address

To quickly look up a bookmarked address in Google Maps, tap the blue Bookmark icon on the right of the search box. The Bookmarks screen will slide up from the bottom of the screen with your list of bookmarked addresses (as shown in Figure 10-2). If instead you see the Recents or Contacts screen, tap the Bookmarks button on the bottom left of the screen. Tap the bookmark

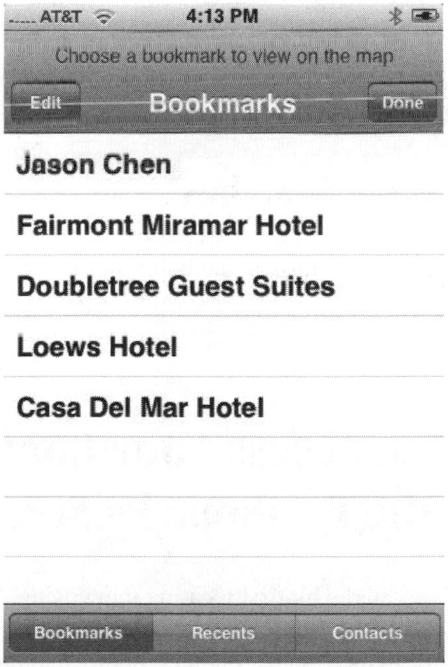

FIGURE 10-2   The bookmarks pane lets you keep track of frequently searched locations without adding them to your contacts.

you want and Google Maps will instantly drop a pin into your bookmarked address in Google Maps. If you change your mind and want to go back to the map without selecting a bookmark, just hit the Done button on the top right of the Bookmarks pane.

Edit Bookmarks

You can delete, rename, and reorder your bookmarks by tapping the Edit button on the top left of the Bookmarks pane (see Figure 10-2). Once you do, you can delete any bookmark by tapping the red minus sign (–) icon next to the bookmark and confirming the delete by pressing the big red Delete button. To rename a bookmark, tap the gray arrow (looks like a greater-than sign) and type a new name for the bookmark. Finally, you can reorder your bookmarks by tapping and dragging the bookmark's drag bars (three horizontal bars) on the far left of the bookmark entry (much the same way you reorder favorites in the Phone app). When you're finished editing your bookmarks, tap the blue Done button.

Find a Location by Contacts

If you've taken the time to enter in address information for your contacts, you're about to be rewarded for your diligence. You can actually look up an address by contacts. Start by tapping the blue bookmark icon in the Google Maps search box, and then tapping the contact button on the bottom right of the new screen. You'll see a list that looks very familiar—that's because it's your alphabetized contact list. Tap a contact you want to locate in Google Maps. Assuming you've entered an address for that contact, the contacts list will drop away and Google Maps will locate your contact's address. The red pin will be identified with that contact's name rather than the long address.

SHORTCUT *You can also look up an address in Google Maps from the Phone application at any time by tapping an individual contact's address field.*

Find a Location by Recent Searches

You can browse all of your recent Google Maps searches by tapping the Bookmarks button in the search box, followed by the Recents button at the bottom of the screen. Every search you've

Did you know?

You Can Access Your Contacts' Details from the Bookmarks Screen

If you add a contact to your bookmarks by first locating them using the contact method described previously, that bookmark's Info screen (remember the blue arrow?) will include all of that contact's info, including their phone number, photo, and email address. This provides you with a handy way, for example, to call a contact once you've made it to their place! (Or, if you're Jason, to tell them you're lost.)

conducted through the search box, including contact search, bookmark search, or even directions you've looked up (see below for more on directions) is available in the Recents section. To perform any of those searches on Google Maps again, just tap the search you want to perform.

Use the Keyboard for Quick Lookups

The Google Maps search box isn't just for searching full addresses. It also gives you quick access to the bookmarked addresses, contact addresses, and recently-searched addresses we discussed previously. For example, if I were to tap the Google Maps search box and start typing the name Jason Chen rather than Jason's street address, Google Maps' as-you-type search results would comb all of the potential addresses I might be looking up—including contact addresses—for a quick match. That means by the time I get to 'J', I'm already looking at Jason's name and address in my search results. By the time I get to 'Jas', he's the only result left. (What can I say, I only know one Jason.) Any time you can see the address you're looking for in the Quick Lookup results, just tap it and you're there. (See Figure 10-3 below for an example of what Quick Lookups look like.)

  Quick Lookups give you a quick way to find contacts, recently searched addresses, or bookmarks.

Likewise, if I wanted to use the Quick Lookup search to find my house, which I've bookmarked as Home, I could just start typing home. And if I had just looked up 1600 Pennsylvania Ave, Washington, D.C. a day or two ago, and I wanted to show a buddy the satellite images of the White House again, I could just start typing 1600 and then tap the Quick Lookup result after a few keystrokes, rather than typing out that whole address a second time (though, as you learned earlier in the chapter, searching White House would also work). Rather than sorting through your bookmarks, contacts, and recent searches, you'll find that using the search box for Quick Lookups is much quicker in most instances. (In fact, it'd be nice to see the same Quick Lookup option for contacts in the Phone app).

Switch Between Map and Satellite View

Google Maps on the iPhone provides two different ways to look at your maps: Map view and Satellite view. The former, which looks like a regular street map (see Figure 10-1), is the more informative view, complete with street names. The latter is best used for showing off close up satellite imagery of an address (I've enjoyed looking up nearby landmarks with iPhone-interested parties on several occasions) and looks like Figure 10-4. Switching between the two views is easy:

 FIGURE 10-4   The satellite view lets you see what something would look like if you were orbiting the planet from space and had really good eyesight.

For Map view, tap the Map button on the bottom left of the map screen. Likewise, to toggle to Satellite view, tap the Satellite button on the bottom middle of the map screen.

Search for and Call Local Businesses

There are basically two places most of us generally need to find maps and directions for: homes and businesses. Searching for addresses by contacts covers the first with ease, but shouldn't there be an equally easy way to find a local business; and then map and call that business? There is! And it's right on your iPhone.

Search for a Local Business

Finding a local business is simple with the iPhone's Google Maps search. Let's say you're in a city you're not familiar with, and you're looking at the hotel's address on the map. Your stomach starts to grumble and you decide you're in the mood for a big slice of pizza. Just tap the Google Maps search box, clear the input, and type in **pizza**. Google Maps will search the area around your hotel for pizza joints, and then drop a handful of red pins into the map with the locations of several local restaurants as shown in Figure 10-5.

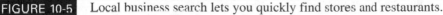
FIGURE 10-5 Local business search lets you quickly find stores and restaurants.

Tap the different pins to see the names of the different pizza places Google Maps located in your area. Of course, you're not limited to just food, and you're not limited to general searches like, pizza. If you know specifically what business you want to look up, just type the business name.

To see all of your search results by name in one window, tap the List button at the bottom left of the map window. The screen will flip over and show you every local pizza result as text search results. Tap any of the results to see it on the map, or tap the blue arrow next to the result to see its Info pane.

Call a Business or Visit Its Home Page

If you want more information on any of the businesses in your search results, tap the blue arrow to view that business's Info pane. Google Maps will display the phone number, website, and street address for that business in a screen similar to your contacts' Info panel (see Figure 10-6). If you decide, for example, that you want to go ahead and order your pizza, just tap the phone number. Google Maps will drop away and your Phone app will take over, calling the business. On the other hand, if you want more information on the business, just tap the Home Page field. Your iPhone's web browser, Safari, will take over and route you straight to the website for that business.

FIGURE 10-6   The info pane for a business lets you easily call them, locate them on the map, or just visit their website.

The Info pane also gives you the option to use the address for the business as a start or end point for turn-by-turn directions. You can also add the business to your bookmarks, create a new contact complete with all of the business's info, or add the info for that business to an existing contact. (See below for more on turn-by-turn directions and creating contacts from an address.)

Create a New Contact from an Address

Once you've found an address, location, or business in Google Maps, it's likely that you'll want to save this address as a contact so you can locate it easily at another time (that is if you haven't bookmarked it already). If the contact in question is a business (for example, your mechanic or dry cleaner), Google Maps will include a phone number along with the address in the Info pane. Since you may want to call the business occasionally—and you won't want to go into the Maps application every time you need to check if your dry cleaning is ready—creating contacts from businesses is especially handy. To create a new contact from an address, first type in an address, and then find a business or select a location from your Bookmarks or Recents lists.

Now that the address is on the screen and pinpointed, click the Right Arrow button found next on the location name. This will pull up the address Info screen. Now, scroll down and hit the Create New Contact button.

A new contact pane will now come up. If you've read Chapter 3, you'll be familiar with this screen, since it's the same New Contact screen you see in the phone application. In any case, fill in the name of the location (or if it's a person, type in their name). Some contact details may be filled in for you automatically, depending on how much information came up with the Google Maps search (if you did indeed find this location with a Google Maps business search). You can fill in the phone number, email address, and various other contact details as you would any other contact. When you're done, hit the Save button on the top right. It's now one of your contacts.

TIP *If you want to add an address you've looked up, to an existing contact, just tap the Add to Existing Contact button on the address Info screen rather than Create New Contact.*

Get Turn-by-Turn Directions

Turn-by-turn directions allow you to use your iPhone as an interactive map to get you from one place to another. Because your iPhone doesn't actually have a GPS receiver, it doesn't know exactly where you are in the world. But, you can still use your iPhone to get directions by manually telling it where you're starting from, where you're going to, and when you've reached a turn.

To start turn-by-turn directions, click the To/From button on the bottom left of your screen to go into Directions mode. It's the button that looks like an up/down arrow in Figure 10-7. Once you go into directions mode, the single search box at the top of your screen will turn into two boxes labeled Start: and End:.

First, tap the Start: box and then find your starting point. You can get an address by any of the methods we described previously: by searching for a business, choosing an address from your

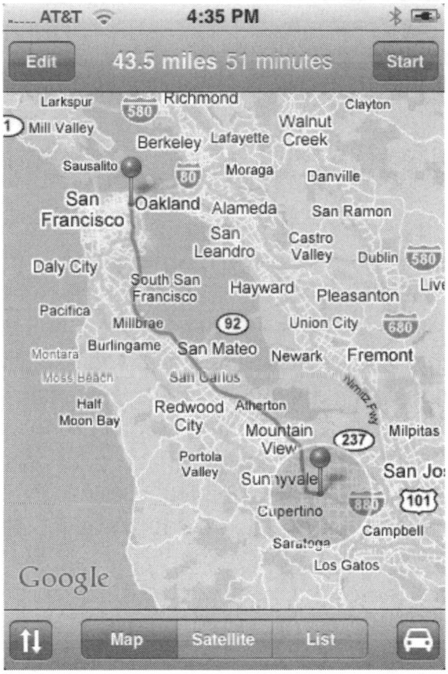

FIGURE 10-7   Turn-by-turn directions guide you conveniently from point A to point B.

bookmarks, choosing a contact, picking one of your recent searches, or even manually typing in an address if you know it. Once you've selected an address for your start point, the cursor will automatically move to the End: box. Repeat the same process here to choose your stop address. Once you've chosen an endpoint, Google Maps will start calculating your driving directions.

When it's finished, you'll see two pinpoints on the map and a blue line connecting them. (The time it takes will depend on your data connection as always, and Wi-Fi will generally be faster than EDGE.) The pin circled in blue represents your starting point; the other represents your end point. You can tap Satellite to view the map in Satellite view, or List to view a list of your entire trip written out in a turn-by-turn fashion. You can even click the car icon on the bottom right to view traffic information. See the section on traffic for more information on what the traffic symbols mean.

TIP   *Combining turn-by-turn directions with real-time traffic information is a good way to save time on a trip. If your turn-by-turn directions take you through a congested stretch of highway, you can take a detour and avoid getting stuck in traffic.*

How to ...   **View Your Travel ETA**

If you turn on the traffic data when you use turn-by-turn directions, Google Maps will actually give you an estimated time to arrival. This time reflects how bad the traffic is on your current route, and will actually change and update every time you reroute your current directions. It's an easy way to get an estimation of how long it'll take you to get where you're going, or give you an idea of whether or not you should wait until the traffic dies down before leaving.

To get started using your turn-by-turn driving directions, hit the Start button on the top right of the screen. The map will zoom in on starting location. The top of your screen will change to Directions, telling you to head in a specific direction on a street. This is your first turn. Google Maps even gives you the distance you need to travel between turns. When you reach your first turn, click the right arrow on the top right of your screen to advance to the next set of directions. The map will shift and the directions will change to the next step in your list of turn-by-turn instructions. If you've accidentally advanced to the next step before you've reached the turn, you can hit the left arrow in the top left corner to go back a step. You can cycle through all the steps of your directions by hitting these two buttons. To jump to a specific turn, click the List button on the bottom and click a direction. Your map will readjust to that turn.

Once you've reached your last direction, the right arrow will be replaced with an Edit button. If you press this, you can edit the starting and ending locations to start a new set of directions.

TIP   *If you've scrolled and flicked around the map to get a better sense of where you are, you'll notice that there's no button to recenter your view on your current location or turn instruction. That's because the iPhone doesn't know where you are! But you can do the next best thing. Either press the List button on the bottom, then click on your current turn, or click the left or right arrows at the top. The map will recenter itself on your current direction step, leaving you back where you were before you scrolled and flicked around the map.*

View Traffic Information

Google Maps tracks traffic information for major interstates and highways, and you can actually view traffic congestion on those roads on Google Maps using your iPhone. To toggle the traffic information, tap the Car icon on the bottom right of the map. The traffic information shows up as an overlay on both the map and satellite views (see Figure 10-8).

FIGURE 10-8   Traffic data is provided free of charge from Google Maps online as long as you have an active data connection.

If traffic is moving along smoothly at more than 50 mph, the overlay is green; if traffic is moderately congested (moving from 25-50 mph), the overlay is yellow; if traffic is at a highly-congested standstill (less than 25 mph), the overlay is red. Sometimes Google won't have current traffic data for a road. In those instances, the overlay is displayed as gray.

Chapter 11

Watch YouTube, Check Weather, and Monitor Stocks from Your iPhone

How to...

- Navigate and watch YouTube videos
- Check the weather forecast
- View the latest stock information

Apart from the marquee applications—like the phone, the iPod and Safari—that make the iPhone such a breakthrough mobile device, your phone also has simple, single-use applications that put weather forecasts, YouTube videos, and stock market information at your fingertips.

Navigate and Watch YouTube Videos

Instead of going to YouTube with Safari to view videos, you've got a dedicated YouTube client built right into the iPhone. This means you get higher quality videos even compared to the desktop version of YouTube, thanks to the fact that clips are encoded especially for the iPhone. Don't worry about those details though—all you need to know is that it's super easy to browse and watch videos. First, tap the YouTube application from the Home screen.

Navigate YouTube

When the YouTube application starts up, you'll notice a big list of videos you can navigate using the scroll and swipe gestures. To pick a video, all you have to do is tap either the screenshot of the video or the text next to it. Tapping the blue right arrow takes you to the info screen for this video. And those navigation buttons on the bottom row of Figure 11-1? They're just like the ones in the iPod application. Let's start with them.

Navigate Using the Bottom Row

The bottom row on every YouTube list view has a set of icons you can tap to navigate around YouTube. It's similar to the various sections of YouTube on the desktop version, but condensed down to fit onto your iPhone. Here's what they all do.

- **Featured**   YouTube selects videos each day to add to their featured section. These can be interesting or funny videos, and are usually worth checking out.

- **Most Viewed**   These are the videos that have been viewed the most times. There are actually three sub-tabs in this option: All, Today, and This Week. Tap each one of those to see videos that were the most viewed of all time, just for today, or for the week. If there are more than 25 results, you'll be prompted to tap the Load 25 More... option to see the rest.

- **Bookmarks**   These are your bookmarked videos, available here in list form for you to easily view again. To remove videos from the bookmarks, tap the Edit button, then the − symbol next to the video you want to remove, and finally the Delete button.

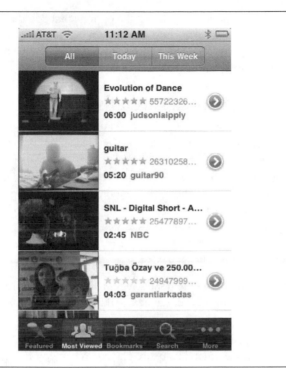

FIGURE 11-1   The most viewed YouTube videos of all time

- **Search**   Here's where you go to search for a specific video you don't have a link to. If there are more than 25 results for a search, you'll be prompted to tap the Load 25 More... option to see the rest.

- **More**   Brings up the rest of the views and provides access to the Edit button, which lets you customize which four buttons are on the bottom bar.

- **Most Recent**   These are the most recently uploaded files. They're not guaranteed to be good (or even watchably bad), but you may be able to find a gem here before any of your friends forward it to you in an email.

- **Top Rated**   The most highly rated videos of all time. These are the videos that people have chosen to be the best, which may or may not be the videos that have been watched the most.

- **History**   All the videos that you've previously watched on the iPhone are listed here. This view is especially useful if you forgot to bookmark a good video you recently watched and want to go back and find it. Tapping the Clear button on the top right will wipe out the entire history.

By pressing the More button, you'll bring up the options that couldn't fit into the Default screen. To change the views that are present in the bottom bar, tap Edit on the top right. This will bring up a screen with all the possible view options. Just drag the view you want to add to the location you want on the bottom, and it will replace whatever view was there before.

Play Back and View a Video's Details

Now that you know how to find videos, let's move on the exciting part: watching them.

Watch a Video

To play back a video, just tap on the video in any list. This will bring up the video playback screen and automatically start playing the video as soon as there's enough of it downloaded. YouTube videos are only available in landscape mode, so you'll have to rotate your iPhone to the left when watching. Once the video has started, you can bring up the playback overlay (See Figure 11-2) by tapping anywhere on the screen. The overlay lets you control, manage, and share videos as follows, starting from the top left:

- ■ **Done** Tap this button if you are done watching a video to return to its Info page. We'll cover more about the Info page in the next section.
- ■ **Playback bar** You can skip forward and backward in a video by dragging the silver dot around the progress bar. As the dot moves, the progress bar turns blue behind it to signify how much of the video is already played. When you first start playing a video,

FIGURE 11-2 The playback control overlay lets you control videos while watching.

that video needs to be downloaded from YouTube before you can actually watch it. The silver bar on top of the playback bar moves forward as the video downloads to indicate how much of the video has been downloaded.

■ **Shrink/Grow**   The Shrink/Grow button on the top right allows you to fit the video to the iPhone's not quite widescreen and not quite 4:3 aspect ratio. Tapping this again will zoom out and allow you to view the entire video without chopping bits of it off to fit the screen. You can also shrink or grow a video at any time without bringing up the control overlay by double-tapping the screen.

■ **Bookmark**   The book icon on left of the bottom overlay lets you bookmark this video. If the icon is gray, as opposed to white (like the other four buttons on the row), that means you've already bookmarked this particular video.

■ **Back/Rewind button**   Tapping the button once will skip to the beginning of this video. Tapping it again will skip to the previous video in the list that you were browsing to get to this clip. Holding the button down will rewind the video. The longer you hold it down, the faster the video will rewind

■ **Play/Pause**   Tap once to pause, tap again to resume playback.

■ **Forward/Fast-forward button**   Tapping the button once will skip to the next video in the list you came from. Holding down the button will fast-forward the video, and the longer you hold it down the faster it goes.

■ **Email**   Tapping the envelope icon will bring up a new email message with the link to this YouTube video in the body (and the title of the video as the subject). All you have to do is type in an email address or choose a contact, and you'll send a link of whatever you were watching off to your friend.

Did you know?   **YouTube on the iPhone Is Different**

Not only was YouTube the last application revealed on the iPhone, it's actually quite different from the desktop version. This is because Apple and YouTube struck a deal to have the latter reconvert all their videos into H.264 format—something both the iPhone and AppleTV understand—as opposed to Flash format, which is the format you watch YouTube videos in on your computers. This in turn means both a higher quality video experience and conserved battery life when watching on the iPhone than if Apple went with Flash format support.

View a Video's Details

Whenever you're finished watching a video or if you click the blue arrow next to a video, you'll be forwarded to the video's Detail screen (Figure 11-3). Here you can see some of the video's details, such as its title, its rating, how many views it has, and the tags its uploader tagged it with. There are a few other things you can do from this screen as well.

- **Watch the video again**   To do this, just tap the section with the screenshot and the title. Tapping anywhere in this area will take you back to the video.

- **Bookmark**   Tap the Bookmark button to save this video to your bookmark list.

- **Share this video**   Tap the share button and to open and compose an email message with a link to this video. This is the same email screen, described above, that you can reach while watching a video.

- **Watch related videos**   A list of related videos on YouTube that share the same tag, similar description, or are in someway related to the video you just watched. Tap any related video to watch it, or tap the blue arrow to go to its Info page.

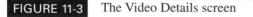

The Video Details screen

How to ...   Maximize Your YouTube Experience

Playing back YouTube videos over Wi-Fi doesn't just mean the videos download faster; it actually gives you a higher-quality video than playing it over EDGE. The lower-quality EDGE videos allow YouTube to stream over the relatively slow EDGE data network, so you can still watch videos, but you get a noticeably worse quality version so you won't have to wait five minutes for the clip to download. You should try and use a Wi-Fi connection to view YouTube videos whenever you can, both for the quality and for the ability to receive incoming calls while watching videos. So to recap, that's faster downloading, better quality, and less chance you'll miss a call. Sounds like a win, win, win situation.

Check the Weather Forecast

The iPhone Weather application gives you a quick overview of the current weather conditions, along with a six-day forecast for up to twenty cities of your choosing. The first time you launch Weather from the Home screen, you'll see the a screen similar to Figure 11-4, with current weather conditions and forecast for Cupertino, CA, home of Apple Inc. The picture on top of the weather screen displays the current conditions (it varies between day or night, sunny or cloudy, rain or snow, and so on). Below the city name is today's high and low (in Fahrenheit, by default), and on the right you'll see the current temperature.

Below the current conditions, Weather displays the six-day forecast from today. On the very bottom of the screen, you'll see a series of dots (or just one, if you're only tracking the weather in one city). These dots correspond to how many cities you've added to the Weather application, and the white dot tells you which one you're currently viewing.

Add a New City

Tap the small i icon at the bottom right of the Weather screen. The forecast will flip over to reveal the Weather preferences. To add a new city, tap the + button on the top left and begin typing in the name of the city you want to add. Weather will dynamically search Yahoo Weather for a match to your city, and the results will display in a list. Once you find a match, just tap it to add that city to Weather.

When you're done adding cities, tap the blue Done button on the top right. The Weather screen will flip back over and you'll now have access to the weather of any city on your list. Navigating between cities works just like moving between photos in a photo album. Swipe the screen horizontally to move between cities. On the other hand, if swiping's not your thing, you can tap the bottom left or right half of the dots to move back and forth between cities. There are no visible buttons (just the dots indicating how many cities you've added), but it still works.

FIGURE 11-4   The Weather application

Remove a City

In Edit mode, you can remove a city at any time by tapping the – button to the left of the city name, and then tapping the red Delete button.

TIP   *If you prefer viewing temperatures in Celsius rather than in Fahrenheit, tap the i icon and then tap the °C button at the bottom of the screen. Likewise, you can switch back to Fahrenheit at any time by coming back to this screen and tapping the °F button.*

View City Information with Yahoo

The Weather application's forecast is pulled from the Internet using Yahoo. When you're viewing a city's weather forecast, you can tap the small Y! button on the bottom left of the screen to open a Yahoo oneSearch of that city in Safari, with links to city guides, local news, weather (though you've already seen that), photos, and more. It's a handy way to take a quick look at what's going on in the city to help you plan your activities now that you know what the weather will be like.

View the Latest Stock Information

The Stocks application gives you a quick overview of the latest trends for any stock in your portfolio. To try it out, go to the Home screen and tap the Stocks button. You'll bring up the stock list as shown in Figure 11-5.

Navigate Stocks

The Stocks application displays individual stocks in a list. From the left, you see the stock's abbreviation, the price for a share, and how many points the stock has risen or fallen in the course of the day (see Figure 11-5). By default, Stocks tracks the Dow Jones Industrial Index (^DJI), Apple, (AAPL), Google (GOOG), Yahoo (YHOO), and AT&T (T). (We'll show you how to add or remove stocks from your portfolio next) If a stock has gone up in the course of a day, the points on the far right will be highlighted in green. If they've fallen, they're highlighted in red.

Below the list of stocks in your portfolio is a line graph of the stock's performance over time. You can adjust the time over which the stock performance graph displays by tapping any of the different durations on top of the graph. Your choices are: performance over one day, one week, one month, three months, six months, one year, and two years.

The stock list

You can view the performance graph of any stock in your portfolio by tapping that stock in the list.

Add Stocks

Unless by some uncanny coincidence you've invested exclusively in Apple, Google, Yahoo, and AT&T, you probably want to add different stocks to your portfolio. Adding stocks works almost exactly the same way as adding cities to your Weather app. Tap the i icon on the bottom right to flip the screen over to the Stocks preferences and click the + button on the top left of the screen. In the Add Stock search box, type either the name of the company or its stock symbol (if you know it), and then tap Search. When you see the stock you want in the list, tap it to add it to your portfolio. When you're finished adding stocks, click the blue Done button to return to the main Stocks screen and view your new stocks.

If you prefer to see your stock's performance by percentage rather than numbers (the default), go to the Stocks preferences screen and tap the % button at the bottom of the screen.

Remove Stocks

To remove stocks from your portfolio, simply tap the i button on the main screen to go into the Stocks preferences. This will bring up the editing options you see in Figure 11-6. Find the stock you want to remove from the list, tap the − button to the left of it, and then tap the Delete button.

View Related News with Yahoo

The Stocks app is powered by information provided by Yahoo Finance. If you want to see more detailed information about the currently highlighted stock from Yahoo, tap the Y! button on the bottom left of the main Stocks screen. A Yahoo oneSearch of the stock will open in Safari, providing you with breaking news and other information that might explain the drastic spike in your portfolio.

Not only can the iPhone keep you entertained and informed on the go, but you can also use its clock, notes, and calculator features to keep yourself on time and organized as well. We'll cover these, and more, in Chapter 12.

FIGURE 11-6   The Edit Stock screen

Chapter 12

Get Organized and Productive with Your iPhone

How to...

- Stay Organized with Notes
- Manage Your Time with the Clock
- Do Math with the Calculator

Along with revolutionary features like the iPod and Safari, the iPhone comes with several tried and true productivity and organization applications, including Notes, Clock, and Calculator. Although not as flashy, the advanced clock, notes, and calculator applications packed into your iPhone let you get stuff done no matter where you are.

Stay Organized with Notes

While you can view Microsoft Word attachments you receive in Mail, you can't actually create or edit them on the iPhone. What you've got is Notes, a very feature-light text editor that provides a sandbox for you to write drafts, make lists, and perform other very simple word processing tasks. The notes you make in Notes can't be formatted or synced, but they can still provide a good place to jot down an idea or add to your grocery list on the go. So launch the Notes app from the Home screen and dive in.

Write, Edit, and Navigate Notes

If this is the first time you've run Notes, you'll see an empty legal pad without any notes. To create a new note, tap the + button on the top right of the screen. The new Note screen will appear, and you can start typing your new note using the virtual keyboard, shown in Figure 12-1. When you're finished scribbling down your thoughts, tap the Done button.

From this point, you can add another note by tapping the + button again, edit the note you're currently viewing by tapping anywhere inside the legal pad, or view all of the notes you've created in a list by tapping the Notes button.

Tapping the Notes button will take you back to the Notes Home screen, where you can view how many notes you've written (following Notes in parenthesis), start a new note with the + button, or view any of the notes you've already created. You'll notice that notes are listed by the first written line, meaning that while you can't exactly name a note in the traditional file sense, you can control how it's listed by adding a name to the top of the note (for example, Groceries).

When you're viewing but not editing an individual note, you'll notice four buttons on the bottom of the screen as shown in Figure 12-2. These buttons are described in the following list:

- **Back/Forward** You can navigate backward and forward between notes by tapping the left and right arrow icons on the bottom of the note. When you move to another note using one of these buttons, you'll see a snazzy tear-off animation that moves to the next note on your Notes list. They provide a quick way to move between notes without going back to the main Notes screen.

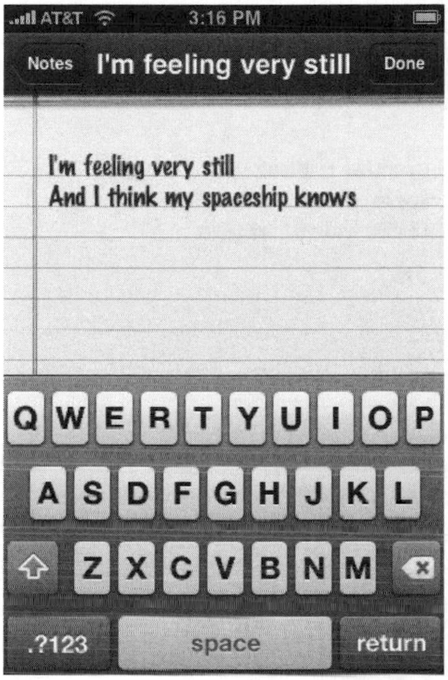

FIGURE 12-1   Writing a note

- **Envelope**   You can share any note you've written via email by tapping the envelope button. When you do, a new email message will slide into view with the first line of the note (that is, the note's name as you see it on the main notes screen) in the subject and the entire contents of the note inside the email body. All you have to do now is add people to the To and Cc fields. Since Notes don't currently sync to your computer, sending them via email is the best way to get a note from your iPhone to your computer.

- **Trash**   You can delete any note while you're viewing it by first tapping the Trash icon, and then tapping the Delete Note button on the Confirmation dialog that slides onto the screen. If you change your mind, tap the Cancel button. When you delete a note, it'll shrink into the trash can with a snazzy animation. You won't be able to recover a deleted note, so make sure you really don't need it anymore before you confirm.

TIP   *If syncing notes to and from your iPhone is an absolute necessity, you can create dummy contacts in your address book and add notes in their Note field. This way you can edit notes on the iPhone—under the dummy contacts—but still sync them to your computer, and vice versa.*

Note editing

Manage Your Time with the Clock

You can do a lot of fancy things with your iPhone, but one of the simplest yet most useful applications on the iPhone is the Clock. With the Clock app, you can get a quick glance at current times in various cities around the world, create alarms, time tasks with the stopwatch, or set quick countdown reminders with the timer.

Track Time Around the Globe with World Clock

Whether you do business across the globe or you just like keeping an eye what time it is where your aunt lives, the World Clock displays a simple dashboard overview of the current time in cities all over the world. As shown in Figure 12-3, it displays cities in a list and provides useful information you can take in at a glance. On the far left, you'll see the name of the city. Next to that is an analog clock view of the time. The face of the clock is either white or black, indicating day or night, respectively. On the far right, the time is listed digitally and indicates whether the time is AM or PM. Below that, World Clock indicates whether the time in that city is still part of the same day as you (Today), or whether it's that time Tomorrow or Yesterday.

FIGURE 12-3   You can easily see the times of four locations at once.

Add a City to the World Clock

Tap the + button on the top right of the screen to search for a city you want to add to the World Clock. This city search provides instant, dynamic as-you-type search results for cities. Unlike the Weather app, the World Clock searches from a limited set of large world cities. If the city you're searching for isn't available, you'll see No Results Found in the results. When you do find the city you want (or at least a city that's close), just tap that entry in the list to add it to your World Clock.

Only four clocks fit on the World Clock screen at one time, but you can scroll your list to view all of your cities if you have over four (the maximum is 24).

Manage Your Cities

You can delete or reorder cities on your World Clock by tapping the Edit button on the top left of the screen. World Clock will go into Edit Mode, displaying the – delete icon to the left of every city and the drag bars to the right.

To delete a city, tap the – button and then confirm the delete by tapping the red Delete button. To reorder your list of cities, touch and drag the city by the drag bars (the three horizontal lines on the right) and release when you've got the city where you want it.

Get There on Time with Alarms

You can use your iPhone as a fancy alarm clock—a feature that you'll find especially convenient when you're on the road. Under the Alarms tab, tap the + icon on the top right to add a new alarm. Now you can set options such as Repeat (this indicates the days of the week your alarm should repeat), the alarm sound (one of your ringtones), whether Snooze is enabled (tap once when the alarm's going off for 10 more minutes of sleep), and what the label for this alarm will be ("Wake up," or "Pick up kids from street fighting practice"). Then just choose a time for the alarm to go off using the dial on the bottom of the screen. When you're finished, tap the Save button shown on the top right of Figure 12-4.

You can enable and disable individual alarms without deleting them by tapping the On/Off switch on the right hand side of each alarm. This way you have a rotating set of alarms programmed into your phone without having to set up each one again whenever you need to use it. To scroll through your list of alarms, just use the normal swipe and flick gestures you're already accustomed to.

TIP

If you dock your iPhone to an iPod dock at night, your morning alarm will actually play back through your iPod dock's speakers—assuming you haven't turned off your iPod dock and have the volume set to an appropriate level.

FIGURE 12-4   The Add Alarm screen

Time Tasks with the Stopwatch

If you're already listening to music with the iPod application on your iPhone while you're working out, you can use the stopwatch function to time yourself as well. It's a pretty standard stopwatch that counts up in deciseconds (tenths of a second) as soon as you tap the Start button. To pause the count, just tap Stop. You can start it up again from where you left off by tapping the Start button. To clear the time and start the counter at 0, tap the Reset button when the counter is stopped, as shown in Figure 12-5.

You can use the stopwatch to keep track of your lap times as well. While the counter is going, tap the Lap button to start a new lap. Your previous laps will be displayed in the list below, and you can use the standard gestures to scroll through the laps.

Countdown with the Timer

If counting up doesn't quite suit your purpose, you can count down with the Timer in order to alert yourself after a certain time has passed. Take a look at the options in Figure 12-6. By turning the large dial on top, you can count down from anywhere between 1 minute to 23 hours and 59 minutes, in one minute intervals. By tapping the area labeled When Timer Ends, you can select a ringtone to play back when the clock runs down to 0. When you're done setting options, tap Start to start the timer.

FIGURE 12-5   Stopwatch lets you time yourself when you're running.

FIGURE 12-6   Unlike alarms, there can only be one timer going at a time.

How to ...   Sleep Your iPod with the Timer

You can actually use the Timer application to rig up a type of sleep mode for the iPod application. This is useful when you want to fall asleep listening to your music, but don't want it playing all through the night. To do this, start playing back a song. Now open up the Timer tab inside the Clock app, choose a time, and pick Sleep iPod under the When Timer Ends option. When the timer runs down to 0, the iPod music will stop without affecting any of your iPhone's other functions.

Do Math with the Calculator

The Calculator app works just like any simple calculator you've ever used. In fact, after you launch it from the Home screen, your iPhone may even look like a calculator (Figure 12-7) you've used before (see the Did You Know? sidebar covering this later in the chapter).

There are a few small tweaks that Apple made to the calculator to make it a bit friendlier for your touchscreen. For example, since you won't be touching physical hardware buttons like you're used to on a calculator, the iPhone provides feedback by highlighting buttons with a white glow when they're pressed. Also, to help you remember which operation you're performing, the iPhone will display a white circle around the operator (divide, multiply, plus, or minus) that you pressed last.

TIP *The Calculator will remember the last number you entered or the results of the last calculation even when you leave the application. This can come in particularly handy, for example, if you're working off figures someone sent you in an email or off a web site.*

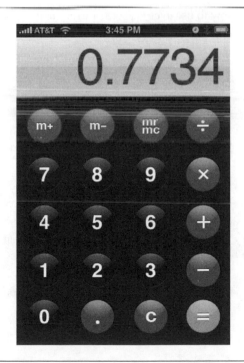

FIGURE 12-7 The calculator

The memory buttons at the top of the calculator (m+, m−, and mr/mc) provide you with a simple place to hold one number at a time in the calculator's memory (if you've used these functions on a calculator before, this won't be new to you). To add the currently displayed number to memory, tap m+. Like the operators, mr/mc now has a white circle around it indicating that you've placed a number into memory. You can now use that number at any time by tapping the mr/mc button. For example, if you wanted to multiply 5 times the number you just placed into memory, you would enter 5, press the × multiplier, and then tap mr/mc followed by the = sign.

If you're just performing simple addition and subtraction to and from the number in memory, you can do that using the m+ and m− buttons. For example, if I had 30 in memory, I could subtract 5 from 30 by pressing 5, then pressing the m- button. My memory will now hold the result of that operation, in this case 25. The m+ button works exactly the same way, except it would add 5 to the number in memory.

You can clear the memory at any time by pressing the mr/mc button twice in succession. Alternately, the memory will be cleared any time you leave the Calculator app.

NOTE   *The iPhone calculator only displays a maximum of nine digits and won't display any more, even if you keep on hitting numbers.*

By now you should know how to use every aspect of every application your iPhone has to offer. Now we'll take a closer look at how to tweak your iPhone settings to make your iPhone work exactly how you want it to.

Did you know?

The Calculator Looks Like a Braun ET44

If you're old enough, you may be wondering why the iPhone's calculator looks so familiar. That's because it looks very similar to a Braun ET44 calculator made in the 1970s. For a comparison image, see the following URL.

http://tinyurl.com/2kc8rl

Part V

Troubleshoot and Master
Your iPhone

Chapter 13

Tweak Your iPhone Settings to Fit Your Needs

How to...

- Tweak iPhone connectivity settings
- View your usage information
- Adjust volume and sound notifications
- Get a better view by adjusting brightness
- Customize your iPhone with wallpapers
- Modify General settings
- Modify Mail settings
- Modify Phone settings
- Modify Safari settings
- Modify iPod settings
- Modify Photos settings

Apple thought of just about everything when they created the iPhone, but what they couldn't account for is each person's personal preferences (they haven't perfected mind-reading just yet). The iPhone is a great mobile device out of the box, but we've all got our own way of doing things, and your iPhone has consolidated all of those options into the Settings application. Everything in this chapter will take place in Settings, so from the Home screen, tap Settings, load up the screen shown in Figure 13-1, and let's get started.

Did you know?

You Can Use Your iPhone on an Airplane

We've all heard that you need to shut off your cell phones when you're flying, but what you actually need to turn off is the wireless communication going on inside your phone. That's why your iPhone makes it simple to switch into Airplane mode, a mode that turns off all of the wireless communication and lets you use your phones other functions—like the iPod—while you're in a plane.

To switch your iPhone to Airplane mode, tap the On/Off switch next to Airplane mode in the first screen of the Settings app. Turning on airplane mode will completely shut down all your iPhone's wireless connectivity—including phone calls, Wi-Fi, Bluetooth, and EDGE downloads. To break it down into what you can't do: this means you can't make or take calls, use your Bluetooth headset, browse the Internet with Safari, check your email, download weather and stock updates, connect to Google Maps, or watch YouTube videos. All applications that don't rely on a wireless connection will work the same as always.

The main Settings screen

Tweak iPhone Connectivity Settings

Although you own an iPhone because you want to be connected all the time, there are some occasions where you need to unplug completely—for example, on an airplane.

Set Up Wi-Fi

When you want to get connected, we recommend that you use Wi-Fi rather than EDGE whenever possible. It's faster, and as we've mentioned before, you won't miss any calls when you're actively downloading data over Wi-Fi (as opposed to EDGE). Tap Wi-Fi from the first screen in Settings, and your iPhone will scan the local area for wireless access points (see Figure 13-2). You want to make sure the switch to the right of the Wi-Fi setting says ON. A list of those local Wi-Fi access points will show up below, allowing you to connect to the one you want. Choose a network, and if it's a secure network (a lock will appear to the left of the signal strength meter if it is), you'll be prompted to enter a WEP, WPA, or WPA2 key. If you don't know the password, ask your network administrator or the person responsible for the Wi-Fi hotspot.

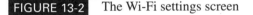

Wi-Fi settings screen with:
.ı111 AT&T 6:26 PM ✳ ▭
Settings **Wi-Fi Networks**

Wi-Fi ON

Choose a Network...

2WIRE345 🔒 📶 ⊚
2WIRE884 🔒 📶 ⊚
✓ BERSERK 🔒 📶 ⊚
NETGEAR 📶 ⊚
vivisky 🔒 📶 ⊚
Other... ›

Ask to Join Networks OFF

FIGURE 13-2 The Wi-Fi settings screen

TIP *Your iPhone can only use 802.11b and 802.11g. If you have a wireless access point that uses 802.11b/g, then you'll be fine. However, if you have one that supports 802.11a or 802.11n, you need to make sure it's configured to allow 802.11b/g access. If this is not on, your iPhone won't be able to connect.*

Once you've connected to a wireless access point, you can change its connection details. Tap the blue arrow to the right of the access point entry to see its details page.

There are three options at the top: DHCP, BootP, and Static. These options determine the way you obtain an IP address, which is how the router and other computers on the network locate your iPhone. Unless you have a specific reason to change these settings, we recommend leaving them alone. The same goes for the HTTP Proxy options on the bottom, which should not need to be changed unless your network or your network administrator require it.

The last option, Ask to Join Networks, allows you to disable the prompts your iPhone gives you when it can't find any preferred networks and wants to join an unprotected network. By turning this off, you won't be able to automatically join open networks when you're on the go, but you also won't be bugged by prompts when you're walking down the street and checking email. If you do want to be notified of networks you can join, set this to On.

View Your Usage Information

The very cool and very useful Usage section of the Settings application displays just how much you've used the iPhone, both as an Internet device and as a phone. Here's what the numbers in the Usage section shown in Figure 13-3 all mean:

- **Time since last full charge**   The two numbers under this entry show you how much time has elapsed since you last fully charged the iPhone. You have to add up both Usage and Standby to get the exact time of use, but if there is a note that says iPhone has been plugged in since the last full charge underneath the two entries, then the measurement is fairly useless in terms of knowing just how long you can go without charging. These numbers go back to 0 the next time you fully charge your phone.

  - **Usage**   This measures how much time you've spent with the iPhone actively being used. Active is a relative term, since talking on the phone, playing the iPod, and leaving your iPhone idle at the Home screen all count toward increasing the Usage number.

  - **Standby**   This is the amount of time your iPhone has been on, but in the locked position and not doing anything.

FIGURE 13-3   Usage information

- **Call Time**   This shows how many minutes you've used of your AT&T call plan.

  - **Current Period**   This shows the number of minutes you've used in this current period. That may sound like it's your current AT&T billing month, but it's not. It just means how many minutes you've used since you last hit the Reset Statistics button at the bottom of this screen. If you manually reset stats every month at billing time, this can be a great tool to keep track of how many minutes you've used in order to keep from going over.

  - **Lifetime**   The amount of time you've talked on the phone for the lifetime of your iPhone. This stat doesn't get reset when you hit Reset Statistics, so you don't have to worry about losing your lifetime data.

- **EDGE Network Data**   Sent and Received measure how much data you've sent over the EDGE network. This really doesn't usually affect anything, since AT&T gives you unlimited data, but if you take your iPhone to another country and start roaming on their network, you'll find this *very* useful in keeping your bill low.

- **Reset Statistics**   Hitting this button will reset the Current Call Time Period and the EDGE Network Data to 0. Your Lifetime call time and the time since the last full charge will be untouched.

Adjust Volume and Sound Notifications

The Sounds settings pane shown in Figure 13-4 is where you can adjust all the sound-related options on your iPhone. If you're sick of the noises your phone makes when a new text message or voicemail comes in, this is where you go to shut them off.

- **Silent Vibrate**   This option lets you choose whether you want your phone to vibrate when you get a call or alert when the phone's on silent mode.

- **Ring Vibrate**   This is similar to the silent vibrate, but Ring Vibrate also lets you choose whether you want the phone to both ring and vibrate when the phone is in standard mode (ring active).

- **Volume Slider**   Adjusting your ring volume here is the same as adjusting it using the side volume keys, but this allows you to quickly pull it to either the loudest or softest setting.

- **Ringtone**   Tapping this option will take you into the sub-menu, where you can choose a universal ringtone for all your calls. After you've chosen one, tap the Sounds button on the top left to go back to the main Sounds menu.

- **New Voicemail**   This is the alert sound that plays when someone has left you a new voicemail.

- **New Text Message**   This is the new text message alert sound. Although the iPhone actually plays back two different sounds—one when the phone is locked and one when you're in the actual SMS conversation screen with the recipient—this switch enables and disables both.

- **New Mail**   The alert that plays when you receive a new mail message. Unless you use Yahoo Mail or have your email set to automatically check for new mail, you won't hear this sound unless you launch the Mail application to manually check for new email.

FIGURE 13-4   Sound settings

- **Sent Mail** This is the whoosh sound that plays whenever you successfully send an email.
- **Calendar Alerts** This is the sound that accompanies Calendar alerts when the go off. Shutting this off will just shut off the sound, but the alert will still pop up.
- **Lock Sounds** This is both the Click noise that goes off when you press the On/Off button to lock your iPhone, and the click noise that goes off when you slide the unlock bar to unlock your iPhone.
- **Keyboard Clicks** These are the click noises you hear when you type on the keyboard in any application. They're useful when you want to know if you hit a key correctly, but the keyboard sounds can get annoying once your typing speed goes up.

Get a Better View by Adjusting Brightness

The iPhone's screen can be really bright, but using it at full brightness all the time will drain your battery faster than usual. We recommend moving the brightness slider to a level where you can easily see all the details on your screen, but not too high that it hurts your eyes when you stare at it for a long time.

The Auto-Brightness option is fantastic as well. The iPhone actually has a light sensor on board that detects how much light is in its surrounding environment. This allows it to automatically get brighter when you're outside in the sun, as well as dim itself when you're in the dark. We recommend leaving this On unless you have a need to manually set the iPhone to a really bright or really dim mode.

Customize Your iPhone with Wallpapers

Apple included fifteen photos with your iPhone that you can set to be the wallpaper in your standby screen. The only place you'll see this wallpaper is in that screen (which you probably won't see much of) and when you get a call from someone who doesn't have a contact picture (which you probably will see a lot of unless you've already set up everyone's picture).

If the Apple-provided wallpapers under Wallpaper don't suit you, you can also set your wallpaper using any picture from your Photo library. All the albums in your photo library, including the Camera Roll, are present under the Wallpaper option. Choose an album, select a picture, move and scale the photo, and then tap Set Wallpaper. Moving and scaling the photo will let you make sure the most interesting part of the picture is in the frame, and it can help you make the shot big enough to fill the iPhone's frame—useful if this is a picture you shot in landscape mode.

Modify General Settings

Apple placed all of the configuration options that don't belong to a specific application into the General settings. Let's start from the top of Figure 13-5.

See Your iPhone's Information in About

The About screen lets you quickly glance at your iPhone's statistics. The only ones that are generally useful to you are the Songs, Videos, Photos, Capacity, Available, and Version. The first three show you how many songs, videos, and photos you have on your iPhone. Capacity displays how much storage your iPhone has in total (the 4GB model will say 3.3GB and the 8GB model will say 7.3GB because the iPhone's operating system takes up 700MB of space). Available shows you how much space you have left on your iPhone for new songs, photos, and videos. If this number is running low, you might think about deleting some videos in order to make sure you have enough space for new emails to come in. You can always re-sync these videos to your iPhone the next time you dock with your computer.

Tapping the Legal button on the bottom brings up the Legal Notices associated with the iPhone. This screen is very long and very dry, so unless you're an insomniac, a lawyer, or very curious, there's not much reason to go here.

Adjust the Date & Time

The Date & Time option allows you to change options that relate to your iPhone's internal clock.

- **24-Hour Time**   This switches the display on the top of your iPhone screen from, for example, 7:01PM to 19:01. If you're using 24-hour time in your work, this can be a handy way to quickly use your phone to get military time.

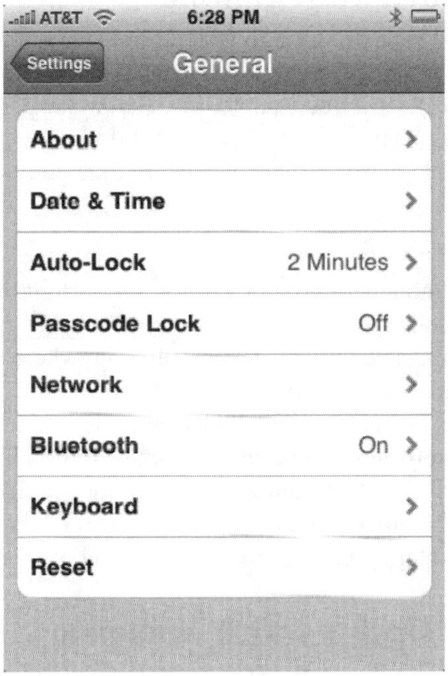

FIGURE 13-5   The General settings screen

- **Set Automatically**   Turning this on will automatically update your iPhone's internal clock using the cellular network. This means that if you travel from San Francisco to New York, your iPhone will automatically change its clock to Eastern time when you land and connect to a cell tower. Turning this off will bring up two more options.

  - **Time Zone (Optional)**   This is only active when Set Automatically is turned off. This lets you manually set the time zone you want your iPhone's clock to use.

  - **Set Date & Time (Optional)**   This is only active when Set Automatically is turned off. You choose the date and time using a set of dials.

You can also adjust time zone settings for your Calendar as well. If your calendar on the desktop (like iCal) supports multiple time zones, you may have set some events to one time zone and some events to another. By turning on Time Zone support, your iPhone Calendar will show the event times for the time zone that's selected. If you turn the option off, the time zone for your calendar will default to your current time zone, which you set (or automatically fetched) under Date & Time options.

Set a Time to Auto-Lock Your iPhone

Auto-Lock lets you choose how long you have to wait before the phone automatically shifts to Locked mode when not in use. You can choose between 1, 2, 3, 4, and 5 minutes, or you can choose to avoid Auto-Lock altogether if you want to, say, always keep the iPod display active when listening to music. This last option is especially useful if you've got the iPhone plugged into an iPod dock, so you don't have to wake the phone up every time you want to change a track.

Set a Passcode Lock

When you set a passcode, the iPhone will prompt you for a four-digit code every time you wake the phone. After you set a passcode, you'll see new options in the Passcode Lock screen. You can set the phone to prompt for a passcode immediately, or after anywhere between 1 to 60 minutes of usage. By setting a longer interval, you can use your phone and not have to worry about putting your password in all the time, but still protect your phone from being used when stolen. If you set it to prompt immediately, you can protect it from unauthorized use altogether.

Turning Show SMS Preview to On will allow you to see the preview of a new SMS message in your standby screen without having to go unlock your phone (and therefore enter the passcode). This saves you from having to enter in the code for messages that you don't need to respond to.

Change Connectivity Options with Network

Network has two options: VPN and Wi-Fi. Wi-Fi just points you to the same screen you reach from the Wi-Fi option under the Settings main screen, which we've already described. VPN allows you to securely connect to a network at work. Your office may require you to use a Virtual Private Network (VPN) connection before you an access your work email, or before you can access internal web pages. To configure your VPN, just tap the option and switch it to On.

Once the VPN is set to on, the account information pane will pop up. The iPhone supports both L2TP and PPTP protocols, which both have their upsides and downsides in network security. Ask your network administrator for information on how your iPhone will connect to the VPN network and enter the details in the appropriate fields. When you're finished, hit Save.

Set Up a Bluetooth Device

The Bluetooth option, when turned on, allows you to hook your iPhone up with a Bluetooth headset for hands-free conversations. Turn this on and the iPhone will start searching for nearby Bluetooth devices. You may need to consult your Bluetooth headset's instructions on how to set it on Discoverable mode. Once the device has been discovered, an entry will show up under Devices. Tap the entry, and the iPhone will prompt you to enter in a password. Search your Bluetooth headset instructions again for its passcode and enter it in here.

Once your headset is paired (it will show the word Paired on the right side of its entry under Devices), the Bluetooth icon on the top right of the phone will turn Blue. If it's not currently paired, the icon will be grey. It's a good idea to make sure this icon is blue before you make a call—in other words, make sure your headset is paired if you want to use it to have a conversation. Consult your headset's instruction manual again to see which button you need to press to activate or answer a call. For more on answering and making calls with a headset, see Chapter 3.

Adjust Keyboard Settings

The two options under Keyboard let you choose whether you want to enable auto-capitalization of words and whether you want to enable caps lock. Once enabled, Auto-Capitalization is transparent, but to activate caps lock you have to tap the Shift key twice. The key will turn blue and all the subsequent letters you type will be capitalized.

Reset Content and Settings

The options under Reset should generally be left alone unless you have a specific reason to use them, such as if you want to delete all of your settings before you give or sell your iPhone to someone else (which we would recommend). Here's what the options in Figure 13-6 do:

- ■ **Reset All Settings**   This erases all preferences from your iPhone and reverts it to just about the way it was when you purchased it. The only difference is that your photos, videos, and songs will still be on board. This is because they are considered content, as opposed to settings. To delete content as well, see the next option.

- ■ **Erase All Content and Settings**   This will delete both your settings and your content, so your phone will be erased of all knowledge that you were ever there. This is super useful if you're going to sell your phone or give it to a family member when you upgrade to the second generation iPhone.

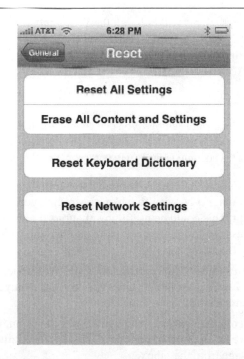

 Reset screen

How to ... **Start from Scratch with Your Settings**

If you went on a tweaking binge and now your iPhone is behaving abnormally and you don't know how to fix it, you can reset all of your settings and start from scratch rather than digging through your settings looking for where you went wrong. To do so, open the Settings application from the Home screen, tap General, Reset, and then Reset All Settings. Confirm the reset by tapping the Reset All Settings button. Your iPhone, settings, are now as fresh as the day you bought it.

■ **Reset Keyboard Dictionary**   When you're typing in the iPhone keyboard you actually train the internal dictionary every time you type in a word or name that's not already inside—for example, when you type in a word and the iPhone auto-suggests another word and you reject that word by tapping the little x to tell it that you want to use your word. If you do this twice, the iPhone will place this word into the internal dictionary. If you accidentally do this too many times with words you didn't intend to add to the dictionary, just reset.

■ **Reset Network Settings**   This will erase all the Wi-Fi network settings you've programmed in—handy if you've just traveled and connected to a bunch of Wi-Fi hotspots on the road that you will never use again.

Modify Mail Settings

If you're not happy with the default Mail settings, you can change them to fit your needs. First, we'll touch on accounts. By going into each account, you can change your displayed name, the outgoing server address, or even disable the account entirely. Here are some of the more advanced features:

■ **Outgoing Server**   You can change the outgoing server of an account to the outgoing server of another account, if you want to make it seem like you're sending messages from the other account. This could be useful in situations like Hosted Gmail, or where you're forwarding messages from one account to another and trying to make it seem like messages are coming from the first.

■ **Removing deleted messages**   Under Advanced, you can set messages to never delete, or delete after a day, a week, or a month. This frees up space on your iPhone, especially if you get a lot of messages with large attachments.

■ **Deleting messages from the server**   Another Advanced option, this allows you to set your iPhone to remove an email from your email server never, after seven days, or after you remove the message from the inbox.

- **Mailbox Behavior**   Again under Advanced for certain mail accounts (like .Mac), you can assign the location to store drafts or sent messages—either on your iPhone or on the server.

It's best not to fiddle with your mail account's settings unless you or your network administrator have a reason to, but you should feel free to change other mail settings to customize your experience however you like.

- **Auto-Check**   Change the interval for your iPhone to automatically check your accounts to see if there are any new messages.

- **Show**   This lets you decide if you want to display the 25, 50, 75, 100, or 200 most recent messages in your Inbox.

- **Preview**   Changing this option will change the amount of lines displayed from each message in your Inbox list view. Setting it higher means that sometimes you won't even have to open up a message to read the contents, but it makes scrolling through large lists take slightly longer.

- **Minimum Font Size**   If the default font size for messages is too small, you can increase it here to make text easier to read.

- **Show To/Cc Label**   Turning this on will show a To or Cc icon next to messages that are actually addressed to you. This helps if you're on a lot of mailing lists or you get bulk email by letting you discern important messages right away.

- **Always Bcc Myself**   This lets you send a Bcc of your messages to yourself whenever you send mail. Bcc stands for blind carbon copy, which means the person you're sending the message to will have no idea you're sending a copy to yourself.

- **Signature**   By default, your signature is "Sent from my iPhone," and will be attached at the bottom of every message you send. Feel free to change this to anything that suits you.

- **Default account**   Choose the default account you want your messages to send from. This is used when you click the Share button from Photos and YouTube, for example.

Modify Phone Settings

You can make a number of simple yet very useful tweaks to the Phone application through the Settings. In addition, the Phone Settings gives you quick access to AT&T services, so you can check your balance and pay your bill with the touch of a button. Inside the Phone settings in Figure 13-7, you'll see:

- **International Assist**   Normally, when you're traveling abroad, you'd need to dial an international calling code in front of your US numbers to reach your contacts. With the International Assist option turned on, the iPhone will recognize when you're dialing from outside the country and automatically add the appropriate prefix to your US numbers.

- **Sort Order**   You can sort your contact list alphabetically by last name or first name. The iPhone defaults to the Last, First sort order.

FIGURE 13-7　Phone settings screen

- **Display Order**　You can change the order in which individual contacts are listed by adjusting the Display Order. A Display order of First, Last would display a contact as Jason Chen, while an order of Last, First would display a contact as Pash, Adam. Most likely you'll want your Display Order to match your Sort Order.

- **Call Forwarding**　Forward your calls to another phone number. This is useful when you don't have cell coverage or your phone's running out of batteries. Note that call forwarding still uses up your anytime minutes. To turn it on, tap the On/Off toggle and enter the number you want to forward calls to.

- **Call Waiting**　If turned off, any call you receive while you're already on the phone will go directly to voicemail instead of notifying you with the standard call waiting beep.

- **Show My Caller ID**　This displays your name and phone number to the people you call when turned on. Most of the time you'll want your contacts to know you're calling—in fact, a lot of people don't answer their phone when they can't see who's calling. However, you can turn your Caller ID off if you want some privacy.

- **TTY**　Turn this on to enable teletype machine compatibility, a technology used by the hearing impaired to communicate textually.

- **SIM PIN**   If you turn this on, your SIM chip (the small, removable card inside your iPhone) can't be taken out and used in another phone without the password. This is a useful setting to enable if you're worried about your phone being stolen.

- **AT&T Services**   Check the status of your AT&T account right on your phone with the tap of a button. Check Bill Balance will send an SMS message to your phone with the balance of your current bill; Directory Assistance dials the familiar 411; Pay My Bill calls AT&T's express pay line phone number; View My Minutes will send an SMS message to your phone displaying your remaining anytime, nights and weekends, and mobile-to-mobile minutes; and Voice Connect lets you access and set up AT&T's voice-activated information service, Voice Connect. Tapping AT&T My Account loads your AT&T account page in Safari, but you need to have signed up for an online account and enter your phone number and password.

Modify Safari Settings

Just like in a regular desktop browser, there are some settings in Safari you can tweak to enhance or speed up your browsing session. Here's a quick look at what they are and what they do (Figure 13-8):

- **Search Engine**   You can switch your search engine from the default Google to Yahoo if you favor it.

- **JavaScript**   Many websites, including sites that host the web applications for your iPhone that we covered previously in the book, use JavaScript. Disabling this will speed up browsing slightly, but make some pages behave oddly and other pages completely unreadable. We recommend leaving this on unless you have a specific reason to turn it off.

- **Plug-Ins**   This allows you to play Quicktime movies and various audio files inside your browser. You should leave this on unless a specific movie or audio file is crashing Safari, which will happen very rarely.

- **Block Pop-ups**   This prevents web pages from opening up new windows uninvited, which are usually the pop-up ads that you're already familiar with. Imagine how fun those could be on the iPhone! Make sure to leave this on.

- **Accept Cookies**   Cookies are little pieces of data that websites use as storage bins for information. This info can be your login (to automatically log you in to a site when you visit), so we recommend leaving it set to From Visited. This lets sites you're actually viewing leave cookies, but blocks cookies from the ad sites that you're not directly visiting.

- **Clear History**   If you're like Jason and you're ashamed of the sites you've been browsing, click Clear History. This will prevent any wandering eyes from accidentally seeing your surfing habits. The downside is that you won't be able to go into your history to find a page you viewed a few days ago but forgot to bookmark.

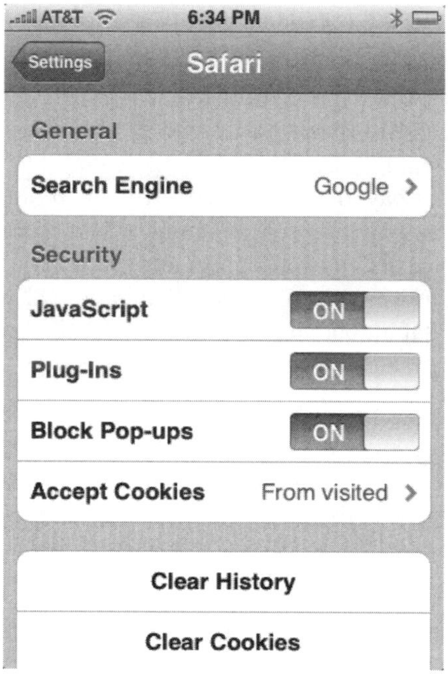

FIGURE 13-8   Safari settings screen

- **Clear Cookies**   Not a huge deal if you've been accepting cookies by default, but if you want to clear your login info from certain websites, you can do so here.

- **Clear Cache**   The iPhone stores web page data, such as images, in its internal memory to speed up subsequent visits to the same website. If you're running low on space, you can clear the cache here to free up some more room to take pictures or receive emails.

Modify iPod Settings

There are a couple tweaks you can make your iPod experience even more enjoyable, including setting a maximum volume limit and adjusting the equalizer to optimize sound. This is what the options in Figure 13-9 do:

- **Sound Check**   This option allows songs recorded at different volume levels to be played back at the same volume. If you have a playlist with two albums, one recorded really loudly and the other softly, you may find yourself fiddling with the volume every time the track changes. Sound Check equalizes the volume between tracks so you don't have to. To turn it on, open up iTunes preferences on your computer (Mac or PC), go to Playback and select Sound Check. Then, in your iPod Settings, make sure Sound Check is switched on.

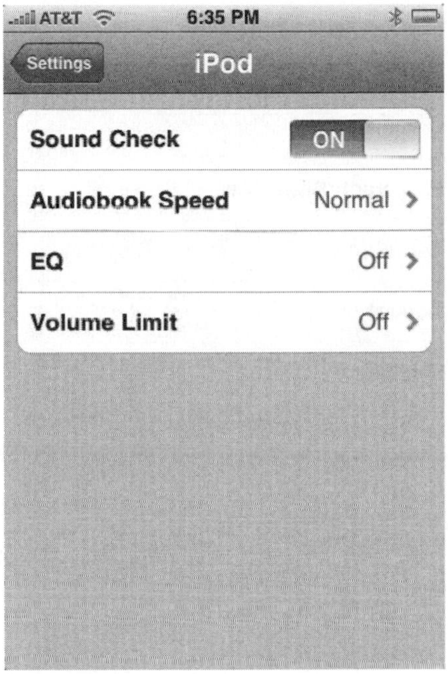

FIGURE 13-9   iPod settings screen

- **Audiobook Speed**   You can speed up audiobooks to play back faster, if you want to save time, or slower, if you want to make out words more clearly.

- **EQ**   The EQ customizes the sound output to accommodate a certain music style or speaker type. For example, Small Speakers is a good option to choose if you're playing back music through the iPhone's built-in speakers, and Spoken Word is a good option for audiobooks.

- **Volume Limit**   To prevent music and videos from being accidentally played back at a really loud volume when you have your headphones on, drag the volume slider under Volume Limit. To prevent anyone else from changing this volume limit, click Lock Volume Limit and type in a four-digit code.

Modify Photos Settings

You can adjust slideshow playback for the Photos application through the Photos settings, as shown in Figure 13-10. You have four options for adjusting Slideshow settings:

- **Play Each Slide For**   Adjust how long the slideshow displays one photo before advancing to the next. You can set playback times at 2, 3, 5, 10, or 20 seconds.

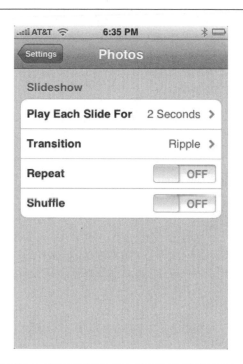

 **FIGURE 13-10**   Photos settings screen

■ **Transition**   The slideshow moves between photos using one of several transition effects. The Cube effect rotates from one picture to the next as though your images are displayed on a rotating cube. Dissolve slowly fades from one photo to the next; Ripple uses a water-ripple effect to move between photos; and Wipe Across and Wipe Down slide the new picture over the top of the previous one.

■ **Repeat**   When Repeat is off, your slideshow will stop playing back once it reaches the last picture. If repeat is on, the slideshow will continue playing until you manually stop it by tapping the screen, sleeping the phone, or pressing the Home button.

■ **Shuffle**   When shuffle is on, your slideshows will play back randomly rather than sequentially.

Customizing the settings of your iPhone to fit your needs is a great way to improve your iPhone's functionality, but in Chapter 14, we'll cover some really advanced usage so you can wield your phone like a pro.

Chapter 14

Advanced Usage: Wield Your iPhone Like a Pro

How to...

■ Use your iPhone like a pro

■ Master the iPhone keyboard

■ Control the iPhone with your headphones

■ Get new email as soon as it's sent

■ Take advantage of web applications made for the iPhone

If you've read through the entire book up until this chapter, you'll have learned pretty much all you need to know about using your iPhone. There are, however, many shortcuts and usage tips that can both save you time and let you do things with your iPhone you didn't even know were possible!

Use Your iPhone Like a Pro

In the following sections, we'll discuss several advanced methods for taking full advantage of your iPhone's multi-touch gestures and hardware buttons. Then we'll discuss a few other advanced methods for operating with your iPhone from sending MMS messages to syncing with multiple computers.

Master Gestures and General Usage

Although the basic swipe, flick, and pinch gestures are old hat by now, here are a couple advanced gestures that you may not know about.

Swipe Right to Left to Delete Messages

Although we've been recommending that you swipe from left to right to delete email messages (and videos) on your iPhone, you can actually swipe from right to left as well. This gesture could useful for left-handers, even though you have to hit the Delete button on the right to confirm deletion.

Double Tap to Zoom Smartly

Although pinching and spreading lets you zoom in just about every application that supports zoom, there are three places that support double-tap to zoom in and out: Safari, Photos, iPod, YouTube, and Google Maps (though in Google Maps, however, you have to two-finger-tap in order to zoom out). The double-tap zoom is especially useful in Safari, where double tapping on a section, column, or area makes Safari automatically fit that section into the width of the view. This lets you focus your attention on just one section, ignoring everything else.

Two-Finger Scroll

Sometimes a web page will have a scrollable section that you need to scroll separately from the contents of the page as a whole. If you want to scroll that section only, and not the rest of the page, place two fingers on the screen and swipe up and down to scroll only the contents of the frame. The two-finger scroll is probably the most esoteric gesture on the iPhone, and it's currently only supported in Safari.

The two-finger scroll is used in a few iPhone web applications, namely chat applications like FlickIM and anything with an embedded, scrollable frame on the page.

Take a Self-Portrait

Most phones have a small mirror on the back in order for you to see yourself when taking self portraits, but the only thing on the back of your iPhone is the Apple logo (which is quite lousy as a mirror, in case you were wondering). To take a good picture of yourself, just place your finger on the shutter button, hold it, turn the phone around, and let go when you think you've framed it correctly. You can delete the picture you took and try again until you've got it right.

Use the iPhone's Sensors

You may not know this, but the iPhone has three invisible sensors in it designed to make your life easier. First, there's the light sensor, which automatically raises the screen brightness when you're outdoors and lowers it when you're in the dark. Then there's the proximity sensor that automatically turns off the screen (both the display and the touch interface) whenever you have the phone up to your face during a call so you won't accidentally push the phone's virtual buttons. Lastly, you have the accelerometer that knows when you've twisted the phone into Landscape mode and turns accordingly.

Utilize the iPhone's Advanced Hardware

Even though the software is what makes the iPhone so revolutionary, its hardware buttons and features hold their own as well. Here are some of the cool, advanced things you can do with the iPhone's hardware buttons shown in Figure 14-1.

Use the Hardware Buttons to Control Calls and Alarms

The On/Off hardware button on the top of the iPhone is actually a very useful multi-purpose button that can perform several subtle actions in addition to the power on/off and lock/unlock functionality you've probably used it for so far.

Ignore or Silence Calls with the On/Off Button   When you receive an incoming call on your iPhone, you can instantly silence the ringer from the call by tapping the On/Off button once. The call will continue ringing on the caller's end, and you can still pick up the call even though the ringer is silenced.

Let's say, on the other hand, the call is from Jason and you don't want to hear more about the great new jeans and sweater vest he just bought. You can route the call directly to voicemail by tapping the On/Off button twice in succession. On your end, the ringer will stop and the call will no longer be available to answer. On the caller's end, the phone will stop ringing and go straight to your voicemail.

End Calls with the On/Off Button   Rather than use the big red End Call button at the bottom of the screen when you're in a call, you can actually end a call and instantly lock your phone by

FIGURE 14-1   The iPhone's hardware buttons

pressing the On/Off button instead of tapping the End Call button. This shortcut works from anywhere, whether you're on the call screen or you're multitasking and in another program altogether. If you're making the call using headphones, however, pressing the On/Off button will not end the call—it will, however, lock the phone as usual.

Control Alarms and Timers with the Hardware Buttons

If any alarms you've set in the Clock application are going off, tapping the On/Off button once will turn off the alarm while you're actively using your phone. However, if your phone is locked and in your pocket, tapping the On/Off button will only sleep the alarm, meaning it will go off again in nine minutes. To turn it off completely when the phone is locked, you'll need to use the onscreen software slider to turn off the alarm.

When a timer you've set goes off, the On/Off button will turn off the timer's alert.

Amplify Your iPhone's External Speakers

After making a few calls using your iPhone's speakerphone feature, you may have noticed that the call volume on the iPhone speaker is a bit on the quiet side. You can amplify the sound coming out of the speakers (which are located on the bottom of the iPhone next to the dock connector), by cupping your hand at the bottom of the speaker to reflect the sound up toward your ear. This method isn't ideal, but you'll notice that under the right conditions, it can dramatically improve the volume of the call.

How to ...   Use Your iPhone's SIM in Another Phone

If your phone ever breaks and you don't want to pay the $30 for a loaner iPhone while it's getting repaired, you can actually transplant your contacts into another cell phone. Before you send the iPhone in for repairs, you can take out the SIM chip. First make sure it's powered off, then take a small paper clip, stick it into the hole on the top of the iPhone (next to the headset jack) and pop out the SIM. Take this chip and place it into a spare GSM-capable phone (any phone that's AT&T-compatible should work) and it will contain the contacts you've programmed into the iPhone.

Alternately, you may have noticed that your iPhone dock has holes and a grill in the bottom of the dock. This is so that the sound from your iPhone speakers can travel through the dock and reflect off the surface of whatever the dock is sitting on and up toward you. Again, this won't go a long way toward amplifying the overall volume of the iPhone, but it's useful in the right circumstances.

Listen to Music with the Line Out

The dock Apple included with your iPhone actually has a stereo line-out port in the back, which you can use to pipe music to your speaker system. It's essentially the same as plugging the speakers into the headphone jack of your iPhone, but it's slightly easier since you can play music on your stereo and charge it at the same time (provided the dock is also plugged into your computer or the AC adapter).

Listen to Voicemail on the Bluetooth Headset

There's actually a third way, other than using the iPhone's built-in speakers, to listen to your voicemail. To pipe sound through the Bluetooth headset, first pair it with your iPhone. Then, under the Voicemail screen, tap the Source button on the top right. This will give you a choice, like you have during a call, of playing sound through the iPhone, the Speaker, or the Bluetooth headset. Choose headset, then start playing a voicemail.

iPhone General Usage Tips

Here are a few general usage tips for your iPhone that you can put to good use every day.

Fix a Stuck Program

If you need to force a program to shut down because it's unresponsive, you can hold down the Home button for six seconds. This should stop the program and force your phone back to the Home screen. If this doesn't work, hold down the On/Off and Home buttons together until the phone turns off and the Apple logo shows up again. Let go, and when the phone finishes booting, you should be back to normal.

Sync with Multiple Computers

If you regularly use more than one computer, you may have your music on one machine and your contacts on another; or you may have work contacts on your work computer and personal contacts on your personal computer. The solution to keeping all these things on your iPhone is simple. All you have to do is dock your iPhone with each computer, then check the sections (music, contacts) that you want to sync. You can choose music on one machine and contacts on another. Or, if you choose contacts on two or more machines, they will all be mixed together on your iPhone.

Use Email with Your Computer and Your iPhone Simultaneously

If you're checking email on both your iPhone and your desktop mail client, sometimes a message may show up only on your iPhone and not your desktop, or vice versa. To avoid this problem, you want to make sure your iPhone always leaves a copy of the email on the server when it's accessed. Here's what you do in the screen shown on Figure 14-2:

1. Open up the Settings application from the Home screen.

2. Tap Email.

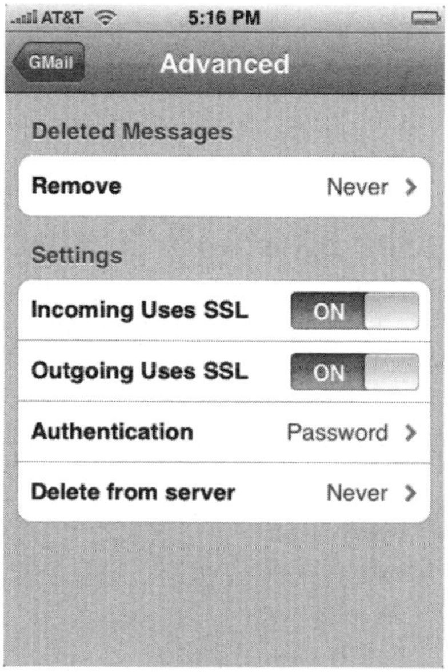

FIGURE 14-2   If you're using multiple email clients, set your Mail settings to leave email on the server.

3. Choose an email account.

4. Scroll down to the bottom and tap Advanced.

5. Tap the Delete from server option at the bottom and make sure it says Never.

By doing this, you can make sure that reading your email on the iPhone won't affect your desktop email. You have to do the same thing on your desktop as well. Find your account information on your email client there and then set the option to either never delete messages from the server or delete messages when they're moved from your Inbox. The second way ensures that you can still have two clients (your desktop and your iPhone) receive messages, but won't have to redownload old messages when you've already removed them from the desktop.

Make Fun Contact Pictures for Your iPhone

We already know that the larger iPhone-assigned contact pictures are better than the desktop-assigned thumbnails, but here's a way to make fun contact pictures that look like people are stuck inside your iPhone. Just tell your friend to put her face up against a window or glass, then take her picture with your iPhone—it'll look like you've shrunken her inside.

```
http://tinyurl.com/ywu8sn
```

Send MMS Messages Through Email

Even though the iPhone doesn't support pictures messaging (MMS), you can still send photos to your friends' phones. How? By sending messages to their phone numbers over email, where they automatically be converted into picture messages. Each cellular provider assigns an email address to each phone number in the following form: 5554445555@wireless.service.com (where, obviously, you replace 5554445555 with their number; the domain varies by carrier, as described later on). By tapping Email Photo and creating an email to this address, your email will be

Did you know?

You Can Save Money on International Calls with Jajah

Calling internationally on your iPhone with AT&T's rates is anything but cheap, but you can actually use a service called Jajah to make international calls for the same cost as regular calls. If both you and the person you're calling are members of jajah.com, you can start a Jajah call from the iPhone's Safari browser, essentially turning that international call into a domestic call, which just uses up the minutes on your AT&T plan. This isn't completely free (you still use up your minutes), but it's better than paying standard international rates.

converted to an MMS message and delivered to your friends' phone. Instead of remembering all your friends' numbers, we suggest you create an email address under each contact with their number and appropriate email domain so you can send MMS pictures easily. Here's a list of providers and their email addresses:

- **Alltel**   5554445555@message.alltel.com
- **AT&T/Cingular**   5554445555@mms.att.net
- **Boost Mobile**   5554445555@myboostmobile.com
- **Helio**   5554445555@messaging.sprintpcs.com
- **Nextel**   5554445555@messaging.nextel.com
- **Sprint**   5554445555@messaging.sprintpcs.com
- **T-Mobile**   5554445555@tmomail.net
- **Verizon**   5554445555@vtext.com
- **Virgin Mobile**   5554445555@vmobl.com

If you don't know what cellular provider a particular contact uses, you can actually send messages through a service called Teleflip at 5554445555@teleflip.com. When sent to Teleflip as shown in Figure 14-3, Teleflip will convert your message and forward it to the correct provider. They only allow 100 messages per month for free, so if you want more than that you'll have to sign up for one of their pay plans.

Use the iPhone with a Pay-As-You-Go Plan

Although you probably already signed up for a two-year AT&T plan when you bought the iPhone, you can actually use the phone on a pay-as-you-go basis without having to sign a contract. It's called the GoPhone plan, and it's AT&T's month-to-month pay-as-you-go service. To get this, you still have to start by purchasing an iPhone and activating it. When you're in the iTunes iPhone activation screen, choose any service plan, but use the Social Security Number 999-99-9999. This isn't a valid SSN, so it will fail the credit check. That's the vital step. When you fail the credit check, AT&T will offer to sign you up for a GoPhone plan. Enter in all your normal (real) information here, and you'll be using your iPhone sans contract in no time.

```
http://tinyurl.com/yrc5uf
```

NOTE   *You can actually use the iPhone without a contract on any other GSM network around the world. See the Spotlight section of this book for more details.*

Beef Up iTunes with Advanced Features

There are a few advanced tricks you can use in iTunes to make organizing and syncing your music and video even smoother.

FIGURE 14-3   Send MMS messages with Mail

Increase Your Video Encode Speed

Encoding videos to an iPhone-compatible format can be a strain on your computer. If you've got an older computer, or if you just want your videos to encode faster than they are now, you can purchase an external H.264 encoder from Elgato. Elegato's USB encoders offload the workload from your CPU to the encoder, which not only frees up your computer to do other stuff like browsing and emailing, but manages to get the job done about five times faster. The Elgato Turbo.264 encoder costs $99.

```
http://elgato.com/index.php?file=products_turbo264
```

Authorize Multiple Computers with iTunes

Songs purchased from iTunes can only be authorized to play back on five computers at once, but that should be enough to allow your whole family to listen to the same song at the same time. To authorize another computer to play back your purchased music, copy the file over to another computer, and then import it into iTunes. When you try to play it, you'll be prompted with a message asking you to enter in your name and password (the same one you used to buy the song) in order to authorize this computer to play it (see Figure 14-4).

Authorize Computer

This computer is not authorized to play "Modern Romance". Would you like to authorize it?

To play this song you must authorize this computer to play songs purchased using the account "drew@drewreynolds.com". You may authorize up to 5 computers for each account.

○ ❤️

Apple ID:

adam@lifehacker.com   Example: steve@mac.com

Password:

●●●●●●●●●●●●   (Forgot Password?)

○ AOL 🔊

(?) (Preview)   (Cancel) (Authorize)

FIGURE 14-4   The iTunes authorization screen

If you've already authorized a total of five computers—some may be old machines that aren't in use anymore—you can still authorize another computer. The trick is that you have to deauthorize all your previous computers and start fresh. Just go to your iTunes account page by clicking on your iTunes login in the iTunes Store. Now, deauthorize all the computers, and try to play the file again. You'll be prompted with the login and password, which will then authorize this current computer to play back the file. You'll have to redo the process again on all other computers that want to play back this song, but you'll have cleared the authorization of the computer that's no longer in use.

Master the iPhone Keyboard

The iPhone's onscreen software keyboard has been a source of much debate. Some people—like Jason and myself—love it, while others aren't so keen on the lack of hardware buttons. Our contention is this: Most iPhone owners will be able to type just as fast—if not faster—on their iPhone as they ever did on their previous phone provided they take advantage of a few of these tips and the great features the iPhone has to offer.

Trust the Autocorrect

First and foremost, if you really want to improve your typing speed on the iPhone, you need to learn to trust the iPhone's smart Autocorrect feature. Believe us when we tell you that this trust, in time, will lead to outright love. The iPhone Autocorrect feature analyzes what you're typing and looks for common words and misspellings and then automatically corrects errors and replaces misspelled words with the correct word. This isn't a terribly new idea; in fact, you've probably seen a similar feature in desktop word processing applications like Microsoft Word. What's so special about the iPhone's Autocorrect, though, is that it's very smart. It takes into account hundreds of different possibilities for the word you may have been typing based on the proximity of letters that you may have miskeyed to other letters nearby, as you can see in Figure 14-5.

To put Autocorrect into practice, try mistyping a word—like trust, for example. Open up an email or note and type in something like "ttist." First, notice that just because you're getting things wrong from the start, you don't need to stop. Don't worry about being perfect (and don't obsess about typing ttist correctly), just type, and get as close to the letters you want as possible. If you do in fact type out the letters t-t-i-s-t, you'll notice that by about the third letter, the iPhone is already suggesting possible corrections. You can accept a suggestion at any time by pressing the space button or adding punctuation, or if you're not finished yet, just continue typing. By the time you get to the final 't', you should see the word—trust—in the Autocorrect box. Like I said, typing a space or any punctuation will automatically replace your misspelled word with the correct word.

SHORTCUT *Autocorrect will also take care of your contractions so you don't have to go looking for the proper punctuation. For example, rather than typing* **can't**, *just type* **cant** *and let your iPhone take care of the grunt work. For contractions using the word "will" (like he'll or she'll), you actually need to type a third 'l' to the end of the word to get the correct suggestion—like* **shelll**.

On the other hand, if you've reached the end of the word and don't want to accept the suggestion, tap the Autocorrect box to dismiss the suggestion.

FIGURE 14-5   The iPhone's Autocorrect in action

When you're typing full speed with Autocorrect, you shouldn't get hung up on what you're seeing at the moment. Instead, trust that by the end of the word, even if you miskeyed a few of the letters, Autocorrect will have found the word you wanted to type. However, the iPhone only autocorrects words that have the same number of letters, so if you type in **ttisst** for trust, your iPhone won't know what word that was supposed to be.

The one time you won't want to rely on Autocorrect is when you're typing a word or phrase that you wouldn't normally see in a dictionary. In those cases, accuracy is important because your iPhone is not yet aware of those words. The cool thing is this: if it's a word the iPhone does not understand and you dismiss the Autocorrect suggestions just twice, the word will be added to your Autocorrect dictionary.

Improve Your Typing with Different Methods

There are a few different methods for typing on the iPhone, and the most appealing method will depend on what works best for you. However, you may also find that different situations call for different typing styles, so learning a few alternate methods of typing can help improve your speed and accuracy. These include

- **One-finger tap** Probably the most common method of typing on the iPhone, the one finger tap consists of holding the phone in one hand while pecking at the keys with the fingertip of your index or middle finger on the other hand.

- **Two-thumb typing** If you really want to fire off email messages and the like on your iPhone with lightning speed, you need to master typing with two thumbs. Cradle the phone in your hands and position your left and right thumbs over the phone. Your left thumb takes care of all the letters on the left side of the keyboard and vice versa for your right thumb. If you have a good grasp of the keyboard layout, you want to just start pecking with fairly reckless abandon. This is where trust in the iPhone's Autocorrect feature comes in very handy. Focus more on the keys than the output, assuming that the iPhone is correcting any miskeys. When you've finished typing a sentence, look back over what you've typed and, if necessary, fix any errors.

- **Touch-and-drag method** If you've never gotten the hang of pecking the software keys and you really have no faith in Autocorrect, the touch-and-drag method is probably for you. Rather than tapping away at individual keys, try pressing your finger against the keyboard and then dragging your finger to the letter you want to type. This allows you to see exactly what keystroke will be made before you release the key (just watch the magnified letter) so you can hit exactly what letter you want every time. This may sound fairly slow, but it can actually be a surprisingly fast method of typing. When I touch-and-drag type, I generally touch near the middle of the keyboard and drag to the letter I want every time I type a new letter.

You can even apply the touch-and-drag method to punctuation. To do so, press the keyboard switch key on the bottom left of the keyboard to switch to the punctuation keyboard and drag your finger to the desired punctuation mark. When you get there, release your finger to type the punctuation and return to the main keyboard. Unlike typing punctuation the normal way (by tapping the Keyboard Toggle button, tapping the punctuation mark, and then tapping the Space button or Keyboard Toggle button), a lot of people find using the touch-and-drag method for typing punctuation much faster.

Like we said previously, one method for typing might stand out above the rest for you, but there are instances where each method can be useful in its own right. For pure speed, you can't do much better than two-thumb typing. But there are times when you can't rely on the Autocorrect—like when you're typing in a web address, a word that's not yet in the iPhone dictionary, or a password that doesn't show up on the screen—and for those times, nothing works better than the touch-and-drag method.

Deleting text with the Delete button moves a little slowly at first, but if you hold down the Delete button, it starts removing whole words at a time, making it the quickest way to delete a lot of text at one time.

Additionally, the touch-and-drag method works extremely well if you've only got one hand free for typing. You can use your thumb to touch-and-drag with one hand while hailing a cab with your other.

Train the iPhone's Dictionary

As we've already mentioned briefly, your iPhone's built-in dictionary can actually be trained to learn words that aren't already available to your Autocorrect. When you type a word that isn't already in your dictionary, the iPhone will likely assume you've misspelled that word and suggest an alternate. Once you reject the Autocorrect suggestion for the word just two times, that word will automatically be added to the iPhone dictionary and actually included in Autocorrect suggestions.

Control the iPhone with Your Headphones

If you're using the earbud headphones and microphone included with your iPhone (or certain third-party iPhone headsets), you can actually control calls and the iPod using the microphone button without any interaction with the iPhone. First, it's worth pointing out that the inline microphone on your headset is actually a button—give it a squeeze and you'll notice a small click. You can control the iPhone using either one or two clicks of the microphone button. For controlling calls, you can use the following features:

- **One click**   Answer incoming calls with one click of your inline mic. When you've finished with a call, click once again to end the call.

- **Two clicks**   While you're in a call, you can answer another call in call waiting by clicking the inline mic button twice in succession.

When you're using your headphones with the iPod, the inline mic button can control playback so you don't have to take your iPhone out of your pocket whenever you want to change tracks. Here's how it works:

- **One click**   Play or pause your iPod. Since one click also answers calls, keep in mind that an incoming phone call will always take precedence over the iPod. However, your iPhone is smart and will automatically pause the iPod when someone calls, then resume playing after you end the call. If someone isn't calling, clicking the Mic button will always toggle the Play or Pause button on the iPod.
- **Two clicks**   Skip to the next track by clicking the Mic button twice in quick succession.

Play Streaming Video Inside Safari

As we mentioned in Chapter 7, Safari can handle streaming video provided it's encoded in an iPhone/iPod-compatible format. Apple's trailers website, shown in Figure 14-6, has a great selection of streaming trailers optimized for your iPhone.

Since the iPod is so popular, you'll actually find that some online video sites like Google Video (which you can watch on the iPhone already) actually offer iPod-compatible video downloads. Since iPods and iPhones both require the same video formats, any site that offers

FIGURE 14-6   Apple's trailers page

a link for iPod-compatible video will work on your iPhone as well. In Google Video, for example, just select Download for Video iPod/PSP from the dropdown menu and then tap the Download link. You can then put these videos onto the iPhone via iTunes.

Check Your Voicemail from Another Phone

While it'll never match up to the accessibility of visual voicemail, you can check your voicemail from any phone the old fashioned way by calling your iPhone number and pressing the asterisk (*) key once your voice mail message begins. Next enter in the PIN you set up for your visual voicemail and then press pound (#). You've now got traditional access to your voicemail. Here are a few shortcuts you can use from here:

- **Save the message**   Press 9
- **Delete the message**   Press 7
- **Replay the current message**   Press 4
- **Skip the current message**   Press #
- **Get delivery date**   Press 5
- **Rewind 10 seconds**   Press 1
- **Rewind to start of message**   Press 1, 1
- **Pause playback**   Press 2
- **Fast-foward 10 seconds**   Press 3
- **Go to end of message**   Press 3, 3

TIP   *If you don't like your visual voicemail, you can access the traditional voicemail from your iPhone by pressing and holding 1 from the keypad. Your phone will automatically call voicemail.*

Know if You've Silenced Your iPhone

A lot of the time—often due to necessity—you'll want to silence your phone without taking it out of your pocket. You could memorize the on/off positions of the mute button, but the iPhone provides a simpler cue for telling you your iPhone has been silenced: one short vibration. Whenever you flip the mute switch to silence, your iPhone will vibrate once. When you flip the mute button to the off position, the phone provides no feedback. Just remember, even when your iPhone is muted your alarms will still sound, so if you've got alarms set and you want to mute your phone, be sure to manually turn the volume on your phone all the way down.

Get New Email as Soon as Its Sent

As we described in Chapter 6, most email services require that you check your email periodically in order to download new messages. That means that you could have new email messages sitting on your email server from anywhere between 15 minutes (the smallest auto-check interval) to hours (if you only check email manually). If you want to make sure you always receive new email as soon as it arrives, you may want to consider signing up for a Yahoo Mail account, which supports push email. With push email, messages are delivered to your phone as soon as they're received.

As an added bonus, when you read a message on your iPhone, it's marked as read in your Yahoo Mail account. Likewise, when you delete or file a message to a folder on your iPhone, your changes are reflected in your Yahoo Mail (and vice versa). All of the perks associated with Yahoo Mail are turned on automatically, so all you need is a Yahoo Mail account.

If you want the benefits of push email but you don't want to ditch your old email address, you might want to consider forwarding email from other accounts to your Yahoo Mail account. For example, I've set up a filter in my Gmail account that forwards important messages to Yahoo. The added benefit of push email is that you don't need to waste your battery auto-checking for emails. They'll come to you whenever they arrive.

Take Advantage of Web Applications Made for the iPhone

When the iPhone was first released, Apple CEO Steve Jobs announced that software developers should build applications for the iPhone using the Internet and Safari on the iPhone. As a result, there are loads of really great web applications on the Internet specifically designed for the iPhone. Covering the gamut from games and instant messaging, to application launchers and RSS readers, here are a few of our favorite iPhone web applications, grouped by category:

 **FIGURE 14-7**   MockDock

Application Launchers

- **MockDock** `http://mockdock.com/` (see Figure 14-7)
- **Mojits** `http://www.mojits.com/`
- **Appleopolis** `http://appleopolis.com/`

Games

- **Sudoku for iPhone** `http://soduko.myiphone.pl`
- **Bejeweled** `http://static.popcap.com/iphone/`
- **iChess** `http://ichess.morfik.com/`
- **Battlefleet** `http://www.rogerkenny.com/battlefleet/`
- **iMineSweeper** `http://iminesweeper.com/`
- **Blackjack** `http://mynumo.com/iphone/bj/blackjack.htm`
- **Texas Hold 'Em Poker** `http://iphone.scenario.com/`
- **Solitaire** `http://www.digiwidge.com/solitaire/solitaire.html`
- **Avalanche** `http://tinyurl.com/3axx18`

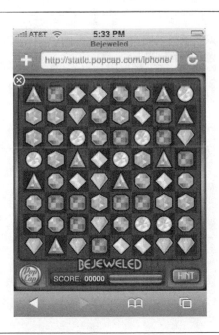

 FIGURE 14-8   Bejeweled

News/RSS Readers

- **Google Reader**   An iPhone optimized version of Google's very popular online RSS reader. `http://google.com/reader/`

- **Newsgator**   Another online RSS reader that syncs with popular desktop RSS readers FeedDemon (Windows) and NetNewsWire (Mac). `http://m.newsgator.com/`

- **iActu**   Newstand-like interface for accessing popular news sources like the New York Times, Wall Street Journal, and USA Today. `http://www.widgetinfo.net/iphone/`

- **Digg**   This is an iPhone-optimized interface for the popular technology and news aggregation web site. `http://digg.com/iphone`

- **Netvibes**   This is the iPhone version of the popular online start page. `http://m.nv1.netvibes.com/`

Social

- **Facebook**   Bar none, this is one of the best applications for the iPhone. You'll feel like you're using a real software application and not just a web app when browsing Facebook (see Figure 14-9) for the iPhone `http://iphone.facebook.com/`.

- **iPhlickr**   Search and view photos from the popular photo sharing site, Flickr. `http://www.chandlerkent.com/iphlickr/`

FIGURE 14-9   Facebook

Word Processing

- **iZoho** Create documents, spreadsheets, presentations, and databases from your iPhone using the mobile version of the Zoho online office suite: `http://www.izoho.com/`
- **gOffice** No one would accuse this site of being beautifully made, but you can actually create and save real Word documents from your iPhone using gOffice. Since you can't actually save a Word file anywhere on your iPhone, gOffice lets you email the result of your work as a Microsoft Word attachment. `http://goffice.com/`

Information

- **Showtimes** Browse movie listings and showtimes by zip code and theater, then map the results or call the theater for more information. `http://optimalconnection.net/`
- **Gas.app** Find the cheapest gas near you by zip code, then open a link to find the gas station in Google Maps. `http://www.gasapp.com/index.html`

To-do

- **OneTrip Shopping List** `http://onetrip.org/onetrip/` (see Figure 14-10)
- **Remember the Milk** `http://rememberthemilk.com`

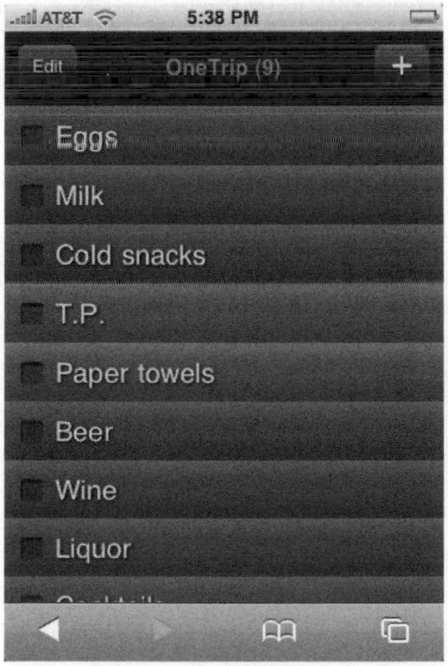

FIGURE 14-10 OneTrip

- **Ta-da Lists** `http://tadalist.com/`
- **Nozbe** `http://nozbe.com/`

Instant Messaging

- **Beejive** `http://iphone.beejive.com/`
- **FlickIM** `http://flickim.com/`
- **Meebo** `http://meebo.com/` (see Figure 14-11)
- **Skype IM** `http://skypeforiphone.com/index_iphone.jsp`

Remote Control

- **Remote Buddy** `http://tinyurl.com/24e6wx`

Now that you *really* know everything there is to know about using the iPhone, let's take a look at the accessories you can get to make the iPhone even better in Chapter 15.

FIGURE 14-11   Meebo

Chapter 15

Accessorize Your iPhone

How to...

- Know whether an accessory will work with your iPhone
- Familiarize yourself with iPhone accessories
- Buy official Apple accessories
- Use recommended accessories
- Shop for more accessories

Some people will be happy with the standard headphones, charger, and syncing dock that come with the iPhone. Others love to accessorize. Whether you're looking to protect your iPhone from damage with a screen protector or case, integrate it into your home with a stereo dock, or improve your iPod experience on-the-go with a better set of headphones, you can't go wrong if you're searching in the right place. In this chapter, we'll highlight some of our favorite accessories along with our favorite places to get them—as well as what you should look for in your own iPhone gear.

Know Whether an Accessory Will Work with Your iPhone

Although many accessories—including iPod accessories—will work flawlessly with the iPhone, the only way you can be absolutely sure an accessory was designed specifically for the iPhone is if it carries the Works with iPhone label. This label ensures that there's minimal interference between an accessory's functions (docking, music speakers) and the iPhone's communication functions (calling, Internet).

Did you know?

Many iPod Accessories Work with the iPhone

If you already own iPod docks and iPod speakers, then you can find out whether they work with the iPhone by just plugging them in. The dock connector on the iPhone is the same as on the iPod, so plugging it into an iPod accessory won't damage your phone at all. The worst that will happen is that your speakers will give out a lot of static interference caused by the phone's wireless operation. The static interference can usually be remedied by enabling Airplane mode, but doing so means you'll miss calls and won't be able to access the Internet until you turn Airplane mode off.

Familiarize Yourself with iPhone Accessories

The iPhone has many different types of accessories designed to do different things. Here's a brief, consolidated list:

- ■ **Headphones**   The iPhone actually comes with a fairly decent set of headphones. As a headset for making calls, it's quite good, but as headphones for audio, it's not all that great. We recommend that you use your own third-party headphones from companies like Shure (with the Shure iPhone adapter) and V-Moda in order to get the highest quality audio out of your iPhone. Models like the V-Moda Vibe Duo Control are made especially for the iPhone's recessed headset jack. If you already have a favorite pair of headphones, the recessed headphone jack rules out plugging in many headphones directly into the iPhone, but there are a few headphone adapters available that fix this oversight.

- ■ **Headphone Adapters**   Because of the recessed headset jack on your iPhone, most headphones just won't fit in all the way. Adapters from Belkin and Shure have a male end that goes into the iPhone and a female end that allows you to plug in any headphones. The Shure adapter also has an on-board microphone, which essentially turns any headphones you have into ones that can make calls as well.

- ■ **Docks**   iPhone docks, such as the one that comes packaged with your phone, allow you to connect the phone to your computer easily without having to fiddle with a cable each time. You can both sync your phone and charge its battery while it's docked. The dock usually consists of two pieces: the dock itself and the USB to iPhone connector cable that goes into your computer. There's even a line-out port on the dock that comes with your iPhone, and that allows you to connect your iPhone to a set of speakers when it's docked. If you own an official Apple Bluetooth headset, it also comes with a special dock that charges both the iPhone and the headset, and actually automatically pairs the two together when they're both docked.

- **Dock Adapters**   Many third-party speaker docks have interchangeable dock adapters so you can fit different sized iPods (each generation is a slightly different size than the last) into them snugly. Apple sells dock adapters for the iPhone as well, so if you want your phone to fit just right in your iPod dock, you can get a pack of three adapters from the Apple store.

- **Car Kits**   Just like with traditional iPods, car kits allow you to charge your iPhone, broadcast music over FM to your car's radio, or hook your phone up to your car's stereo system. Not all of the existing iPod car kits work with the iPhone, and the ones that do may give you some static interference. Check to make sure the Works with iPhone tag is on a car kit before you buy a new one.

- **Bluetooth Headset**   The iPhone works with just about all Bluetooth headsets, not just the official iPhone Bluetooth headset. If you already own a Bluetooth headset that works well with another phone, chances are that it will work just as well with the iPhone. Just follow the directions in Chapter 3 to see how to connect and use your headset. If by some chance your current headset doesn't work with the iPhone, see the "Recommended Accessories" section later in this chapter.

- **Chargers**   You don't have to use your computer to charge your iPhone all the time because Apple actually includes an AC adapter charger that works with the iPhone connector cable. If you happen to lose this charger, you can purchase a replacement one from Apple. You can also use any USB charger—Internet retailers are full of them—as long as you have the iPhone connector/USB cable.

- **Mobile Chargers**   There are two types of mobile chargers that you can use with your iPhone. The first is a cigarette adapter charger that you can use in the car. This lets you use the iPod in your iPhone with your car's audio system without worrying about running out of power for calls. The other type of mobile charger is a mobile battery pack that you can take along to augment your iPhone's battery life until the next time you can plug in.

- **Cables**   If you misplace the iPhone Dock Connector to USB cable, Apple sells a replacement for $19. It's quite useful to have multiple cables so that you don't need to carry a cable with you wherever you need to charge your iPhone. Any standard dock connector to USB cable will work, so if you've already got one for your iPod, or if you bought a third-party cord for cheap, those will work just fine.

- **Cases**   There are already many third-party cases for the iPhone on the market. If you want to protect your phone from drops and scratches, you can invest in any number of cases, all with various build qualities and materials. If you buy a case, make sure it fits your iPhone correctly and leaves enough space for the Home button, the On/Off button, the volume buttons, and the camera. Not all cases are created equal, and some may unintentionally cover up one or more of the hardware buttons.

- **Screen Protectors**   The iPhone's glass screen is fairly scratch-proof, but if you want to ensure that no damage will come to your screen, you can purchase one of the transparent screen protectors that people have been using on their iPods for a while. The good ones will protect your screen but won't interfere with finger inputs. The bad ones will leave the screen shiny and reflective, which is bad for visibility, and makes it hard to interact with your touchscreen. Check out reviews online before you decide to stick one onto your iPhone.

- **Wireless Access Points/Routers**   If you don't already own a wireless access point or router for your home or office, you should think about getting one so your iPhone can use Wi-Fi to access the Internet. This will allow you to check your email and surf the Web much faster than using EDGE, but it also means you'll never miss a call because you tied up the line using the EDGE connection.

- **Cellular Repeaters**   Although the iPhone's reception is quite good, you may live in an area where AT&T's reach doesn't quite meet its grasp (also known as dropped call city). In this case, you may want to purchase a wireless repeater and signal booster, which grabs the AT&T (along with T-Mobile, Sprint, and Verizon) signal and boosts it internally. Cellular repeaters actually boost everyone's cell phone signal, not just yours, so your family or roommates will be able to get crystal clear reception as well.

- **TTY Adapters**   Apple sells an iPhone TTY adapter for the hearing impaired that allows you to link your phone with a TTY device. This adapter is just $19 from the official Apple store.

How to ... Apply a Screen Protector

If you buy a clear protective screen for your iPhone, you should be aware of a few important steps for properly installing it. First, clean your screen so it's free of any debris, grease, or oils. You'll also want to make sure your hands are free from dirt and oils so you won't leave any fingerprints on the bare screen before you cover it up with the protector. Remove the screen protector from its packaging and peel the protector from its backing. Now carefully line up one edge of the protector with the corresponding edge on your iPhone. Once the edges are lined up, gently apply the protector to the surface of your screen. You may see some small air bubbles under the protector after it's been applied. To get rid of them, take a soft cloth and smooth over the top of the screen until the bubbles are no longer visible. If you decide to remove or replace the screen protector, you can remove your old protector by applying a piece of clear tape to a corner surface of the protector and using that to peel it off.

- **Paint Job**　If the default silver and black paint scheme on your iPhone is wearing a little thin, there's a company called Colorware that will custom-paint your iPhone for $149. All you have to do is design a color scheme on their website and send them your iPhone. Their paint jobs are high quality and won't damage your phone in any way. If you want to purchase a pre-painted iPhone, you can also do that from their website:

```
http://www.colorwarepc.com/products/Select_Iphone.aspx
```

Buy Official Apple Accessories

If you want to be absolutely sure that an accessory will work with your iPhone, you can purchase official iPhone accessories from the Apple store. If there isn't an Apple store near you, you can visit the online apple store for iPhone accessories as well.

```
http://www.apple.com/iphone/accessories/
```

Although there are only a handful of iPhone-compatible accessories from third-party manufacturers as of this writing, within a few years you'll find that buying non-official accessories will be cheaper and work just as well as the ones from Apple (just like we've seen with the iPod).

Use Recommended Accessories

There are a lot of accessories you *can* buy for your iPhone, but there are only a handful that are actually *worth* buying. Here are a few we recommend:

- **Headphones**　V-Moda Vibe Duo and Vibe Duo Control—V-Moda makes great mid-range headphones that retail for around $100. These earbuds provide excellent sound quality for a reasonable price. Both fit neatly into the iPhone's headset jack without the need for an adapter, and the Vibe Duo Control features an in-line button that controls both calls and iPod playback.

- **Headphone Adapter**   If you want to use your own headset or line-in speakers—but your iPhone's recessed headphone jack won't allow it—Belkin's headphone adapter is just the thing. They cost only $9, but they do add a few inches onto the iPhone's length. This means it's great for the home and the car, but it's fairly unwieldy for carrying around in your pockets.

- **Headphone Adapter w/ Mic**   The Shure headset adapter acts as a standard adapter (makes regular headphones work with the iPhone) and a microphone, so you can have a conversation using any pair of headphones you own.

- **Bluetooth Headset**   Although the Apple Bluetooth Headset works great with the iPhone, it doesn't have noise cancellation and some of the fancier functions that other Bluetooth headsets do. We recommend the Aliph Jawbone, which has military grade noise cancellation and works perfectly with your phone.

- **Screen Protector**   Shieldzone invisibleSHIELD—The invisibleSHIELD line of screen protectors are arguably the best for the iPod and other portable devices, and they don't disappoint on the iPhone. These protect your screen from straight-on key scratches and don't inhibit finger presses and gestures.

- **Armband**   Belkin Sport Armband for iPhone—Because the iPhone stores data using flash memory instead of a hard drive, it's safe to take it jogging or exercising. The Belkin Sport Armband allows you to keep your iPhone attached to your arm (along with a house key) and protects your phone from the sweat and dirt that accumulate during exercise.

Shop for More Accessories

Besides popular electronics outlets like Best Buy and Amazon.com, there are a few iPhone-centric shops online where you can find just about every accessory imaginable for your phone. Here are a few stores that you can take a look at for all your iPhone needs:

- `http://store.everythingiphone.com`
- `http://www.thegadgetlocker.com`

The following manufacturers are well known for their iPod accessories and have started creating great accessories for the iPhone as well:

- `http://dlo.com`
- `http://www.griffintechnology.com/devices/iphone/`
- `http://www.belkin.com/ipod/iphone/`
- `http://www.xtrememac.com/byipod/iphone.php`

These stores specialize in either cases or screen protectors, and they have different styles to fit your needs:

- `http://www.myincipio.com/`
- `http://www.iskin.com/`
- `http://ifrogz.com/iphone/cases/`
- `http://www.marware.com/PRODUCTS/iPhone-Products`
- `http://www.macally.com/`

Even with all these accessories protecting your iPhone, you may still sometimes run into problems. Chapter 16 will show you how to troubleshoot and resolve any hiccups you may run into.

Chapter 16

Troubleshoot and Care
for Your iPhone

How to...

- Find a solution for your problem
- Reset the iPhone
- Erase your iPhone settings
- Install software updates for your iPhone
- Restore the factory defaults with iTunes
- Restore saved settings to an iPhone
- Recover synced data
- Contact Apple and AT&T
- Care for your iPhone

The iPhone is a remarkable piece of computing equipment, but like all gadgets, your iPhone may hit a snag in operation every now and then. In this chapter, we'll discuss how to troubleshoot your iPhone for problems and—if you don't have any luck doing that—contact Apple and AT&T for help. We'll also give you a few pointers for taking good care of your iPhone to help avoid problems in the first place.

Find a Solution for Your Problem

We've compiled a list of some of the most common problems you may run into while using your iPhone, arranged into hardware problems, usage problems, and syncing problems. The hardware section covers everything related to your iPhone's hardware, from battery problems to accessory issues. The usage section covers problems you might experience while using any of the applications inside the iPhone. Last, the syncing section covers issues related to syncing data—such as contacts, notes, or music—to the iPhone.

Some solutions to your problems will be very simple and can be answered in a few sentences. However we've extracted more complicated problems—or problems with solutions that apply to several potential problems—into their own sections. In those cases, we'll direct you to the appropriate section.

Find a Solution for Your Hardware Problems

If you're having problems with your hardware, such as battery issues or accessory issues, this section will help you find a solution for most of them. If you don't find a solution here, we'll point you in the right direction to contact Apple tech support so you can get help from the source.

- **My iPhone battery doesn't charge all the way**   When the iPhone was first released, a software bug sometimes prevented the battery meter from showing up as fully charged. If this happens to you, you may be using an old version of the iPhone firmware. See the "Install Software Updates for Your iPhone" section.

- **My iPhone doesn't charge at all**   See "Perform a Hard Reset." If that doesn't work, see "Contact Apple."

- **My iPhone doesn't turn on**   Make sure there's at least some power in your phone first. Charge it up with the AC adapter instead of the USB port on your computer, because there's a slight chance the USB port could be not supplying enough/any power to your iPhone. If this doesn't work, see "Perform a Hard Reset."

- **I got my iPhone wet**   See the sidebar "How to Save Your iPhone from Water Damage."

- **My headphones don't fit the jack**   The iPhone has a recessed headphone input that makes it difficult for many headphones to plug in. See Chapter 15 for a look at both iPhone-friendly headphones and accessories that will allow you to plug in your old headphones.

- **My battery doesn't hold a charge**   See the "Condition Your Battery" section. You may want to use the AC adapter for this, in case your USB port on your computer is damaged. If this doesn't help, see "Contact Apple."

- **My battery only lasts a fraction of what it used to**   See "Condition Your Battery."

- **My iPhone is getting really hot**   Turn the phone off and on again. If the phone is unresponsive, see the section called "Perform a Hard Reset." The iPhone does get warm when charging, so if it gets hot while plugged in, that's fairly normal. But if you think the phone is too far out of normal operating temperature range, see "Contact Apple."

- **This accessory is not made to work with iPhone**   You're using the iPhone with a dock or an adapter that's made for the iPod. It's usually all right to do this, but you may run into some static from the speakers whenever your iPhone communicates with the cell network. If you don't mind possibly missing calls, you can put your phone into Airplane mode and eliminate the static.

- **I want to buy insurance for my iPhone**   See "Contact Apple."

- **Nothing is working!**   See "Contact Apple."

Find Solutions for Your Usage Problems

If you're looking for solutions to problems you're having with iPhone operation, chances are they fall into one of four areas: general problems that aren't specific to any application, phone problems, Internet and email problems, and iPod problems.

Fix General Problems

- **My iPhone is stuck in a program**   See "Force an Application to Close."

- **My iPhone won't turn on/off**   See "Perform a Hard Reset."

- **My iPhone is very slow**   See "Restart the iPhone."

- **I forgot my password**   See "Restore the Factory Defaults with iTunes."

- **My bill shows a lot of roaming charges**   See "Contact AT&T."

- **My bill shows a lot of data charges**   See "Contact AT&T."

How to ... Save Your iPhone from Water Damage

If fortune frowns on you and you accidentally take your iPhone on a cool water plunge, don't lose heart—things may not be as dire as they appear. It's actually not uncommon to get a cell phone back in working condition—even after it's taken a swim—as long as you follow a few steps. First, don't try turning on your iPhone or plugging it in. While it's still soggy, putting electricity to the phone will only cause harm. Instead, let the water evaporate by keeping your phone in a warm, dry place for a few days. If your phone still appears wet after a few, give it more time—you want to make sure it's completely dry. Once you're sure it's dry, try plugging it in and powering it back up. With any luck, you'll be making calls and surfing the Internet like nothing happened. If it doesn't work and you have to ask Apple for a replacement, tell them the truth. They can tell if your phone has suffered water damage.

- **I got a new iPhone and I want to transfer my old settings** See "Restore Saved Settings to an iPhone."
- **Nothing is working!** See "Contact Apple and AT&T."

Fix Phone Problems

- **My iPhone won't make calls** Check the signal bars on the top of your phone to make sure you have a strong enough cell signal. If not, wait until your signal strength increases and try again. Also, make sure you're not in Airplane mode. If all else fails, try restarting the phone.
- **The iPhone isn't receiving text messages** Make sure you're not in Airplane mode and you have a strong enough cell signal. If you were sent an MMS text message, you won't receive the message on the iPhone. Instead, you'll receive an SMS message with details for accessing the MMS message online.
- **The iPhone can't send text messages** Make sure you've entered a valid cell phone number, complete with area code. Also be sure you're not in Airplane mode and you have a strong enough cell signal.
- **Nothing is working** See "Contact Apple and AT&T."

Fix Internet and Email Problems

- **My iPhone won't connect to the Internet** Make sure your iPhone is not in Airplane mode. To connect to the Internet, you either need an EDGE or Wi-Fi network connection. See Chapter 13 for more on setting up a Wi-Fi connection. If a Wi-Fi hotspot is unavailable, check to see if the EDGE icon (the small 'E' next to your phone signal) is visible and you have a strong enough signal. If it is not, you won't be able to connect to the Internet until either Wi-Fi becomes available or you pick up an EDGE signal. If you aren't connected to the Internet and you receive a Could Not Activate EDGE error message, it means that one of your programs, like Mail, has tried accessing the Internet with no luck.

■ **The iPhone can't send/receive email**   Make sure you've set up your email account properly (Chapter 6), and be sure you have an active Internet connection (over either EDGE or Wi-Fi). If you can receive email but you can't send it, try changing the Outgoing Mail Server to a different port. To do so, go to that email account's settings and add :587 to the end of the address you've already entered into the Outgoing Mail Server section. Some ISPs only allow outgoing SMTP messages through this port.

■ **I got a Could Not Activate EDGE message**   See "My iPhone Won't Connect" to the Internet.

■ **The call volume is too soft**   When you're in a call, try increasing the in-call volume using the hardware volume button. If the in-call volume is turned up all the way and it still seems unreasonably quiet, see "Contact Apple."

■ **Nothing is working!**   See "Contact Apple and AT&T."

Fix iPod Problems

■ **Music and videos are missing from my iPhone**   Be sure the music and videos are selected for syncing in the iPhone sync settings, and double-check that the music and videos are working on your computer and in the proper formats. If that doesn't help, see "Contact Apple."

■ **I can't hear music playing back**   Make sure your volume is turned up by either using the volume rocker button on the side of the iPhone or by setting the volume in the iPod application. If you're expecting to hear music from the iPhone speakers, make sure you don't have any headphones plugged in, as this will disable the external speakers. If you were listening to headphones and you unplugged the headphones, the music will automatically pause (this is actually a feature to save you embarrassment). Go back to the iPod application and press Play.

■ **There's no video in my video podcast**   As we discussed in Chapter 4, if you launch a video podcast from the podcast screen, it will display a still image from the video and play back the audio only. This feature allows you to listen to the podcast audio while doing other tasks on your iPhone, like reading your email or browsing the Internet. To watch the audio with the video, launch the video podcast from the Videos screen.

■ **My video skips**   Try playing back the video on your computer. If playback on your computer is smooth, try deleting the video from your iPhone and resyncing. If playback on your computer is jumpy as well, the video file is corrupted. If you ripped it from a DVD or encoded it from another video format, try ripping it again. If you bought the video from Apple, see "Contact Apple."

■ **Nothing is working**   See "Contact Apple and AT&T."

Find Solutions for Your Syncing Problems

■ **My iPhone doesn't show up in iTunes**   Check to make sure the iPhone is seated properly in the dock or is connected properly to the cable. Then check to make sure the USB cable is connected properly to your computer. If this doesn't work, make sure the iPhone has enough power in it—you may want to charge it up a bit using the included AC adapter first. You can also perform a hard reset—see the "Perform a Hard Reset" section for more information. If that doesn't work, make sure you're connecting to a computer that has the latest version of iTunes, and if you're on a Mac, running an OS version of at least version 10.4.10.

■ **I want to stop my iPhone from syncing with my computer when I've got auto-sync on**   Hold down the COMMAND and OPTIONS keys on the Mac, or the SHIFT and CTRL keys on the PC when you connect your iPhone. Once it's connected and not syncing, you can open iTunes and uncheck the Auto-Sync option. You can turn off auto-sync altogether in the iPhone section of the iTunes preferences.

■ **Information—like contacts or settings—have vanished from my iPhone**   See "Restore Saved Settings to an iPhone."

■ **My phone was repaired and all the settings are gone**   See "Restore Saved Settings to an iPhone."

■ **All my Notes are missing**   See "Recover Synced Data."

■ **I accidentally deleted one very important Note and I need it back**   See "Recover Synced Data."

■ **I accidentally deleted an important contact/calendar appointment and I need it back**   Connect your iPhone to your computer, but don't sync. See the previous section on stopping a sync. Now, in iTunes, under the Info tab of your iPhone, check the appropriate section under Advanced. This will overwrite your iPhone's calendar/contact with the information on your computer, which presumably has the contact/calendar appointment that you want to recover.

■ **My music doesn't sync**   Check to make sure the music still exists on your computer. If your music is on an external USB hard drive or stored over the network, check to make sure those drives are connected. Also make sure that the total amount of synced music isn't larger than the amount of free space you have on your iPhone. Newly synced videos and pictures may have lowered the amount of free space past this point.

■ **Nothing is working**   See "Contact Apple."

Reset the iPhone

If your iPhone freezes up on you, you have a few of options. If it freezes in an application, you can try forcing the application to close. Alternately, you can restart the phone, and last, you can perform a hard reset.

Force an Application to Close

First, if you're frozen in an application, try holding the Home button for at least six seconds. This will force the current application to close, and if it works, will take you back to the Home screen. Next time you start the application, it should be back to normal operation. If that doesn't work, try restarting the iPhone.

Restart the iPhone

To restart the iPhone, hold the On/Off button for a few seconds and, when it appears, swipe the red power slider as shown in Figure 16-1. Then restart the iPhone by holding the On/Off button for a few seconds until the Apple logo appears on screen. If you've been having problems with a glitchy iPhone, a simple restart may solve the problem. If restarting doesn't help, try performing a hard reset.

Perform a Hard Reset

If your iPhone is completely unresponsive to the previous methods, or you can't even turn on your iPhone to try either method, you'll need to hard reset the iPhone. To do this, hold down the Home button and the On/Off button simultaneously for around ten seconds. If the hard reset worked, the Apple logo should appear onscreen and the phone should start up.

FIGURE 16-1   iPhone power-off screen

Erase Your iPhone Settings

Whether you're experiencing persistent problems with your iPhone or you want to remove your personal information before you give your phone away, it's easy to erase your settings from the iPhone. You can either delete just your preferences, or you can delete your preferences and all of your content (like music, videos, and pictures).

Delete Your Preferences

Should you continue to have problems with your iPhone freezing up after you perform a reset, you should try resetting your preferences in the Settings application. Open Settings from the Home screen. Next tap General, Reset, and then Reset All Settings (see Figure 16-2). This will reset all of your personalized settings but keep all of your data intact on your iPhone.

Delete All the iPhone's Content

You can delete all of the content from your iPhone by opening Settings from the Home screen, tapping General, Reset, and then Erase All Content and Settings (see Figure 16-2). Like Reset All Settings, this will reset your preferences, but it will also delete all content from the iPhone, including your photos, music, and video.

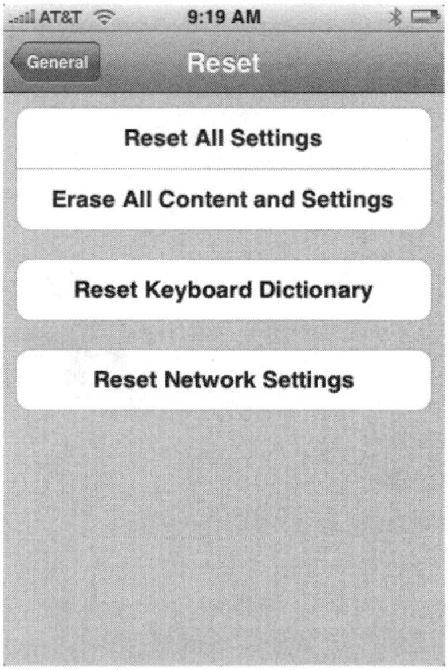

FIGURE 16-2   You can reset many of your iPhone's settings, or you can completely remove all settings and content from the iPhone.

A new iPhone software version (1.0.2) is available for the iPhone "Adam Pash's iPhone". Would you like to download and install it now?

☐ Do not ask me again

Cancel   Download Only   Download and Install

iTunes will automatically check for and alert you of new software updates for the iPhone.

Install Software Updates for Your iPhone

Installing software updates on your iPhone is very easy—in fact, iTunes will automatically check for updates every few days so you don't have to keep on top of it. As long as you regularly dock your iPhone, you'll receive prompts to download and install the latest and greatest software as soon as it becomes available (see Figure 16-3). If you're eager to check for a new update, you can manually check for updates on the Summary screen when you dock your iPhone by clicking the Check for Update button. If and when an update is available, follow the iTunes prompts to download the software and update your iPhone.

Restore the Factory Defaults with iTunes

If you continue to experience problems with your iPhone even after you've reset all of the iPhone settings and cleared all the content from the phone, it's time to perform a system restore.

To reset your iPhone software, dock the iPhone and then open the Summary tab of the iPhone information in iTunes. In the section labeled Version, click the button labeled Restore, as shown in Figure 16-4. Before you do so, it's a good idea to click the Check for Update button above it, just in case a newer version is available. Either way, after you click Restore you'll be prompted to confirm that you want to restore your iPhone to factory settings. Click Restore on the prompt and iTunes will restore your iPhone to a completely fresh state.

Restore Saved Settings to Your iPhone

Each time you sync your iPhone, iTunes backs up all of your phone's settings. That way if you buy a new phone, you don't have to go through the time-consuming process of entering in your settings and preferences all over again. In fact, the only content you'll need to re-sync to your new iPhone after you restore a backed up profile is the music, photos, and video. You'll also need to set up passwords and your Visual Voicemail again.

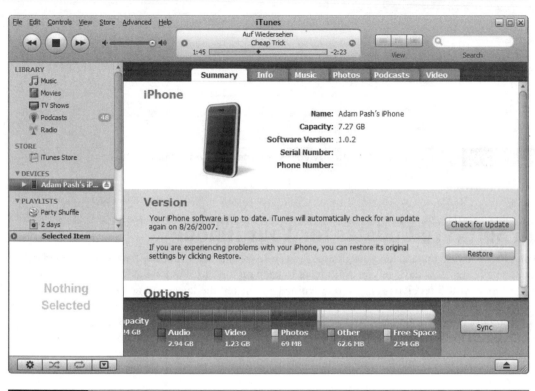

FIGURE 16-4   You can restore or check for updates to the iPhone software in the Summary tab of iTunes.

Restoring settings to a new iPhone works just like restoring the iPhone to factory settings. Plug in your fresh iPhone and click Restore in the Summary tab in iTunes, then follow the prompt to restore your old settings. The label in iTunes may say that you're restoring to the iPhone's original settings, but you're actually restoring to your last saved backup. This means all your Notes, your SMS messages, and even your Recently Called list will be transferred back to your iPhone. The only thing that won't be transferred back are your Camera Roll photos, so make sure to grab photos off of your iPhone before you do a restore.

Recover Synced Data

If you've accidentally deleted a really important note and you really, really need it back, it's possible to recover it. First, you have to be sure this particular note was on your iPhone the last time you synced with iTunes. If it was, continue. If it wasn't, then there's nothing you can do—the note is lost.

Dock your iPhone, but don't sync it with iTunes. If you've got the Auto-Sync option checked, you'll have to manually prevent syncing. To do this, hold down the COMMAND and OPTIONS keys on the Mac, or the SHIFT and CTRL keys on the PC when you connect your iPhone. This will prevent syncing for this one time. Now perform a factory restore by following the instructions in the previous section. Once you've restored, sync your phone normally, and your notes (along with everything else) will come back to your phone. You will, however, lose some content—like the pictures in the Camera Roll—if you haven't already synced that with your computer.

Contact Apple and AT&T

If troubleshooting has gotten you nowhere—or you just need to ask a question of an actual person—you can always contact either Apple or AT&T.

Contact Apple

For iPhone issues related to hardware and software—ranging from a broken button to a completely dead iPhone—you should contact Apple. You can reach Apple's iPhone technical support hotline at: 1-800-MY-IPHONE (1-800-694-7466). You're eligible for complimentary phone support from Apple for up to two years (one without AppleCare) after purchasing your iPhone, as long as you have an active AT&T service plan.

Keep in mind that your iPhone comes with a one-year warranty. You can extend the length of your warranty and your access to Apple's complimentary customer service hotline an extra year by paying $70 for AppleCare. Anything that goes wrong with your iPhone while it's under warranty will be covered by Apple (provided you're not at fault).

> TIP
> *Before you give your iPhone in to Apple for any reason, be sure you've synced the phone to your computer to back up all of your latest data. Many repairs your phone might undergo will clear your iPhone's data, meaning that you're data is completely gone unless you've backed up. If you did, you can restore your latest data to your phone next time you sync it with iTunes. See the previous "Restore Saved Settings to Your iPhone" section for details.*

If you need repairs but your iPhone is out of warranty, Apple charges $200 to $250 to repair the 4GB and 8GB iPhones, respectively. If your battery is the problem (for example, it's not longer holding a charge), you can take advantage of Apple's out-of-warranty battery replacement program. For just shy of $86 you can take your phone into an Apple store or send your phone to Apple to have the battery replaced.

Contact AT&T

If you have questions about your phone bill or problems with your service or visual voicemail, you should contact AT&T. You can reach AT&T customer service at 1-800-888-7600. If you prefer email, online chat, or in-store support, you can find what you're looking for here:

```
http://tinyurl.com/2h7sxw
```

Did you know?

You Can Rent a Replacement When Your iPhone Is Undergoing Repairs

Normally Apple repairs only take a few days, which isn't that big of a problem when you're repairing your iPod. On the other hand, three days is a very big deal when it comes to your phone. If you need to take your phone in for repairs, Apple will rent you a replacement phone for the term of the repairs for a not-so-friendly $30. This probably won't make too many users happy, especially if the fault lies entirely with your phone and/or you've already paid $70 for AppleCare, but it is what it is.

When you get your rental phone, you can move all of your settings to the phone by restoring the phone (see "Restore Saved Settings to an iPhone" above for details). After you're finished with the rental, you should also clear your settings and data from the phone to protect your privacy (see Erase Your iPhone Settings).

You can also check your current balance, pay your bill, view your minutes, and more from the AT&T Services section of the Phone settings, such as is shown in Figure 16-5.

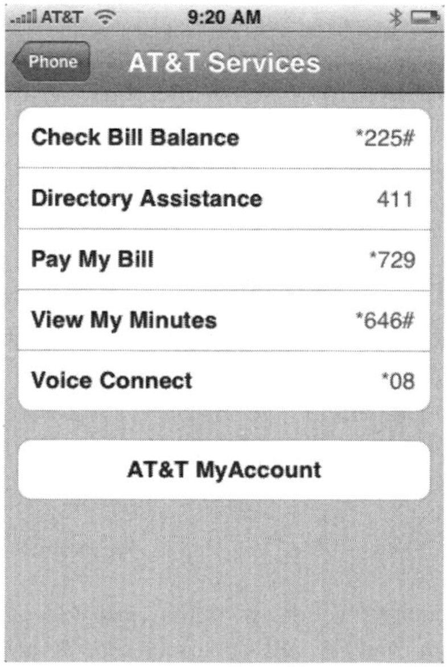

FIGURE 16-5   Access AT&T Services from Settings

Care for Your iPhone

Although you sometimes can't avoid problems, there are a few things you can do to avoid having problems in the first place.

Condition Your Battery

If you've been using your iPhone for a while, you'll notice that the battery doesn't quite last as long as it did when you first purchased it. You can help prolong the life of the battery by conditioning it about once every month.

Step one in conditioning your battery: let it fully charge. Step two: don't plug your iPhone in again until the battery has completely drained. Finally, the third step: Charge your phone until it's reached its full capacity yet again. Most people rarely use their iPhone until it's completely out of power, so it's good to cycle (drain and charge) your battery once in a while to exercise it.

If your battery dies really fast, Apple has a battery replacement program that allows you to send your iPhone in for a new battery. If your iPhone is under warranty, you will receive a free replacement. See the "Contact Apple" section for more details.

Maximize Your Battery Life

Besides conditioning, there are a couple things you can do while using the iPhone to maximize its battery life. This way, you're less likely to be caught on the road with a low battery warning.

- Don't set the screen to maximum brightness. The auto-brightness setting works well, and you usually don't need to set the screen's brightness to maximum to be able to see it. Setting it to slightly higher than halfway, as shown in Figure 16-6, should be enough for most environments.

- Set the auto-lock interval lower. Unless you really need to have it set to five minutes of idle before the iPhone locks itself, setting the auto-lock to one minute can save four minutes worth of battery that's used to power your screen.

- Set the email-check interval above 15 minutes. If your interval is 15 minutes, the iPhone never actually enters Sleep mode, even if there aren't any messages when checking. This causes significantly more drain on your battery than if the interval were higher, or if you check mail manually.

- Use Wi-Fi instead of EDGE for Internet access. Not only is Wi-Fi faster, it consumes less power on the whole than EDGE does. This can partially be attributed to the fact that your iPhone needs to be on longer for you to finish what you're doing using EDGE, but Wi-Fi is slightly more efficient as well.

- Turn off Wi-Fi and Bluetooth altogether when you're not going to use them.

- Lock your iPhone when you're not using it.

- Cut down on playing music and video. We're not saying that you should stop watching music and video on your iPhone entirely, but if you need that last bit of power to last you through the rest of the day, media playback will drastically decrease your battery life.

FIGURE 16-6   You can drastically increase your battery life between charges by adjusting your brightness levels.

Clean Your iPhone's Screen

Since your iPhone is a touchscreen phone, it's quite easy to get it dirty with both fingerprints and facial grease (it goes up to your cheek after all). Here are a few tips to help keep your phone as clean and shiny as possible.

- **Don't put it into the same pocket as your keys**   The screen is sturdy and will stand up to a few scratches if you accidentally mix your keys and phone, but try not to do this often.
- **Don't clean it with Windex or any non-approved cleaner**   The harsh solvents may harm the screen.
- **Do clean it with the included soft felt cloth, an eyeglass cloth, or any bit of soft clothing**   Rubbing the screen on your sleeve or on your pants is actually a decent way to clean it on the go.
- **Consider buying a case**   This is not for everyone, but if you're prone to dropping your iPhone, a protective case will not only help keep the screen, but also the sides and back, scratch free.
- **Consider buying a screen protector**   Like cases, not everyone likes screen protectors. However, a good screen protector will keep scratches off the face while not interfering with the standard touchscreen inputs.

Index